The American Crisis Series

Books on the Civil War Era

*Steven E. Woodworth, Associate Professor of History,
Texas Christian University*
SERIES EDITOR

∾ The Civil War was the crisis of the Republic's first century
—the test, in Abraham Lincoln's words, of whether any free government could long endure. It touched with fire the hearts of a generation, and its story has fired the imaginations of every generation since.
This series offers to students of the Civil War, either those continu-
ing or those just beginning their exciting journey into the past, concise overviews of important persons, events, and themes in that
remarkable period of America's history.

Volumes Published

James L. Abrahamson. *The Men of Secession and Civil War, 1859–1861*
(2000). Cloth ISBN 0-8420-2818-8   Paper ISBN 0-8420-2819-6

Robert G. Tanner. *Retreat to Victory? Confederate Strategy Reconsidered*
(2001). Cloth ISBN 0-8420-2881-1 Paper ISBN 0-8420-2882-X

Stephen Davis. *Atlanta Will Fall: Sherman, Joe Johnston, and the
Yankee Heavy Battalions* (2001). Cloth ISBN 0-8420-2787-4
Paper ISBN 0-8420-2788-2

Paul Ashdown and Edward Caudill. *The Mosby Myth: A Confederate
Hero in Life and Legend* (2002). Cloth ISBN 0-8420-2928-1
Paper ISBN 0-8420-2929-X

Spencer C. Tucker. *A Short History of the Civil War at Sea* (2002).
Cloth ISBN 0-8420-2867-6   Paper ISBN 0-8420-2868-4

Richard Bruce Winders. *Crisis in the Southwest: The United States,
Mexico, and the Struggle over Texas* (2002). Cloth ISBN 0-8420-
2800-5   Paper ISBN 0-8420-2801-3

Ethan S. Rafuse. *A Single Grand Victory: The First Campaign and
Battle of Manassas* (2002). Cloth ISBN 0-8420-2875-7
Paper ISBN 0-8420-2876-5

John G. Selby. *Virginians at War: The Civil War Experiences of Seven Young Confederates* (2002). Cloth ISBN 0-8420-5054-X Paper ISBN 0-8420-5055-8

Edward K. Spann. *Gotham at War: New York City, 1860–1865* (2002). Cloth ISBN 0-8420-5056-6   Paper ISBN 0-8420-5057-4

A Single Grand Victory

To Dad, Mom,
Jon, and Stephen,
with thanks for
every thing.

Ethan
West Point, NY 10996
10 Apr 2002

A Single Grand Victory
The First Campaign and Battle of Manassas

The American Crisis Series
BOOKS ON THE CIVIL WAR ERA
NO. 7

Ethan S. Rafuse

A Scholarly Resources Inc. Imprint
Wilmington, Delaware

© 2002 by Scholarly Resources Inc.
All rights reserved
First published 2002
Printed and bound in the United States of America

Scholarly Resources Inc.
104 Greenhill Avenue
Wilmington, DE 19805-1897
www.scholarly.com

ALL MAPS BY FRANK MARTINI.

Library of Congress Cataloging-in-Publication Data

Rafuse, Ethan Sepp, 1968–
    A single grand victory : the First Campaign and Battle of
Manassas / Ethan S. Rafuse.
        p. cm. — (The American crisis series ; no. 7)
    Includes bibliographical references (p.) and index.
    ISBN 0-8420-2875-7 (alk. paper) — ISBN 0-8420-2876-5
(pbk. : alk. paper)
    1. Bull Run, 1st Battle of, Va., 1861. I. Title. II. Series.

E472.18 .R34 2002
973.7'31—dc21   2001045762

⊗ The paper used in this publication meets the minimum require-
ments of the American National Standard for permanence of paper for printed library materials, Z39.48, 1984.

To Rachel

ABOUT THE AUTHOR

Ethan S. Rafuse received his Ph.D. in history and political science from the University of Missouri–Kansas City and has contributed essays, articles, and reviews to numerous publications, including *The Human Tradition from the Colonial Era through Reconstruction*, *Ohio History*, *Civil War Generals in Defeat*, and *The Oxford Companion to American Military History*. He has taught history at the University of Missouri–Kansas City and Johnson County Community College, Overland Park, Kansas, and is currently assistant professor of history at the United States Military Academy at West Point.

ACKNOWLEDGMENTS

Next to the actual appearance of one's book, journal, or maga-
zine article on the shelves of the neighborhood bookstore or college library, there is probably no aspect of the process of writing
for publication more gratifying than the acknowledgment and
expression of gratitude to the people without whose assistance
completion of the project would not have been possible. I would
first like to express my great appreciation for having had the pleasure and good fortune to study the Civil War under Charles P.
Poland Jr., Joseph L. Harsh, and Herman M. Hattaway. If this work
meets the high standards these three superb teachers, scholars,
and gentlemen endeavored to instill in me, I will be quite satisfied. Among Professor Hattaway's many contributions to my efforts was introducing me to Steven E. Woodworth, who invited
me to contribute a volume to the American Crisis series and who
has been a valuable source of advice and encouragement for this
project and several others. At Scholarly Resources, Matthew R.
Hershey and Linda Pote Musumeci possessed all the qualities an
author looks for in editors: rigorous but encouraging eyes, congenial personalities, and, above all, patience.

At Manassas National Battlefield Park, Edmund Raus, Chris
Bryce, and Terri Bard made invaluable contributions to my knowledge and understanding of the events of July 1861 and the fields
upon which the campaign was decided. William D. Young of
Maple Woods Community College, Kansas City, Missouri, read
the entire manuscript and offered a number of helpful comments
and suggestions. The manuscript also benefited immeasurably
from conversations about the Civil War with good friends and
colleagues such as Bill, Ronald G. Machoian, and Eric B. Fair.

During the five years I taught at Johnson County Community
College, Overland Park, Kansas, the chair of the Division of Arts,
Humanities, and Social Sciences, Doreen Maronde, and her staff
were a constant source of support and encouragement, as were
History Department chairs Dennis Merrill, Louis W. Potts, and
Patrick Peebles during the semesters I taught at the University of

Missouri–Kansas City. The staff at the Miller Nichols Library there, especially the interlibrary loan department, displayed marvelous efficiency and infinite patience as they handled my many requests for materials necessary for the completion of this book. My efforts have also benefited from the support and advice I have received from the United States Military Academy's Samuel J. Watson and my colleagues in the "Tyrannized Tercio." I also thank Frank Martini for producing the fine maps that accompany the text.

At the 1999 Northern Great Plains History Conference, session commentator Stephen Bourque offered a number of useful suggestions for improving an essay examining Erasmus Keyes's role in the First Manassas Campaign, which was later published in the August 2001 *Civil War Times Illustrated* under the title: "The Man Who Could Have Knocked Down Stonewall." I thank the publishers of *Civil War Times Illustrated* for permission to include portions of that essay in this work.

My parents, Robert and Diane Rafuse, have provided generous support for and encouragement in all my endeavors, even going so far as to walk the battlefield at Manassas with me. To list all the ways my wife Rachel has contributed to my efforts would double the length of this book. Dedicating this book to her is but partial repayment for everything she has done for me.

CONTENTS

INTRODUCTION

IN JULY 1861, Americans eagerly anticipated the first battle of a civil war that was the culmination of more than a generation of conflict over the balance between federal and state power, the direction of the nation's economic development, the character of its people, and the future of its western empire, issues that all in some way revolved around the South's commitment to black chattel slavery. Yet whatever divisions existed in the nation, most Americans, North and South, once the shooting started, agreed on one thing: A single climactic battle would result in a victory that would persuade the enemy to abandon its war aims and settle the conflict. Although a few minor clashes had already taken place at Fort Sumter and elsewhere by the third week of July 1861, it was in Virginia, somewhere in the 100 or so miles that separated Washington, the Union capital, and Richmond, the Confederate capital, that most anticipated the great battle would take place. On July 16 the grand campaign began; four days later along the banks of Bull Run, the Confederacy would claim victory in the first battle of a war that to the vast surprise of the American people would end up lasting four years and claim over 600,000 lives.

The Campaign and Battle of First Manassas, or Bull Run,[1] holds a curious place in Civil War history. Its status as the first major battle of the war makes it a subject of undeniable importance. Yet it has not attracted the sort of attention in the literature on the war that other major campaigns in the eastern theater have received.[2] This is no doubt attributable in part to the scale of the battle. Although it impressed observers at the time, the numbers engaged at Bull Run paled in comparison to later clashes between the blue and the gray at Antietam, Gettysburg, and Second Manassas. The naive assumptions, rampant hubris, and often silly behavior of the amateur soldiers, officers, and political leaders whose actions and decisions shaped the campaign lent an almost comic quality to the war's first major military operation. Consequently, the campaign has often been perceived as simply a curious episode in American history, one in which both sides wore the same uniforms, railroads were used to shift troops about, an eccentric former college professor stood "like a stone wall," and green Union soldiers picked blackberries before racing crowds of curious spectators back to Washington.

I undertook this study with two goals in mind. First, I hoped to provide a thorough and engrossing narrative of this important campaign and battle that would provide the reader with a clear understanding of the men and events that shaped its outcome. *A Single Grand Victory* chronicles the events between the fall of Fort Sumter and the beginning of the Bull Run Campaign to delineate the factors that led Abraham Lincoln to order an offensive against Manassas Junction at a time when his most prominent military men advised against such a move. The descriptions and analyses of the individuals and the operational and strategic factors that influenced the manner in which the campaign was conducted and the critical events and operational and tactical decisions that shaped its course and outcome follow.

This work is intended to go beyond the almost exclusive emphasis of traditional Civil War campaign studies on personalities, strategy, and tactics. Although these earlier chronicles have been valuable for their insights into how particular campaigns were conducted, they usually provided limited information as to how the battle and the behavior of the participants reflected broader themes in Civil War history. Drawing upon the work of recent scholars such as Reid Mitchell, Philip S. Paludan, and James M. McPherson on Civil War America, my second goal was to provide the reader with insights into American life in the nineteenth century by examining what motivated men to fight in 1861 and analyzing the factors that led both societies to expect the war would be a short one. Americans in the North and South did not believe the war's outcome would be determined by a single clash of arms because they all lacked good sense. Rather, as this study delineates, their respective cultures had socialized them to believe that wars were usually decided by a single major engagement, that the outcome of battles was determined by the character of the armies and the righteousness of one's cause, and that the enemy, both in cause and character, was inferior.

Although there have already been a number of works that chronicle this campaign, at present two stand out: William C.

Davis's *Battle at Bull Run*, and John J. Hennessy's *The First Battle of Manassas*.[3] Davis's book is quite good on the campaign as a whole but is not as thorough as Hennessy's in its treatment of the actual battle; nor does it do much to place the campaign in a cultural context. Hennessy's work, on the other hand, is unmatched in its description of the battle's tactics and actual fighting but devotes limited attention to the battle's broader strategic and political context. In its narrative of the campaign, *A Single Grand Victory* seeks to combine the strengths of these two fine studies in a way that will engross and reward those interested in traditional "drums and trumpets" military history, while offering information and insights on the campaign's broader cultural context that will inform and appeal to enthusiasts of the "New Military History" as well.

NOTES

1. This is as good a place as any to address the question of what to call a campaign that, like so many in the Civil War, is known by two names: First Bull Run and First Manassas (after the battle it was also referred to as the battle of Young's Branch). Tradition has it that the North named battles after the nearest physical feature (for example, Antietam Creek or Stones River), while the South named them after the nearest town such as Sharpsburg or Murfreesboro. Although there are those who attach great symbolic importance to this matter, I agree with James M. McPherson that there is no inherent superiority in either name and will use them interchangeably. For the sake of simplicity, the National Park Service has tended to adopt the policy of using the name favored by the side that won the battle, which seems reasonable enough to me.

2. For example, the series edited by Gary W. Gallagher (initially for the Kent State University Press and now for the University of North Carolina Press) which consists of anthologies of scholarly essays on particular campaigns, has ignored First Bull Run, but has devoted a volume to the Fredericksburg, Chancellorsville, Wilderness, Spotsylvania, Peninsula, and 1864 Shenandoah Valley Campaigns; covered the Maryland Campaign twice; published a separate volume on each of the three days of Gettysburg; and currently has in the works volumes on Second Manassas and the 1862 Shenandoah Valley Campaign.

3. William C. Davis, *Battle at Bull Run: A History of the First Major Campaign of the Civil War* (New York: Doubleday, 1977); and John J. Hennessy, *The First Battle of Manassas: An End to Innocence, July 18–21, 1861* (Lynchburg, VA: H. E. Howard, 1989). For other works on the battle, the reader is directed to the Bibliographical Essay that follows the text.

CHAPTER ONE

"AN IMMENSELY POWERFUL IDEA"

FEW AMERICANS IN THE spring and early summer of 1861 anticipated that the shooting war that began at Fort Sumter would last
four years and cost more than 600,000 American lives. Consequently, the period between Fort Sumter and the first major battle
of the war was distinguished by naive assumptions and brash
talk that would appear foolish only a few years later. Perhaps the
most common idea Americans brought to the banks of Bull Run
in July 1861 was that it would take only a single major battle to
decide the outcome of the struggle. A single grand victory, Northerners and Southerners were equally sanguine, would be sufficient to convince the other side of the hopelessness of its cause
and persuade its adherents to abandon their war aims.

Although in retrospect they were horribly short-sighted,
Americans were not completely irrational in their belief that a
single battle could decide the American Civil War if one looks at
the entire military history of the Western world in the nineteenth
century. To be sure, the War of 1812, the Civil War, and the Franco-
Prussian War were long, drawn-out conflicts in which it took several campaigns to determine the outcome, yet the nineteenth
century did not lack instances where a single battle effectively
decided the outcome of a war. Austerlitz (1805), the most spectacular and celebrated of Napoleon's victories, had ended the War
of the Third Coalition. Solferino had decided the outcome of the
Austro-Franco War of 1859, and, one year after the Civil War
ended, a single battle at Könnigrätz (Sadowa), on July 3, 1866,
would give Prussia victory in its war with Austria.

The idea that a single battle could end the Civil War reflected
a general view in the United States that war, as historians Herman
Hattaway and Archer Jones defined the view, "consisted of battles
and military science consisted solely of leadership in combat." It

3

was a lesson Americans had received from the books they read. The most popular of these books was Sir Edward Creasy's *Fifteen Decisive Battles of the World from Marathon to Waterloo*. Published in 1851, Creasy's book quickly became, writes the celebrated British scholar John Keegan, "one of the great Victorian best-sellers . . . [reflected] in the frequency with which it was republished—thirty-eight times in the forty-eight years between 1851 and 1894." Although Creasy intended for his book, in Keegan's words, to be simply "a jolly good read" and thus oversimplified his analysis of matters, the concept of decisive battles quickly became "an immensely powerful idea . . . which has never lost its impetus."[1]

From Creasy's book and other popular military histories, nineteenth-century Americans learned that in a single day on a single battlefield in a single crucial engagement a whole empire could be destroyed, a nation's independence assured, and the fate of millions determined by the actions of a single army led by a brilliant commander. This concept of war almost totally ignored logistics, political factors, strategy, and other aspects of military operations. Instead, war was conceived of almost purely as a test of character. What determined the outcome of the decisive battles that determined the outcome of wars in the popular mind was the brilliance of commanders and the courage of their armies. Victory inevitably went to the side that was superior in character and virtue.

The popular belief that wars were decided by a single battle, the outcome of which would be determined by the respective characters of the contending parties, made it inevitable that, as they contemplated the Civil War in 1861, Northerners and Southerners would base their expectations on their perceptions of the respective virtues of their societies. And when each side contemplated the nature of the enemy, each saw much to inspire confidence that the war would not last long.

～ Northern confidence that the war would be short was rooted in several factors. First, the North possessed overwhelming material advantages over the South, a fact that the Ohio-born superintendent of the Louisiana Military Academy attempted without success to impress upon one of his colleagues after

Lincoln's election. "The North," William T. Sherman pointed out, "can make a steam-engine, locomotive or railway car; hardly a yard of cloth or shoes can you make. You are rushing into war with one of the most powerful, ingeniously mechanical, and determined people on earth. You are bound to fail. Only in your spirit and determination are you prepared for war. In all else you are totally unprepared. . . . If your people would only stop and think, they must see that in the end you will surely fail."[2]

Of the 31,443,321 persons counted in the 1860 U.S. Census, 22,339,989 lived in states that remained loyal to the Union. Only 9,103,332 lived in the eleven states of the Confederacy, of whom 3,521,110 were slaves and 132,760 were free blacks. Although its advantage in total population was impressive, even greater was the superiority the North enjoyed in the number of white males of military age. For every man of military age President Jefferson Davis could call on for service to the Confederacy, U.S. President Abraham Lincoln had almost three. Nor did the North enjoy superiority only in manpower. In 1861 the North had 1,300,000 workers employed at 110,000 manufacturing enterprises; the South could claim only 110,000 workers and 18,000 factories or workshops. These Northern enterprises produced 97 percent of the nation's firearms, 90 percent of its shoes, and 94 percent of its cloth. In coal and pig iron production, the North enjoyed more than a 20-to-1 advantage. The North also possessed over 21,000 miles of railroads and was furiously building more in 1861; the South had only 9,283 miles. In addition, the North produced over 90 percent of the locomotives built in the United States and, unlike the South, possessed the means necessary to repair and build roads quickly. And although unimpressive by European standards, the ninety-ship, 9,000-man U.S. Navy dwarfed anything the agrarian South could hope to scrape together.

Even in agriculture, the North enjoyed great advantages over the South. Although the South consciously identified itself as an agrarian society and cotton was the most celebrated and lucrative of the crops produced in the United States, the North, with Yankee farmers embracing new technologies, such as the McCormick reaper, actually produced more than twice as much wheat and corn. Indeed, in 1860 the value of Northern crops actually exceeded that of crops grown in the South. To make matters worse for the South, her richest agricultural and industrial regions were located in the northernmost provinces and thus were vulnerable to Union invasions.

To be sure, it would take a good deal of time to mobilize all of these resources, longer than most people in 1861 expected the war would last. Nonetheless, the fact that Southerners would challenge the power of the national government when they were so badly outnumbered, suggested to Northerners that wisdom and reason were lacking in the South. Virginia Unionist John Minor Botts spoke for many when, after considering the relative strength of the two sides, he commented: "You ask . . . what I think will be the result of this rebellion? This question is . . . briefly answered. The history of the world in 6,000 years has furnished but one instance of a David and Goliath."[3] Either the South was ignorant of the facts or so deluded by their passions that they were unable to "stop and think" long enough to recognize reality. Nations based on ignorance and/or deluded passion rarely lasted long.

More important than the results of the 1860 census in inspiring Northern confidence that the Union cause would prevail in a short war was a faith in the martial prowess of its young men. As British scholar Marcus Cunliffe has shown, the notion of a uniquely martial antebellum South has been exaggerated and is to a large extent the product of post–Civil War developments. After the war, he points out, Northern intellectuals disillusioned with the shabby materialism of the Gilded Age romanticized the antebellum South as a place of lost agrarian virtues where noble and gallant Cavaliers served a higher cause than money. To assuage the pain of defeat, Southerners embraced this mythological image of their society and the myth of the Lost Cause, which was rooted in a belief that it was superior Northern resources, the treachery of James Longstreet, the mendacity of Southern politicians—anything but the qualitative superiority of Yankee soldiers—that produced defeat. Consequently, after 1865, writes Cunliffe, "Both sides were therefore prepared to subscribe to the semi-legendary version of a Cavalier or militant South. . . . Preoccupied in the Gilded Age by other things than war, the North was willing to permit the South to lay claim to the nation's military tradition. . . . Scholars soothed Southern pride, and did not wound that of the North, by reiterating the hallowed anecdotes of Cavalierdom."[4]

In fact, the North had a strong military tradition before the Civil War. It was Massachusetts troops that had claimed the first major triumph of American arms in an international conflict, the 1745 capture of the French fortress of Louisbourg during King George's War. And although it was a Virginian who was "first in war" during the Revolution, the best of George Washington's subordinates in the Continental Army—Nathanael Greene, John Sullivan, Anthony Wayne, Henry Knox, and Benedict Arnold— all hailed from states north of the Mason–Dixon line. The "Father of the U.S. Navy," John Adams, was also a Northerner, and there was no greater champion of a strong and efficient regular army during the early national period than Alexander Hamilton of New York. Anthony Wayne, the commander of the Republic's first quasi-professional force, the American Legion that won the battle of Fallen Timbers in 1794, was a Pennsylvanian. The first commanding general of the U.S. Army, Jacob Brown, who won his reputation in the War of 1812—a war fought mainly on Northern soil—also hailed from New York. And although Brown's longest-serving successor before the Civil War, Winfield Scott, was a Virginia native, he never considered going with his state when it seceded.

In terms of military education, the South did possess the two most celebrated military colleges in the country, the Virginia Military Institute and the Charleston Citadel. The North boasted several of its own, however, such as the American Literary, Scientific, and Military Academy at Norwich, Vermont, the nation's first military school, whose founder, Alden Partridge, was a former superintendent at West Point. Other highly regarded military schools located in the North included Mount Pleasant Military Academy in New York, the Highland Military Academy in Massachusetts, and the American Classical and Military Lyceum in Pennsylvania.

In addition, the United States Military Academy was located at West Point, New York. The amount of abuse the academy was subjected to during the Civil War by Radical Republicans in the North, who pointed to the number of West Pointers who served in the Confederate army and the reluctance of those graduates who served the Union to conduct a hard war against Southern property and institutions as evidence that Southern influences prevailed at the school, would seem to suggest the academy was a pariah in its own section. The facts belie this impression, however.

Southerners did receive a disproportionate number of appointments to the academy due to the three-fifths clause of the Constitution giving slave states extra members of congress. Yet around 64 percent of West Point graduates prior to 1861 came from free states (not counting the slave states that remained loyal to the Union), with New York producing the largest number of graduates and Pennsylvania the second largest. Indeed, New York alone produced 317, while the total combined number of graduates from Virginia, North Carolina, and South Carolina, the three Confederate states that produced the most West Point graduates, was only 265.[5] Northerners also tended to outperform their Southern counterparts at the academy, dominating the top ranks of class lists at graduation. To be sure, when the war began a disproportionate number of officers were of Southern origin, but this was only pronounced in one arm of the service, the cavalry. Moreover, any consideration of the relative number of Northerners and Southerners still in the army in 1861 must take into account that Northern graduates were more likely to be lured out of the service by opportunities in the civilian economy, which were far greater for those in the Engineers, the elite branch of the service that was open only to top graduates, and that those opportunities were greater in the North.

If Southerners took confidence from the militia organizations that had enjoyed renewed vitality in the aftermath of John Brown's raid at Harpers Ferry, Northerners could take equal pride and confidence in the large volunteer companies that were a fixture of life in communities all over the North. In fact, the largest reviews of American troops in peacetime before the Civil War actually took place at the annual encampments of volunteer militia in the North. At the 1860 Massachusetts encampment, for example, an estimated 6,000 troops participated. To be sure, these events often saw more attention devoted to the cultivation of political and social contacts than to boosting military efficiency. Nonetheless, they belie the notion that Puritan Massachusetts—

often presented as the antithesis to Cavalier Virginia after the war—was deficient in martial spirit.

Indeed, the most celebrated volunteer unit in the entire country before the Civil War hailed from the North—Elmer Ellsworth's Chicago-based United States Zouave Cadets. And certainly no one who witnessed the response in the summer of 1860 to Ellsworth's Zouaves when they went on a tour of twenty American cities—none of which were located in a state that would join the Confederacy—could have seriously doubted that an enthusiasm for things military existed in the antebellum North. Everywhere Ellsworth and his men went they were greeted by huge crowds, who loudly cheered their exhibitions, and by local volunteer companies, who eagerly accepted their challenge to compete in drill and often found themselves swamped with new recruits in the aftermath of Ellsworth's visit.

The North also drew confidence from what it perceived to be the superior masculinity of its men. This perception was rooted in the different ways the two sections developed economically and socially during the antebellum period and how those ways led each section to define manliness. As the North became more industrial and commercially oriented, it came to celebrate the virtues of self-discipline, sobriety, hard work, and the pursuit of material success. In the North's open, competitive, free-labor society, writes historian Nina Silber, "Economic self-improvement demanded moral and religious self-cultivation. . . . 'Respectability' became the new watchword for northern men." In contrast, Northerners believed that in a slave society hard work was denigrated, the incentives for self-improvement were absent, and young men did not develop the manly self-control that came from growing up in a free-labor society. Consequently, Southern men were, like women, governed by their passions. In Silber's words, "The southern aristocrat, whose slaves relieved him of economic responsibilities, was assumed to have little interest in hard work and self-control . . . [and] was assailed for his laziness and licentiousness, qualities which placed him at the opposite pole from the industrious and restrained northerner." During the antebellum period, Northern men interpreted the South's celebration of honor, chivalry, and aristocracy as evidence of the backwardness and stagnation of Southern society. The brashness and boastfulness of Southern men was viewed as merely a facade that, although designed to conceal their deficiency in the self-discipline that defined true masculinity, actually exposed it.[6]

In addition to the image of the North as the rational male disciplining the impassioned Southern female, "Northerners who were pro-war," writes historian Reid Mitchell, "used the image of unruly children who had to be made to obey" in describing the South. In this view, the federal government was considered the source of paternal authority (the development of the Father Abraham image for President Lincoln was inevitable), which flighty and impudent Southern children revolted against because they lacked the maturity to appreciate its beneficence and Northerners defended out of a cool, mature filial obligation. Alternately, the North relied on the image of the schoolhouse. "The South," in Mitchell's words, "needed to be taught a lesson. The North was the schoolmaster, the army the rod, and the South the disobedient child."[7]

Also important in inspiring Northern confidence in the spring of 1861 that a single battle would decide the war was an inability to believe that the people of the South were truly serious about secession. This view had its roots in what was known as the Slave Power thesis. Northerners, especially Republicans, believed that secession was the work of the small minority of Southerners who owned slaves—the so-called Slave Power—who dominated the ignorant masses who resided in their South and had tricked them into secession by inflaming the temporary passions aroused by Lincoln's election. The Slave Power thesis and its underlying analysis of Southern society as a place where the slaveocracy dominated and kept the masses ignorant and degraded had two effects on the Northern mind-set as it contemplated how difficult the task of subduing the rebellion would be.

First, it fueled contempt for the common soldier of the South. "Long before any invasion of the South," writes Mitchell, "Northern soldiers were convinced that the Confederate armies were composed of degraded, intimidated men . . . the dupes of a self-styled aristocracy."[8] Armies composed of such poor timber could hardly be expected to put up much resistance when confronted by the true men in the ranks of Northern armies when they met in battle. Second, because Northerners believed secession lacked true support among the Southern populace, they did not think it would take much effort to persuade the Southern masses to lay down their arms. Since the majority of Southerners were truly loyal to the Union, Northerners believed all they would have to do was nudge them into taking a sober second thought, which would lead them to realize that the North really meant them no harm and thus to revolt against the Slave Power that had hoodwinked them.

Reinforcing Northern confidence was the fact that many had serious doubts that the Slave Power itself was truly serious about secession and destroying the great republic that Southerners had played such a conspicuous role in founding. As they saw it, the threat of secession was merely an elaborate bluff, a tactic that had enabled the slaveocracy to bully the Northern majority—much as they bullied the majority of Southerners who had no interest in slavery—for decades because the North had never called them on it. The actual secession of the Southern states and establishment of the Confederacy was simply designed, in the words of one Northern soldier, "to intimidate the victors [of the 1860 election] sufficiently to procure concessions from them."[9] It was not, Northerners believed, something the South, and especially not those Southerners who did not own slaves, would truly fight to the death for once they realized the North would not back down.

Not all of the 5,449,462 whites who lived in the Confederacy were fully committed to the new nation. In the mountainous regions of western Virginia and eastern Tennessee, the population never supported or accepted the legitimacy of secession. Even in the Lower South the vote for secession had hardly been unanimous. Despite the hothouse atmosphere produced by Lincoln's election, in Georgia secessionist candidates prevailed in elections for delegates to their state convention by only about 2,500 votes out of more than 95,000 cast; in Louisiana, by only around 1,700 votes out of 38,000 cast.[10] In the Upper South, many were either lukewarm about secession or had only reluctantly converted after Lincoln called for troops after Fort Sumter. Of those who supported secession, it is impossible to determine what percentage of Southerners truly believed in the need for Southern independence in 1861 and how many were simply unwilling to swim against the tide of outrage that swept through the South after Lincoln's call for troops. But it was certainly not unreasonable for Union policymakers to be sanguine that secession had been an act of rashness prompted by the unleashing of popular passions, that could be reversed.

Yes, Northerners were certain, the war to preserve the Union would be a relatively short affair. A single decisive victory in battle would demonstrate the folly of resistance to the superior power and manhood of the free states, call the secessionist bluff, and awaken the good sense of the Southern people. Once they were chastised by defeat and became aware of the true steel in the Northern character, the people of the South would take a sober second thought, realize they had been duped into secession and a war they could not win, and return to the Union.

⁓ The belief that the Civil War would be decided by one battle was hardly unique to the North. Indeed, if anything, Southerners were even more extravagant in their confidence that their war aim, independence, could be achieved at a relatively low cost. This attitude was exemplified by the offer of Leroy P. Walker, the first Confederate secretary of war, to "wipe up with his pocket handkerchief all the blood shed as a result of the South's withdrawal from the Union."[11]

Regardless of what the actual facts were, Southerners truly did believe in the martial superiority of their soldiers and society in 1861, and that in a fair fight one Confederate could whip three, four, or even ten Yankees. "The fact is," President Jefferson Davis advised a visitor who expressed amazement at the enthusiasm with which Southerners sprang to arms, "we are a military people."[12] The list of American military heroes who hailed from slave states certainly was impressive. In addition to Washington, Henry "Light-Horse Harry" Lee (the father of Robert E. Lee), Francis Marion, and Thomas Sumter from the Revolution, the South had also produced Andrew Jackson, William Henry Harrison, Zachary Taylor, and Winfield Scott. Confederates also took pride in the fact that the majority of the volunteers who served in the Mexican War had come from the South. (Of course, an objective analysis of the matter would more likely attribute this predominance to the fact that the United States had fought in Mexico largely in defense of Southern interests than to any other factor. It is highly unlikely that Southerners would have so enthusiastically volunteered to help James K. Polk live up to his pledge of "54°40' or Fight" in Oregon.)

The South's self-image as a uniquely martial society was re-inforced when Southerners contemplated the characters of each sector's respective president. Davis was a West Point graduate, a Mexican War hero, and distinguished former secretary of war. Whom had the Yankees chosen as their commander in chief? A railroad lawyer and rail-splitter whose military service was lim-ited to a few weeks in the Illinois militia during the Black Hawk War! This contrast certainly, in the minds of Southerners, spoke volumes about the relative level of each society's military spirit.

The confidence of Southerners in their ability to persuade the North to abandon the effort to restore the Union with relative ease was also rooted in a contempt for Northern manhood. While Northerners were convinced that the way in which their economy and society had developed in the decades prior to the war had created a true masculinity based on self-discipline, Southerners believed it had had just the opposite effect. They saw the North as a place where pious, mother-centered households, material-ism, assertive women reformers, and urbanization had trans-formed the free states into a society of emasculated young men and degraded immigrants who lacked true manly virtues.

Yankee culture, Southerners believed, produced timid, cow-ardly young men. The outright contempt for the courage of North-erners felt by residents of the slave states was manifest in one Southern algebra textbook, written by future Confederate Gen-eral Daniel H. Hill, which presented students with the following information and asked them to calculate relative rates of travel: "The field of battle at Buena Vista is 6 1/2 miles from Saltillo. Two Indiana volunteers ran away from the field of battle at the same time, one ran half a mile per hour faster than the other and reached Saltillo 5 minutes and 54 6/11 seconds sooner than the other."[13]

Southerners believed that this cowardice in the Yankee charac-ter was in large part a product of an unseemly obsession with the pursuit of money and luxury. A popular joke in the South in 1861 asked: "How would a Southerner defeat a well-armed Yankee?"

"Buy his gun from him," was the answer.[14] Although it was impossible to ignore the outburst of martial enthusiasm in the North that greeted Lincoln's call for troops, Southerners rationalized this was merely a manifestation of a streak of unthinking fanaticism in the Northern character that had spawned abolitionism. But because Yankees lived only for money, Southerners did not believe they could long sustain their enthusiasm for abstract notions such as country and honor. Once Northerners recognized that military life meant enduring danger and self-sacrifice against a superior foe for no significant material reward, Southerners were certain the fundamental cowardice and timidity of the Yankee character would once again reassert itself.

In contrast, Southerners viewed their agrarian, patriarchal society as one that produced a true Anglo-Saxon masculinity. Like the feudal knights and Cavaliers they liked to imagine themselves the spiritual descendants of, Southerners embraced a notion of manliness that was rooted in family and personal honor and sanctioned the use of violence in its defense. Certainly, Southerners believed, products of such a society could easily overcome the emasculated refuse of Northern cities and workshops.

If Northerners took confidence in their overwhelming advantage in manpower and resources, Southerners were not impressed on that score. After all, history had taught them that it was not numbers, but the virtues of one's cause and the courage of the soldiers fighting for it that determined the outcome of wars. "The numbers opposed to us are immense," former President John Tyler, now a secessionist, advised his wife, "but twelve thousand Grecians conquered the whole power of Xerxes at Marathon, and our fathers, a mere handful, overcame the enormous power of Great Britain." Mrs. Tyler was no less confident of victory. After hearing of an early Confederate victory, she remarked to her mother: "How can it be otherwise than that? The hand of Providence should assist this holy Southern cause."[15]

In addition to their certainty of the moral superiority of their cause, Southerners were aware that they did not lack advantages of their own from a strategic standpoint. Unlike the North, the South did not have to wage a war of conquest. To win, the Confederacy merely had to offer sufficient resistance to convince the North that it could not be conquered. And in its sheer size, the

South was a formidable obstacle. The eleven states of the Confederacy consisted of three-quarters of a million square miles, more than the total territory of modern Great Britain, France, Italy, Germany, and Spain combined. In addition to its extensiveness, in many places its terrain was rugged, with insufficient roads to support an invading army. Moreover, the South possessed a railroad system that, though quantitatively and qualitatively inferior to the North's, did make it possible for Confederate military authorities to exploit their interior lines and shift supplies and troops to wherever the threat was greater. Southerners also enjoyed the traditional advantages of fighting on the defensive: better knowledge of the land and a sympathetic population that was a source of material and morale support to the officers and men of the Confederate army. "As for conquering us," wrote one Confederate secretary of war, summing up the thinking of his people in 1861, "the thing is an impossibility. There is no instance in history of a people as numerous as we are inhabiting a country so extensive as ours being subjected if true to themselves."[16]

Certainly, conquering this new Confederate nation was a job that few European observers thought the North had the power or will to pull off. After all, when he had contemplated a potential war by the nations of Europe against France, the celebrated Prussian military thinker Carl von Clausewitz theorized it would take 725,000 troops, with an active field army of 600,000, to overcome an anticipated 200,000 French defenders. And even with these overwhelming odds, Clausewitz did not define victory in terms of the complete overthrow of France or the conquest of all her territory. Instead, he believed the goal would be just to teach the French the folly of "that insolent behavior with which she has burdened Europe" by means of the occupation of her northeastern provinces only.[17]

Just as Northerners interpreted the willingness of the South to fight, despite being so badly outnumbered, as a sign that the Southern people lacked the modicum of good sense necessary to succeed as a nation, Southerners believed the inability of the North to recognize the impossibility of conquering them reflected a deficiency in the mental qualities that would be necessary to prevail in a military contest with the South. Only an unthinking fool or abolitionist fanatic could possibly look at the task facing the Lincoln administration and seriously believe the North could win, much less volunteer to serve in an army and risk his life for a cause that was certain to fail. Defeat in battle, it was believed, would awaken the deluded North to reality and force it to have sober second thoughts. Once reason regained its sway, the impossibility of conquering the South would be acknowledged and support for the war in the North would evaporate.

Another factor that inspired Southern confidence that their independence could be secured relatively easily was their expectation of receiving help from overseas. A combination of sentimental and practical factors, it was believed, would compel the nations of Europe to come to the aid of the Confederacy. First, Southerners anticipated that the monarchs and aristocrats of Europe would be glad to see the upstart American Republic divided and its power diminished. Second, Southerners believed that European political leaders would naturally be more sympathetic to a nation led by an aristocracy, such as the South's, than they would be toward the more egalitarian North. Finally, Southerners were confident that Europe's demand for cotton would compel their political leaders to intervene in the conflict on behalf of the Confederacy. Thus, the adoption of a policy of neutrality by the governments of Great Britain and France in April 1861, which implied belligerent status on the Confederacy, was taken as a very positive sign. To be sure, out of a desire to avoid offending the North, the European powers followed up their adoption of a neutral stance by making it clear they had no intention at that point of officially granting recognition to the new Confederacy. But it was deduced that, after the South won a major victory in battle, Europe would feel free to move more aggressively and openly on their desire to see a Confederate victory.

Finally, Southerners found it hard to believe that the North was truly willing to accept the sacrifices necessary to restore the Union by force. After all, antislavery men in the North had spent a generation proclaiming the republic polluted by the existence of slavery. Would not logic lead them not only to accept but also to welcome the departure of the South from the Union? Was it not reasonable to think they would be content, after defeat in battle, as Republican newspaper editor Horace Greeley once suggested, to let the erring sisters go?

Yes, Southerners were certain, one member of their society could whip three or more representatives of the degraded offspring of Yankee culture whenever they met in battle. One battle would prove this hypothesis sufficiently and convince the North that their experiment in unrepublican coercion was not worth the trouble. Once they realized this, Southerners believed, the residents of the free states would be glad to go back to the pursuit of money that defined the Yankee character and let the Confederacy have its place in the community of independent nations.

NOTES

1. Herman Hattaway and Archer Jones, *How the North Won: A Military History of the Civil War* (Urbana: University of Illinois Press, 1982), 85; John Keegan, *The Face of Battle* (New York: Viking, 1976), 56–57. For the sake of simplicity, I will cite only direct quotes in the endnotes. Readers interested in the sources upon which the information in this book is based are referred to the Bibliographical Essay.

2. Brooks D. Simpson and Jean V. Berlin, eds., *Sherman's Civil War: Selected Correspondence of William T. Sherman, 1860–1865* (Chapel Hill: University of North Carolina Press, 1999), 3.

3. Richard Wheeler, *A Rising Thunder: From Lincoln's Election to the Battle of Bull Run: An Eyewitness History* (New York: HarperCollins, 1994), 108.

4. Marcus Cunliffe, *Soldiers and Civilians: The Martial Spirit in America, 1775–1865* (Boston: Little, Brown, and Company, 1968), 381–82.

5. Ibid., 364–65.

6. Nina Silber, "Intemperate Men, Spiteful Women, and Jefferson Davis," in *Divided Houses: Gender and the Civil War*, edited by Catherine Clinton and Nina Silber (New York: Oxford University Press, 1992), 287–88.

7. Reid Mitchell, *The Vacant Chair: The Northern Soldier Leaves Home* (New York: Oxford University Press, 1993), 15.

8. Idem, *Civil War Soldiers* (New York: Viking, 1988), 32–33.

9. Seldon Connor, "The Boys of 1861," *War Papers Read before the Commandery of the State of Maine Military Order of the Loyal Legion of the United States*, 4 vols. (Portland: The Thorston Print, 1898), 1:324.

10. David M. Potter, *The Impending Crisis, 1848–1861*, completed and edited by Don E. Fehrenbacher (New York: Harper and Row, 1976), 496–97.

11. Richard E. Beringer, Herman Hattaway, Archer Jones, and William N. Still Jr., *Why the South Lost the Civil War* (Athens: University of Georgia Press, 1986), 87–88.

12. William Howard Russell, *My Diary North and South*, edited by Eugene H. Berwanger (Philadelphia: Temple University Press, 1988 [1863]), 126.

13. Hal Bridges, *Lee's Maverick General: Daniel Harvey Hill* (New York; McGraw-Hill, 1961), 26.

14. Philip Shaw Paludan, *"A People's Contest": The Union and the Civil War, 1861–1865* (New York: Harper and Row, 1988), 24.

15. Henry Steele Commager, *The Blue and the Gray: The Story of the Civil War as Told by Participants* (1950; reprint ed., New York: Fairfax Press, 1982), 45–46.

16. Hattaway and Jones, *How the North Won*, 18.

17. Carl von Clausewitz, *On War*, edited and translated by Michael Howard and Peter Paret (Princeton, NJ: Princeton University Press, 1976 [1832]), 633–36.

CHAPTER TWO

LIONS AROUSED

THE SURRENDER OF Federal forces under Major Robert Anderson at Fort Sumter on April 14, 1861, ended several weeks of tension over the fate of the fort and its garrison. More important, it answered the question that had gripped the Republic since South Carolina led the states of the Lower South out of the Union in December: Would there be peaceful secession, peaceful reunion, or civil war? In preparation for war, Lincoln issued a call the day after Fort Sumter's surrender for 75,000 3-month militia to deal with "combinations too powerful to be suppressed by the ordinary course of judicial proceedings." Then, on April 19, he proclaimed a blockade of the southern coastline.[1]

In retrospect, Lincoln's call for only 75,000 3-month troops seems terribly shortsighted, especially in light of what would happen during the First Manassas Campaign and the four years of war that followed. Its wisdom fades even more when one considers that over one month before Fort Sumter, the Confederate government had authorized the raising of an army of 100,000 men for twelve months, and more than 60,000 had already enlisted by the time Lincoln issued his call for troops.

When assessing Lincoln's action, however, several factors must be taken into consideration. First, Lincoln, for whom the war was above all a test of the nation's political and constitutional institutions, was constrained by law, specifically a 1795 law that allowed the militia to be called up only for thirty days after a meeting of Congress. Second, Lincoln was as committed a believer in the Slave Power thesis as could be found in the United States in 1861. "It may well be questioned," he would tell Congress in July, "whether there is, to-day, a majority of the legally qualified voters of any State, except perhaps, South Carolina, in favor of disunion. There is much reason to believe that the Union men are the majority in many, if not every other one, of the so-called seceded States."[2] He may have hoped that a call for 75,000 troops would display sufficient firmness to satisfy Northerners outraged by Fort Sumter, assure Southern Unionists that he would not acquiesce in secession, and, in the game of bluff many still believed the South was engaged in, raise the stakes to the point where the secessionists would fold. At the same time, he did not want to call out a force so overwhelming that it would confirm Southern fears that he intended to ravage their society.

It became clear fairly quickly, however, that 75,000 troops and a blockade had done little to cow the secessionists. Indeed, the main effect of Lincoln's actions was to push four more states into the Confederacy. In Virginia, Unionist sentiment vanished virtually overnight, and two days after the proclamation was issued the state convention, which had previously rejected secession by comfortable majorities, passed an ordinance of secession. "The new Confederate flag was hoisted on the Capitol; and from every hilltop," wrote one observer in Richmond, "the excitement was beyond all description; the satisfaction unparalleled. . . . At last Virginia was free from the obligation that bound her to a Union that had become hateful." John Minor Botts, one of the city's few remaining Unionists, found the residents of Richmond in such a state that he complained: "To reason with them would be like darting straws against the wind." In Goldsboro, North Carolina, a British visitor was stunned at the sight of "flushed faces, wild eyes, screaming mouths, hurrahing for 'Jeff Davis' and 'the Southern Confederacy' . . . true revolutionary furor in full sway."[3] Within weeks, conventions in Tennessee, Arkansas, and North Carolina, all of which had resoundingly rejected secession before Fort Sumter, followed Virginia's lead and left the Union in response to popular outrage over the Lincoln administration's determination to use military force to stamp out secession.

Although Lincoln's call for troops had a counterproductive effect in the South, provoking yet another wave of secession without impressing the Southern masses, in combination with the events at Charleston Harbor, it unleashed a tumultuous outpouring of patriotic fervor in the North. "It seemed as if the people had suddenly started up broad-awake from a deep slumber," one man later recalled. "The war news produced a real intoxication.

. . . Thoroughly aroused indignation and patriotism could find no expression that seemed adequate." In communities throughout the loyal states, citizens rushed to their town squares to express their outrage at the firing on Fort Sumter and pledge devotion to the flag and the Union in such force that one astonished Ohio legislator greeted a colleague by gleefully exclaiming, "The people have gone stark mad!"[4]

To the east, in Boston, "pulpits thundered with denunciations of the rebellion . . . ministers counseled war rather than longer submission to the imperious South. Better that the land be drenched with fraternal blood than that any further concessions should be made to the slaveocracy. . . . The same vigorous speech was heard on the streets, through which surged hosts of excited men." In Portland, Maine, a bank clerk reported that "the popular sentiment has changed as if by magic. . . . People are flinging out American flags by the wholesale. Horses and even dogs have little flags fastened on their harnesses or collars. . . . Everybody is aroused." A Union mass meeting in New York City drew a crowd estimated by newspapers at 250,000. "The attitude of New York and the whole North at this time is magnificent," George Templeton Strong recorded in his diary during the heady week after Fort Sumter. "Perfect unanimity, earnestness, and readiness to make every sacrifice for the support of law and national life. . . . Every other man, woman, and child bearing a flag or decorated with a cockade. Flags from almost every building. The city seems to have gone suddenly wild and crazy."[5]

Newspapers that had advocated compromise or were deemed insufficient in their patriotism found themselves confronted by mobs who compelled them to display the flag conspicuously. Republicans and Democrats who for years had waged bitter political campaigns just weeks before came together in a spirit of unity, following the example of the leader of the Northern Democracy, Stephen A. Douglas. Although he had championed compromise during the secession winter and believed that the Lincoln administration should have abandoned Fort Sumter to avoid a fight with the rebels, when news reached Washington that the South had fired on the flag, Douglas rushed to the Executive Mansion to pledge his support to his old rival Lincoln. When Lincoln showed Douglas his proclamation calling for 75,000 troops, the "Little Giant" fully approved the call for troops, but remarked: "I would make it 200,000." After the meeting, Douglas embarked on a speaking tour of the free states, giving speeches that threw more fuel on the fire of Northern determination to uphold the Union. "We must rally to the defense of the government—to the reestablishment of the Union," he told enthusiastic crowds in the old Northwest. "There are only two sides to the question . . . There can be no neutrals in this war, *only patriots—or traitors.*"[6]

Young men throughout the North responded to Lincoln's call for troops by offering their services at recruiting offices. In Massachusetts, one soldier later recalled how the in rush of his neighbors to enlist fostered a salutary "rivalry on every hand as to who should first reach the recruiting office . . . in a veritable sense were all of them in a state of feverish expectation."[7] In Ohio, Governor William Dennison reported to Washington that Lincoln's call for troops had provoked "great rejoicing." Soon Dennison and every other governor in the Union found himself with far more eager young men than the government had requested. When told by Washington that the federal government required only thirteen regiments from the Buckeye State, Dennison immediately fired back that he already had more than enough to fill twenty regiments and feared that to organize any less would dampen the spirit of his constituents. "The lion in us," he crowed, "is aroused."[8]

In July, President Lincoln would reflect on the response to his call for troops and express astonishment that "one of the greatest perplexities of the government is to avoid receiving troops faster than it can provide for them." For all of the problems, Lincoln nevertheless was immensely gratified by the response of the loyal states to his proclamation. "The people," he believed the actions of the North demonstrated, "will save their government, if the government itself, will do its part."[9]

Lincoln's efforts to mobilize Northern resources in the spring of 1861 were not so impressive as those of his Confederate counterpart, however. Although the North had a much larger population base, by July 1861, Davis had nearly an equal number of troops (approximately 120,000) mobilized for the only time in the entire war.[10] This was attributable primarily to the earlier start the Davis administration and the Confederate congress made in raising troops. Yet it must be noted that, for all his faults, the mobilization of his nation's military resources was one area in which Davis would consistently outperform Lincoln throughout the war.

～ In both the North and South, the recruitment of soldiers followed basically the same pattern. The process began at the local level. The first to rally to the flag in any community were of course the preexisting volunteer or militia companies. Additional companies would then be organized from the raw recruits. Usually, a man of prominence in the community or someone from one of the volunteer companies who aspired to a higher rank would go to local authorities and offer to recruit a 100-man company. The tacit understanding was that he would become the captain and the associates who aided him would be commissioned lieutenants, although officers still had to pass a vote of the men in the unit before they held their rank officially. Once a company had been organized, sometimes there would be some cursory instruction in company drill, often times not, before it traveled to the state capital or some other point designated by state authorities for the gathering of troops. There the company would be brought together with nine others to form a regiment whose title would be designated by the order in which it was mustered into the service (for instance, the Seventeenth Virginia, the Eleventh New York, or the Second Ohio). The regiment would be commanded by a colonel with the assistance of a lieutenant colonel and a major, all of whom were appointed by the governor, subject in nearly all instances to the approval of the men in the regiment in an election. The amount of training troops received from their states varied, but usually was only sufficient to provide the most rudimentary instruction in basic drill before, if they were not already there, the regiment was forwarded to the place the U.S. or Confederate government designated for the assembly of larger units. Once there, the regiment would be combined with three or four others to form a brigade, commanded by a colonel or brigadier general appointed by the War Department, sometimes in consultation with the department commander, but always with the approval of the president and his chief military advisers. During the Bull Run Campaign, the brigade would be the largest unit in a Confederate army, although the Union would organize divisions consisting of two to four brigades. Later in the war two or three divisions would be combined to form a corps.

The way that units were raised reinforced the importance of the local community in the lives of Civil War soldiers, a factor that would play as great a role as any other in motivating and sustaining them. Although developments in transportation and communication were in the process of changing everything, the United States in the mid-nineteenth century was still largely a society of what historian Robert H. Wiebe has labeled "island communities."[11] Restricted in their interaction with outsiders, for most Americans in the mid-nineteenth century their world was still the local community. It was the local community whose standards they respected, good opinion they coveted, ideals they embraced, and interests they would go to war to defend.

When soldiers went to war in 1861, they did so as representatives of their local communities. "Soldiers believed," writes historian Reid Mitchell, "that they were fighting for their families and communities. Rallies, public meetings, exhortations from the press and pulpit had encouraged the teenagers and men . . . to enlist; their communities presented them with homemade flags, promised always to remember their bravery, and marched them out of town."[12] In the spring of 1861, communities could not do enough for the young men who rushed to recruiting officers to volunteer in its defense. Small communities raised thousands of dollars for the support of the families whose loved ones went to the front, soldiers were effusively praised by town elders for their bravery and patriotism in public ceremonies, and the women of the community showered the would-be heroes with flowers and treats as they departed for the front.

Nothing so symbolized the enduring bonds between the soldiers and the communities they came from as the flags they carried to the front. In Haverhill, Massachusetts, it only took one word from a member of its company in April 1861 to set Nancy Buswell to work on a flag for the unit in the face of the objections of her soldier brother. "You can't do it, Nancy; you haven't time," the brother complained. "It is now Wednesday, and we shall have to start Friday." "I'll find time," Mrs. Buswell replied, "if I have to work day and night." And she did just that. "Working continuously fifty-six hours, with only two hours to sleep in that long interval," one appreciative man later recalled, "it was 'Stitch, stitch, stitch' . . . fashioning the stars and stripes of her country's flag with her needle, that most delicate of weapons, proving it a fit companion of sword and bayonet."[13] The ceremonies in which companies were presented with their flag were always solemn occasions for both the community and the soldiers. Patriotic oratory reminded the men of their duty to their nation and brought forth pledges on the part of the officers and men to protect the flag always and never bring shame or dishonor to the community.

The sense of fighting for the local community was reinforced by the fact that the company that marched under the flag was composed of friends, lifelong neighbors, and relatives. The soldiers in the company had learned the same patriotic ideals in their local schoolhouses, internalized the same notions of honor and masculinity that prevailed in their local community, and been inculcated with a determination never to bring shame to their families or community. The eyes of their community were constantly on them as well, as soldiers wrote letters home to family, friends, and local newspapers, reporting on their comrades' behavior in camp and in battle. In return, members of the communities sent letters exhorting the men to do their duty and reminding them of the reasons they fought.

Northern soldiers went to war having been taught by their teachers, families, and political leaders that, in the immortal words of Daniel Webster, Liberty and Union were "one and inseparable." By threatening the Union, they believed, the South endangered the institution that guaranteed liberty; in defending the Union, Northerners believed they were defending the liberties of their families and communities that had been won during the Revolution. The patriotism the soldiers felt was rooted in a belief that each man had a mystical bond to keep with his ancestors who had forged a republic for liberty and was obligated to defend the institutions that preserved that liberty for his family, community, and future generations. "Papa is away from you," one Union officer advised his children in 1861, "to fight for our country . . . that you and all the little children of America may have all the blessings that your papas and grandpapas have had."

Another man, looking back on his first days in the army during the heady time of April 1861, recalled: "I felt as if I were 'lining up' with the men of '76."[14]

The antithesis of liberty was slavery, and, although most Northerners who went to war in 1861 did not do so with the intention of abolishing the South's peculiar institution, they did view themselves as engaged in a struggle with an enemy who revolted against the Union out of hostility to liberty. In the view of Northern soldiers, the Slave Power not only enslaved blacks, but Southern whites as well. In the words of historian Reid Mitchell, "Those aristocrats, having destroyed democracy in their own section of the country, now sought to destroy democracy in the North, by denying an open election [and] breaking up a Union that guaranteed free institutions."[15]

Northerners possessed a powerful attachment to the institutions of self-government because they had participated actively in their operation at the local level. Voter participation in the Northern states has never been as high as it was during the second half of the nineteenth century. Turnout of eligible voters usually reached over 80 percent in presidential campaigns and dropped very little in state and local elections. Northerners participated in politics because they were socialized to believe that their republican institutions, although sound, were fragile and always in danger of being corrupted, whether by the Money Power, King Mob, Slave Power, or some other batch of conspirators who sought to take away their liberties and those of their community. In the local community, Northerners had many opportunities to gain direct experience in the defense of their liberties through the process of the making of law and the preservation of order in their communities. "Widespread involvement in the legal and political institutions of Northerners' communities," in the words of historian Philip S. Paludan, "meant that issues of order or respect for the law were not abstract subjects. They were subjects with which Northerners were personally familiar." They ran for office, served on juries, received patronage jobs, and, when necessary, engaged in vigilante activities out of a sense of duty to their community and a belief that they had a personal stake in the political process. "Such involvement in, and devotion to, the political and governmental structure," writes Paludan, "forged a powerful commitment to the survival of the government itself and to the law and order it was said to nurture." Secession was viewed as an attack on the nation's political institutions and thus on the law and order that Northerners felt a personal stake in creating and maintaining.

For Southerners, the decision to fight for the Confederacy came from a basic desire to defend their homes, families, and communities. James Dawson of the Fourth Alabama expressed a sentiment common among Confederate soldiers in May 1861, when he wrote: "The invasion of Va. has stirred my blood, and I think it will be a pleasure to meet our enemy in mortal combat . . . [and] kill all that we can lay our hands on."[16] However they may have felt about secession, Lincoln's call for troops and the prospect of Yankee armies invading the South led white Southerners to conclude that there was no alternative but to support and fight for the Confederacy.

Still, when Southerners explained why they enlisted, they placed the desire to defend their homes in a broader ideological context. Southerners firmly believed they were acting on, as President Jefferson Davis stated when he accepted the presidency of the Confederacy, "the American idea that governments rest upon the consent of the governed, and that it is the right of the people to alter or abolish governments whenever they become destructive of the ends for which they were established." The North's effort to restore the Union was inconsistent with this principle and reinforced, in the Southern mind, an image of a North that was determined to destroy liberty, which Southerners defined as the inalienable right to direct their own affairs free from the interference of others. "All that we ask," President Davis told the world, "is to be let alone."[17]

Indeed, although they were engaged in rebellion against the U.S. government, Southerners considered themselves the true exemplars of the spirit and ideals of the Revolution. They celebrated the Fourth of July just as their Northern opponents did, based their Constitution on the U.S. Constitution, venerated heroes of the Revolution (even to the point of putting an image of George Washington on the official seal of the Confederacy), and adopted a flag so similar to the "Stars and Stripes" that it would be a source of much confusion early in the war. Like the generation that fought the Revolution, Southerners believed they were engaged in a quintessentially American cause, that of preserving republicanism by resisting an oppressive, corrupt, and tyrannical government that sought to take away their liberties. Separation from the North was necessary to save the South from the pursuit of wealth and party politics that had corrupted the free states and transformed the national political culture in a way that was inconsistent with original republican values. The Confederacy, scholar George C. Rable has argued, was an attempt in the eyes of white Southerners to preserve and perfect the pure republicanism of the Revolutionary Era.[18] In this new nation, statesmen, not party spoilsmen would rule, men who were motivated by a commitment to the principles of limited government, individual liberty, white male democracy, and unity, rather than by a desire to corrupt the political system to serve their own personal ambitions.

Southerners also enlisted to defend the institution that was the cornerstone of their economy and society: slavery. In the hothouse atmosphere produced by a generation of abolitionist agitation, such as John Brown's raid and the 1860 election, Southerners found it hard to believe that slavery could be safe with a Republican in the Executive Mansion, no matter how many sincere assurances Lincoln gave that he had no intention at all of attacking slavery where it then existed. "The prospect before us in regard to our Slave property, if we continue in the Union," wrote one Southerner, in words that were echoed throughout the South during the secession crisis, "is nothing less than utter ruin."[19]

Southerners viewed slavery as the key to their society's prosperity and essential to the survival of their distinctive and superior civilization. Although only a small minority of white Southerners actually owned slaves, most believed they had a direct stake in the preservation of slavery in the South and its expansion into the western territories. Many predicted the slave population would double in a few decades, and, unless slavery were allowed to expand westward, Southerners were terrified that, if still concentrated in a small area, slaves would inevitably engage in primal, insurrectionary violence that would destroy Southern civilization. Moreover, contrary to the view of Northern free-labor ideologists, the South did offer opportunities for upward social and economic mobility before the war with slave ownership serving as the most visible symbol of economic success. If most Southerners did not own slaves, they hoped and believed they could. Like Northerners, Southerners saw the western territories as a place where they could pursue their vision of upward mobility. Yet if a federal government controlled by the Northern majority, as Lincoln promised, denied slavery the opportunity to spread westward, the chance for prosperity and upward mobility would be lost and Southern civilization would be doomed.

In addition to its economic function of providing the cheap labor necessary for the production of cotton and other cash crops, slavery was also the foundation of a stable social order. Since before the Revolution, in the words of historian James L. Abrahamson, "planters had wooed the region's yeomen by combining the prospect of future slave ownership with the incredible notion that black inferiority made all white men equal."[20] Incredible or not, it was a fact that slavery fostered a sense of unity and racial solidarity among whites that served to mute tensions rooted in economic and political inequities in Southern society, kept savage blacks under control, and clearly marked blacks as subordinate to and inferior to whites. In the South's Herrenvolk democracy, even the poorest white Southerner could take pride in belonging to the master class. This sense of white supremacy was so powerful that nonslaveholding Southerners would go to war to preserve the institution that fostered it.

Southerners did not believe that Republican abolitionist fanatics would be satisfied just to keep slavery out of the territories. What the North really wanted now that they had control of the federal government, Southerners believed, was to use its power to destroy the South by freeing the slaves and elevating blacks to the level of whites. Every soldier who joined the Yankee army was believed by Southerners to be an abolitionist zealot, another John Brown, who sought to turn slaves against their masters and destroy Southern communities by destroying their enlightened social order. Southerners envisioned the Northern armies, sent to do battle by a government controlled by Republicans under the mantle of saving the Union, as agents of emancipation long before most Northerners did.

Attacking slavery was also viewed by Southerners as merely one manifestation of a larger desire of the fanatical Northern majority to eventually reduce the South to a state of slavery within the Union. For Southerners, the purpose of the war was, as one Alabama woman wrote her fiancé, to "save our country from shame and dishonor, to wrest it from a Tyrant's grasp. . . . We could none of us ever be happy as subjects under King Lincoln, or wish to live if such was the case." Indeed, as historian James M. McPherson notes, "*Subjugation* was the favorite word of Confederate recruits to describe their fate if the South remained in the Union or was forced back into it." There was no way, white Southerners concluded, that their society and the institutions that supported it would be safe if they were part of a Union where the Northern majority was so overwhelming and hostile that it was willing and able to elect a president on a platform that was anathema to the South. Inevitably, "Liberty would be overthrown," historian Randall C. Jimerson noted, "as the majority forced the helpless minority to submit to its will . . . all of southerners' cherished constitutional rights would be endangered." The ultimate goal of the Republican Party, white Southern males believed, was no less than to transform them from masters of their homes and communities to slaves of the degraded, money-grubbing Yankees. "If we should suffer ourselves to be subjugated by the tyrannical government of the North," one Virginian predicted, "our property would all be confuscated [*sic*] . . . and our people reduced to the most abject bondage and utter degradation."[21]

NOTES

1. Roy P. Basler, ed., *The Collected Works of Abraham Lincoln*, 9 vols. (New Brunswick, NJ: Rutgers University Press, 1953–55), 4:331–32. (Hereafter cited as *CWAL.*)

2. Ibid., 437.

3. Wheeler, *A Rising Thunder*, 107–8; Botts, *The Great Rebellion*, 206–7; Russell, *My Diary North and South*, 77.

4. Connor, "The Boys of 1861," *War Papers Read before the Commandery*, 1:326; Jacob D. Cox, "War Preparations in the North," in *Battles and Leaders of the Civil War*, edited by Robert U. Johnson and Clarence C. Buel, 4 vols. (New York: Century, 1884–88), 1:86.

5. Wheeler, *A Rising Thunder*, 104; William B. Jordan, ed., *The Civil War Journals of John Mead Gould, 1861–1866* (Baltimore: Butternut and Blue, 1997), 3–4; George Templeton Strong, *Diary of the Civil War, 1860–1865*, edited by Allan Nevins (New York: Macmillan, 1962), 123–24, 127.

6. Robert W. Johannsen, *Stephen A. Douglas* (New York: Oxford University Press, 1973), 859, 864, 868.

7. Alfred S. Roe, *The Fifth Regiment Massachusetts Volunteer Infantry in Its Three Tours of Duty, 1861, 1862–'63, 1864* (Worcester, MA: The Blanchard Press, 1911), 10.

8. U.S. War Department, *The War of the Rebellion: The Official Records of the Union and Confederate Armies*, 70 vols., in 128 parts (Washington, DC: Government Printing Office, 1880–1901), series 3, 1:101. (Hereafter cited as *OR*; all subsequent citations will be from series 1 unless otherwise noted.)

9. *CWAL*, 4:432.

10. Joseph L. Harsh, *Confederate Tide Rising: Robert E. Lee and the Making of Southern Strategy, 1861–1862* (Kent, OH: Kent State University Press, 1998), 12–13.

11. Robert H. Wiebe, *The Search for Order: 1877–1920* (New York: Hill and Wang, 1967), xiii.

12. Mitchell, *Vacant Chair*, 25.

13. Roe, *Fifth Massachusetts*, 14–15.

14. Robert Garth Scott, ed., *Forgotten Valor: The Memoirs, Journals, and Civil War Letters of Orlando B. Willcox* (Kent, OH: Kent State University Press, 1999), 278; Connor, "The Boys of 1861," 1:327.

15. Mitchell, *Civil War Soldiers*, 32.

16. Steven E. Woodworth, ed., *Cultures in Conflict: The American Civil War* (Westport, CT: Greenwood Press, 2000), 76; Paludan, *"A People's Contest,"* 12, 14.

17. Jefferson Davis, "Inaugural Address" [February 18, 1861], in *The Papers of Jefferson Davis*, edited by Lynda Laswell Crist and Mary Seaton Dix, 9 vols. to date (Baton Rouge: Louisiana State University Press, 1971–), 7:46; James D. Richardson, ed., *A Compilation of the Messages and Papers of the Confederacy, Including the Diplomatic Correspondence, 1861–1865*, 2 vols. (Nashville: United States Publishing Co., 1906), 1:82; Harsh, *Confederate Tide Rising*, 5.

18. George C. Rable, *The Confederate Republic: A Revolution against Politics* (Chapel Hill: University of North Carolina Press, 1994).

19. Randall C. Jimerson, *The Private Civil War: Popular Thought during the Sectional Conflict* (Baton Rouge: Louisiana State University Press, 1988), 8.

20. James L. Abrahamson, *The Men of Secession and Civil War, 1859–1861* (Wilmington, DE: Scholarly Resources, 2000), 83.

21. Woodworth, ed., *Cultures in Conflict*, 76; James M. McPherson, *For Cause and Comrades: Why Men Fought in the Civil War* (New York: Oxford University Press, 1997), 21; Jimerson, *Private Civil War*, 10.

CHAPTER THREE

ANACONDA OR ACTION?

FOR PRESIDENT JEFFERSON DAVIS and the rest of the Confederate high command, the formulation of strategy during the first months of the war was relatively simple. Assuming a defensive posture while mobilizing the military resources of the Confederacy was an appropriate strategy for achieving the South's main objectives of maintaining its territorial integrity and defending the fait accompli of independence from the attacks of Lincoln's abolitionist hordes. To this list of Southern national objectives, historian Joseph Harsh has added a third, a Confederacy that included all the slave states, which would have demanded an offensive strategy.[1] But this was not an objective that demanded immediate action, and setting up a new government and defending its people and territory were accomplishments that Davis and his supporters could be more than satisfied with achieving in 1861. Consequently, it was with the North that the strategic initiative rested in the spring of 1861. The belief that the Civil War could be won relatively quickly naturally played a large role in shaping how the North approached the task of formulating military strategy.

One of the few who doubted the war could be decided by a single battle was Brevet Lieutenant General Winfield Scott, the general-in-chief of the U.S. Army, to whom the task of formulating a strategy for utilizing the North's vast reservoir of manpower and matériel fell in early 1861. Scott was unquestionably the most accomplished American military man of the first half of the nineteenth century. Born in 1786 near Petersburg, Virginia, he became a national hero for his services in the War of 1812, subsequently played a central role in promoting the professionalization of the army during the 1820s and 1830s, and during the Mexican War conducted a campaign of such great skill that it amazed and elicited the admiration of no less distinguished a military figure than the Duke of Wellington.

Although famous primarily for his accomplishments in leading armies in the field, Scott was instinctively a conservative man who was inclined to seek compromise and avoid conflict wherever possible. Republics, Scott believed, could only survive if they were governed by cool reason; war stirred up dangerous passions that were not easily leashed after a first shot was fired. During the Fort Sumter crisis, he had urged Lincoln to surrender the fort rather than risk provoking the firing of the first shot. Even though the president rejected his advice and the war had come, Scott still hoped in early 1861 that heavy fighting and bloodshed could be avoided—and reason regain its sway—if the North pursued a proper strategy.

Scott had evidently formulated the strategy he hoped would govern Union military operations even before Fort Sumter. He did not, however, put it down on paper until he received a letter from George B. McClellan, the commander of Union forces being raised in Ohio, that proposed marching an army from the Ohio River east to Richmond through the mountains of West Virginia. In response to McClellan's proposal, which Scott dismissed as logistically unfeasible and politically unsound, on May 3 the general-in-chief decided to send McClellan the outlines of what the Washington rumor mill was already referring to as "Scott's Anaconda" after the snake that surrounds, then slowly strangles, its prey.[2]

What Scott proposed to McClellan on May 3, and expanded upon a few weeks later, was to utilize the 75,000 troops Lincoln had called for three months' service purely for the purpose of securing the border states and the nation's capital. That was all Scott considered those troops good for. It would be, Scott advised McClellan, "inexpedient either to rely on the three-months' volunteers for extensive operations or to put in their hands the best class of arms." The navy would then establish a tight blockade of the Southern coastline while the government took several months to raise and train a 60,000–80,000-man force from the regular army and 3-year volunteers and assemble a large naval flotilla at Cairo, Illinois. Once thorough preparations had been made, which Scott believed could be accomplished by November, he would then send a "powerful movement down the Mississippi to the ocean, with a cordon of posts at proper points." This movement would be composed of two columns. One would move by land along the river, while the other traveled by boat, flanking any forces that might try to resist the land force. Together, the blockade and occupation of the Mississippi would "envelop the insurgent States and bring them to terms."[3]

"Cut off from the luxuries to which the people are accustomed and . . . not exasperated by attacks made on them," Scott thought the Southern masses would feel compelled to take a sober second thought about secession. Once they did this, Scott believed they would realize that their interests and true sentiments rested with the Union. They would then rise up and regain control of their states from the minority of Southerners who were truly committed to secession but had taken advantage of the temporary passions stirred up by the election of 1860, the failure of compromise efforts in the following winter, and the battle of Fort Sumter to take their states out of the Union. Once his plan was adopted, Scott was certain that, in the South, "the Union spirit will assert itself; those who are on the fence will descend to the Union side."[4]

Before he could go to work in earnest preparing the Anaconda, Scott first had to make Washington secure, a task the passage of a secession ordinance by Virginia's convention on April 17, with a referendum scheduled for May 23, seriously complicated. Scott and Lincoln both decided it would be best to await the results of the referendum before taking action in the Old Dominion. First of all, they did not want to do anything that might lend credence to the argument of Virginia secessionists that the Federal government was a threat as long as there was even the slightest chance that Unionists might prevail. Scott still could not believe that most of his fellow Virginians were truly dedicated to the proposition that the Lincoln administration posed such a threat to their interests that they would destroy the Union that George Washington, Thomas Jefferson, and James Madison had played such a conspicuous role in creating. An immediate and aggressive show of force, he feared, might be enough to push wavering Virginians into the secessionist camp.

Just as important in inducing Lincoln and Scott to adopt a policy of restraint was the simple fact that the Federal government did not

possess the means necessary for an effective military response to
Virginia's actions. Despite the best efforts of Scott and his subordinates to secure Washington since the first winds of secession
had blown in December, what few troops there were in the capital
still lacked effective organization. Moreover, Washington was a
Southern city, and there were serious questions as to the reliability
and loyalty of the city's police and militia forces. So Scott and other
Federal authorities determined to await the referendum in Virginia,
taking advantage of the wait to prepare militarily and deal with a
crisis in Maryland that demanded the immediate attention and
limited resources of the Federal government.

Although many Marylanders were Southern in orientation
and sympathetic toward the Confederacy, most residents of the
Bay State were loyal to the Union. Problems, however, immediately developed for Federal policymakers in Baltimore, a town
as Southern in its culture and political sympathies as any in the
nation, whose residents quickly made it clear that they did not
relish the idea of thousands of Northern troops passing through
their town on the way to Washington

On April 19, four days after Lincoln's call for troops, Colonel
Edward Jones's Sixth Massachusetts Regiment arrived at Baltimore's President Street Station, the terminus for the Philadelphia,
Wilmington, and Baltimore Railroad, the main line over which
troops from the Northeast would have to travel to Baltimore. To
reach the Camden Street Station, where the Baltimore and Ohio
line connected with Washington, Colonel Jones and his regiment
had to pass through downtown Baltimore. When the residents of
the city learned of their arrival, a crowd of several thousand residents gathered along the route and began harassing the Massachusetts men. Rocks were thrown at the troops, and a number of
Jones's men found themselves engaged in wrestling matches with
members of the crowd who sought to seize their muskets. It did
not take long for the Massachusetts men to decide they had taken
all that armed men should take and begin exchanging fire with
the crowd. Somehow they managed to fight their way through
the crowd and reach the Camden Station, but by the time they
boarded their trains bound for Washington "amid the hisses and
groans of the multitude," four soldiers and twelve civilians had
been killed and many more were wounded.[5]

Outraged by what had happened in Baltimore and the prospect of thousands more troops still to come from the North, pro-Southern citizens of Maryland began making even more mischief. With the tacit approval of the Unionist governor, Thomas Hicks, and the encouragement of city leaders in Baltimore, they took steps to prevent any more Federal troops from invading the state. Telegraph wires were cut and railroad bridges connecting Philadelphia and Harrisburg to Baltimore were destroyed. All of a sudden, the residents of Washington found themselves cut off from the loyal states and besieged with rumors of an imminent attack by Maryland and Virginia secessionists on the defenseless city.

The Lincoln administration and General Scott moved vigorously to deal with the treasonous residents of Maryland. When a delegation of Baltimore residents met with the president on April 22 to demand that he not bring any more troops into Maryland, they were exposed to the steel in the new president's character that became evident whenever he faced a crisis. "You would have me break my oath and surrender the Government without a blow," he coolly but indignantly replied when he heard their proposal. "There is no Washington in that—no Jackson in that—no manhood nor honor in that." He then let them go with a message for their constituents and a stern warning lest they be tempted to defy him. "Go home and tell your people," Lincoln stated, "that if they will not attack us, we will not attack them; but if they do attack us, we will return it, and that severely."[6]

Fortunately, Lincoln received substantial assistance from men outside Washington who responded to the situation with vigor and energy. The man to whom Scott first assigned the task of overseeing affairs in Maryland, however, proved to be an unfortunate selection. Although he had served Scott well during the Mexican War, Major General Robert Patterson in April 1861 was a tired and indecisive old man whose vacillating response to the situation might have proved fatal for the Union had not another man who possessed energy and firmness filled the vacuum produced by Patterson's timidity. He was Benjamin F. Butler, an enterprising Massachusetts politician who had been appointed brigadier general and commander of all the units of Massachusetts militia mobilized in response to Lincoln's call for troops.

Butler, accompanied by the Eighth Massachusetts, was in Philadelphia when he learned of the events that had taken place in Baltimore and the disruption of the direct rail route to Washington. With characteristic decisiveness (which on several other occasions during the war would not be accompanied by such good sense), Butler responded by taking his men off their railroad cars when they reached the head of the Chesapeake Bay at Perryville. He then placed them on boats and, bypassing Baltimore, sailed south to Annapolis, where the U.S. Naval Academy was still in the possession of Federal authorities. Upon arriving at Annapolis on April 20, Butler received an enthusiastic greeting from officials of the Naval Academy who had been living in dread of a secessionist raid to seize the prize vessel of the academy, the fabled USS *Constitution*.

Maryland authorities were less than pleased at the arrival of Butler and the Eighth Massachusetts, who were joined the next day by the Seventh New York, at Annapolis. Governor Hicks immediately sent messages to both Lincoln and Butler requesting that "the troops now off Annapolis be sent elsewhere . . . so that the useless effusion of blood may be prevented." Butler landed his troops anyway and advised Hicks that they were "*not Northern troops; they are a part of the whole militia of the United States, obeying the will of the President.*" Since the Naval Academy was property of the U.S. government, Butler added, "our landing on the grounds of the Naval Academy would be entirely proper."[7] With his men safely ashore, Butler immediately turned to the task of reaching the nation's capital.

From Annapolis, Butler planned to travel to Washington by train. However, he found that secessionists had ripped up the tracks of the Annapolis and Elk Ridge line that connected Annapolis to the Baltimore and Ohio at Annapolis Junction and removed all of the rolling stock from Annapolis except for a broken-down locomotive. Fortunately, in one of those incredible coincidences of this war that were too strange for fiction, a man from Butler's command looked over the locomotive and told the general, "That engine was made in our shop; I guess I can fix her up and run her."[8] The man proved to be as good as his word. He and the rest of Butler's unit, which contained a number of men experienced in railroad construction, immediately went to work and soon the route to Washington was open, although for at least a week Federal troops were forced to march part of the way to the capital on foot. On April 25 the Eighth Massachusetts and the Seventh New York arrived at the station on Capitol Hill, where they received an enthusiastic welcome from President Lincoln and the other residents of a very relieved capital.

Two days after the arrival of Butler's troops, General Scott decided to reorganize his command structure by dividing Patterson's command into three separate departments. Scott assigned Patterson to command the Department of Pennsylvania, with headquarters at Philadelphia. Butler was directed to return to Annapolis to take command of the new Department of Annapolis. Butler's sole assignment was to protect the railroad and to this end his command included "the country for twenty miles on each side of the road from Annapolis to the city of Washington as far as Bladensburg, Md."[9] The final command created by Scott, which included the rest of the railroad route from Bladensburg to Washington, was designated the Department of Washington, with Colonel Joseph K. F. Mansfield, a 58-year-old regular army staff officer who was a favorite of Scott's, assigned to the command.

General Butler, however, was not done yet with the people of Maryland. During the first week of May, General Scott directed him to take the Sixth Massachusetts to Relay House to isolate Frederick, where the Maryland legislature was meeting in special session, from Baltimore. After he completed this mission, on May 13, Butler decided to deal with the root of the problem: Baltimore. Without orders from either Patterson or Scott, he marched his troops into the city and seized Federal Hill, which commanded the town. Butler's decision to act without orders infuriated General Scott and led to his transfer to command at Fort Monroe a week afterward, but his actions effectively cowed the secessionists in Baltimore. By mid-June the rail links between Washington and the rest of the North were once again operating, allowing thousands of troops to reach the capital.

It was not just Butler's actions that had secured Maryland, however. Throughout the month of April and May, the Lincoln administration did all it could to make life as uncomfortable as possible for potential rebels and saboteurs. To facilitate this, on

April 27, Lincoln suspended the writ of habeas corpus along the railroads linking Washington to Philadelphia and Annapolis, permitting the arrest of suspected secessionists and mischief-makers without formal judicial proceedings and relieving arresting officers of the obligation to release prisoners when ordered to do so by a judge. This led to the celebrated case of *Ex parte Merryman*, in which Chief Justice of the Supreme Court Roger B. Taney ruled on May 28 that Lincoln had acted unlawfully in suspending the writ. Lincoln ignored the ruling and continued arresting Marylanders suspected of disloyalty.

By mid-May, Lincoln's, Scott's, and Butler's efforts had effectively cowed the Marylanders. Nonetheless, when the Second New Hampshire passed through Baltimore in late June, it was still deemed necessary to take special precautions. When they reached the city, one man wrote: "All preparations were made to force a passage if circumstances should require. With loaded muskets, and accompanied by the Seventeenth New York and a Pennsylvania regiment, the march was taken up. . . . The line of march was kept clear by cordons of policemen across the head of each intersecting street, behind whom pressed a solid mass of humanity, manifestly not of a very friendly character." Thomas Aldrich of the First Rhode Island later recalled being "under strict orders not to take anything to eat or drink while in Baltimore as they were afraid of poison." Even with all the protection afforded, Aldrich recalled that "as we left for Washington a few bricks and stones were thrown after us."[10]

With the capital safe, its connections with the North secure, and with trainloads of enthusiastic troops pouring into the capital every day, by late May, Lincoln and his advisers were free to turn their attention to affairs in Virginia. Although determined to await the outcome of the referendum in Virginia, Scott made preparations to respond appropriately should the voters of the Old Dominion, as most people expected, ratify the work of its secession convention.

The political leaders of Virginia, however, chose not to await the verdict of their constituents and moved with breathtaking speed to prepare the state for war with the United States. On April 18, one day after the convention's vote on secession, Virginia militia took control of the Federal arsenal at Harpers Ferry.

Then, on April 20, they seized an almost completely intact Gosport Navy Yard after a badly bungled evacuation by Federal authorities. Two days later the highly regarded (and events would prove justifiably so) Colonel Robert E. Lee, after turning down a major command in the Federal army, was offered and accepted command of Virginia's military forces with the rank of major general. By the end of April, several weeks before the scheduled referendum, Virginia state authorities had already established a formal alliance with the Confederate States of America and were vigorously raising and organizing forces to defend her sacred soil. Finally, on April 27, the convention invited Confederate authorities to relocate the capital to Richmond, an invitation that was immediately accepted.

On May 22 the voters of Virginia went to the polls and, as expected, ratified the secession ordinance. Scott responded by directing Colonel Mansfield to undertake a 3-pronged operation across the Potomac the two men had put together to secure the Arlington heights overlooking Washington and the port town of Alexandria. The right wing, a column under the direction of regular army Captain W. H. Wood that consisted of the Sixty-ninth, Twenty-eighth, and Fifth New York, would cross the Potomac over the Aqueduct Bridge. Downstream, regular army colonel Samuel Heintzelman would lead the First Michigan, Seventh, Twelfth, and Twenty-fifth New York, and Third New Jersey over the river via Long Bridge. Finally, the celebrated Colonel Elmer Ellsworth and his First New York Zouaves would cross the Potomac via steamer and land at the Alexandria wharves. Because the bulk of the forces crossing the Potomac were from New York, command of the overall operation was assigned to Charles W. Sandford, a major general in the New York Militia.

On May 24, Mansfield ordered Sandford to undertake the operation. Although little resistance was expected, the night before the "invasion" began was an anxious one for many in the Federal camps. "We march before daylight," the commander of the First Michigan wrote his wife after receiving his orders. "Heaven is my shield of War; to God I commit myself, my regiment, my wife and darlings."[11] At approximately 2:00 P.M., the Federals began crossing the river and by the end of the day had achieved every one of their objectives and managed to capture over thirty members of the Virginia militia, including Captain Delany Ball, a collateral descendant of George Washington. The only black mark was the death of Colonel Ellsworth. Along with his colorfully clad Zouaves, Ellsworth stepped off his boat at the Alexandria wharves just as the small rebel garrison was evacuating the historic town. Soon after his arrival, Ellsworth spied a large Confederate flag flying over the Marshall House on King Street and decided it was his patriotic duty to take it down personally. He dashed into the house, ascended to the roof and secured the flag, but as he came back down the stairs, the owner of the building, James W. Jackson, pointed a shotgun at Ellsworth's chest and pulled the trigger. Ellsworth was killed instantly. One of Ellsworth's men then shot and killed Jackson.

The incident attracted a great deal more attention than it deserved. Northerners grieved the loss of Ellsworth, whose exploits as leader of the celebrated Chicago Zouaves and considerable charm had made him a national hero and a special friend of the Lincoln family. Southerners mourned for Jackson and honored him as a symbol of the Confederate defense of property rights against the invasion of an aggressive North.

By the time Union troops established their first footholds in the Old Dominion, the Davis administration and Confederate congress had already publicly accepted Virginia's invitation to relocate the national capital to Richmond. The move was entirely justifiable politically and militarily, for the city's industrial infrastructure and the state's rich agricultural sections and wealth of military talent were critical to the success of the rebellion. "Virginia," in the words of historian Joseph L. Harsh, "was both Ukraine and Ruhr River Basin to the Confederacy."[12] These material considerations, however, paled in comparison to the symbolism of the move in the minds of Northerners. Transferring the Confederate capital from the heart of Alabama, hundreds of miles from the nearest Northern state to a town less than a hundred miles from Washington seemed almost an act of defiance. Having the rebel capital so tantalizingly close—and the fact that in European warfare seizure of the enemy capital was tantamount to total victory—made launching an invasion of Virginia too tempting to resist. It also ensured that throughout the war attention would be riveted on events in Virginia.

Despite the decision to relocate the Confederate capital, Scott remained committed to the Anaconda, which deliberately avoided launching an offensive into Virginia. As the next four years would prove, Richmond was no easy nut to crack, as there were formidable operational difficulties involved in attacking it. Scott appreciated this and believed, contrary to the naive assumptions of most Northerners, that in order to be successful an invasion of Virginia would take time and require large, well-trained—and costly—armies. Moreover, Scott believed an invasion would ultimately be counterproductive to the goal of establishing a harmonious Union. The challenge to Southern honor, the destruction of property, and the bloodshed of a major invasion would, Scott feared, only inflame Southern hostility toward the Federal government.

Although primarily a manifestation of his concern over the effect a major offensive into Virginia would have on the South, Scott's opposition to an aggressive policy in the summer of 1861 was also rooted in a recognition of the limited military means at his disposal. Scott had devoted a lifetime to building the regular army into a disciplined and efficient organization and to promoting a sense of professionalism in its officers. The 90-day volunteers who had been gathering around Washington since April were woefully deficient in these qualities, and Scott had grave doubts about their ability to fight.

As historian Mark Grimsley has pointed out, the traditional notion that the North rose up as one person to demand immediate military action is inaccurate, because there were in fact many people in the free states who appreciated the virtues of Scott's approach.[13] Nonetheless, it did not take long for critics of the Anaconda and a deliberate war policy to let their voices be heard. Within Lincoln's administration, they found a champion in Postmaster General Montgomery Blair. Blair was a West Pointer, which gave him a certain degree of credibility on military matters. More important, he belonged to a family whose service to the Republic dated back to the days of Andrew Jackson and was especially influential with the new president. The Blairs had been battling with recalcitrant Southerners since the Nullification Crisis of 1832–33, when they had watched Jackson, cheered on by Francis P. Blair Sr.'s fiery editorials in the Democratic Party organ, rattle the sword with conspicuous zeal, and compel the South Carolinians to back down. The lesson of this earlier crisis was clear to the Blairs: The Slave Power talked tough, but was really a toothless dragon. Confrontation, not conciliation and compromise, was the way to deal with Southern hotheads. Once confronted by the superior power of the North, the Blairs were sure the slaveocracy would back down without too much of a struggle.

Yet if Scott and the Blairs disagreed on the means to be employed for achieving a solution to the secession crisis, they did agree that the Federal government should pursue conservative ends: the restoration of the status quo antebellum. Neither Scott, the Blairs, nor the vast majority of Northerners had any interest in pursuing any other goal beyond the preservation of the "Union as it was." Scott and the Blairs, like most Unionists, believed secession was the work of the Slave Power minority in the South and did not reflect the true sentiments of most Southerners. Not only did this belief shape their approaches to strategy, it also influenced Northern policy toward the root cause of the conflict, the South's peculiar institution. A permanent and harmonious Union, could be achieved only if the Lincoln administration adopted a conservative policy on slavery.

When Lincoln called for troops to suppress the rebellion of the Southern states, he made it clear that he would not be sending "abolition hosts" marching south. Instead, he asserted that the North's war aims were conservative: to preserve the Union and restore the Southern states to their proper, antebellum relation to the national government with their institutions and rights intact. Lincoln adopted a limited war policy for two reasons. First, he, like Scott and Montgomery Blair, believed the Southern masses were, in their hearts, truly loyal to the Union but had been bullied by their leaders into this new Confederacy. To proclaim war on slavery would be counterproductive to restoring a permanent and stable Union. It would confirm in the minds of the Southern masses the idea propagated by the Slave Power that the North intended to destroy their society, and thus make it impossible to persuade the South to lay down its arms quickly, once defeated on the battlefield, and to accept the authority of the Union. Second, Lincoln wanted to build as broad a coalition of support in the loyal states—including the border states that allowed slavery but did not secede—and he recognized that anything but a conservative war policy that sought solely to restore the Union would undermine this effort.

The question was what military strategy would best achieve the goal of reviving Southern Unionism and restoring Unionists to control in the South. By mid-May, within the Lincoln administration, the two options were clearly laid before Lincoln by Scott and Blair.

Confident that with the passage of time passions would cool and that avoiding a major provocation, such as an invasion of Southern soil, was the key to encouraging Unionism in the South, Scott argued for the Anaconda. If it was adopted, Scott assured the administration, "I will guarantee that in one year from this time all difficulties will be settled." Rushing south into Virginia in search of battle to lay down the gauntlet, on the other hand, would be counterproductive. First, it would be interpreted by Southerners as a challenge to their honor that they would demand a response to. Moreover, it would reinforce the image of an aggressive North that the Slave Power had used to rally the Southern masses around secession. "Invade the south at any point," Scott warned, "and you will be further away from a settlement in a year than you are today."[14]

The Blairs, along with many Republicans, disagreed. They had long believed—indeed it was one of the cardinal principles that motivated the organization of the Republican Party—that the Northern majority had exercised patience and restraint for too long in its dealings with the slaveocracy and that this was the root cause of the entire conflict. Southerners relied on bluff, bluster, and threats for the simple reason that these tactics had worked in the past because the North had never demonstrated firmness. If, however, the Lincoln administration responded to this outbreak of Southern secessionism with immediate, forceful action, the Blairs and other Republicans believed, the South would quickly back down.

Several other factors supported the case for action. First, Lincoln had called out the troops for ninety days, and these enlistments would soon be up. To be sure, in July, Congress would not only grant Lincoln's request for 400,000 volunteers to serve for three years but also authorize 100,000 more. And although those calling for immediate action never mentioned it, they were all well aware that the costs involved in raising and maintaining such massive numbers of men for any length of time would make the money already spent on the 75,000 90-day troops look like a pittance. Moreover, the volunteers already on hand and their communities had rushed to the colors in order to demonstrate their fidelity to the Union on the field of battle and to suppress treason. To send the 90-day men home without giving them the chance to prove their mettle in battle, after all of the patriotic speeches and melodramatic scenes that had been played out in communities throughout the North, would be sure to have a depressing effect on Northern morale.

Advocates of immediate action also believed that putting off an offensive to allow the passage of time would work to the advantage of the secessionists rather than the Union cause in the South. Scott believed time worked in the favor of the Union, as it would cool passions, produce sober second thoughts, and enable reason to regain its sway in the South. The Blairs and other Republicans, however, were convinced that the passage of time would only allow the secessionists time to consolidate their hold on the South. If too much time were allowed to pass, Southerners might become so accustomed to independence that it would become impossible to persuade them that it was in their compelling interest to risk their lives and property and rise up against the slaveocracy. Moreover, it was feared that, without the promise of immediate relief from a firm federal government, Southern Unionists would become dispirited and find themselves persecuted by Confederate authorities. What Unionists in the South needed was not the passage of time and conciliatory measures, but a demonstration of the power of the national government to protect them and the will of the Lincoln administration to use that power to punish treason. On May 16 the leading spokesman for action within the cabinet, Montgomery Blair, presented the argument for an offensive in a letter to Lincoln, which he asserted:

> Genl Scott's system arises from the constitution of his mind and
> is but a continuation of the compromise policy with which his

mind and that of all his political associates is imbued. He does not comprehend the true theory of this contest and for that reason cannot adopt wise military measures. . . . The military look upon the contest as between the whole people of the South and the people of the North. This is a fundamental and fatal error and if our military movements are predicated on it and we fail to go to the relief of the people of the South they will be subjugated and the state of consolidation now falsely assumed will be produced. The Union must then be severed unless we exterminate the people or subject them. Prompt relief will now be hailed with joy by the people of the South everywhere and it can be given with a very inconsiderable part of the force at our command by a forward movement.[15]

In the end, Lincoln agreed with the Blairs that an immediate offensive should be attempted against Manassas. The president no doubt came to share, in the words of Lincoln scholar Don E. Fehrenbacher, that "the widespread belief that the war could be won quickly with a few bold strokes *had* to be tested" and that "there was probably more to be lost by inaction . . . than by action, whatever its result."[16]

It is also clear that Lincoln made his decision for military action well before the *New York Tribune* and other Northern newspapers had begun printing banner headlines urging the army "On to Richmond" on their front pages on June 26. Only three days after Mansfield's forces seized the Arlington heights and Alexandria, the War Department issued orders creating a new military department separate from his Department of the District of Columbia. This new Department of Northeastern Virginia would encompass those regions of northern Virginia then occupied by Federal forces.

The key phrase in the May 27 orders was the provision that the new department's headquarters were not to be fixed, but were to be "moveable according to circumstances," indicating that this was to be no mere administrative command. It was to be a field army. Another sign that this new department was created with an eye to active operations in Virginia was the decision of the Lincoln administration not to give its command to the elderly Colonel Mansfield, whom Scott preferred, but to a 42-year-old brevet major named Irvin McDowell.[17]

NOTES

1. Harsh, *Confederate Tide Rising*, 7–9.

2. Aaron Perry, "Chapter in Interstate Diplomacy," *Sketches of War History, 1861–1865: Papers Read before the Ohio Commandery of the Military Order of the Loyal Legion of the United States, 1883–1886*, 6 vols. (Cincinnati: Robert Clarke & Co., 1888), 1:354.

3. OR, 51, part 1:369–70, 387.

4. Edward D. Townsend, *Anecdotes of the Civil War in the United States* (New York: D. Appleton and Co., 1884), 55–56.

5. Commager, *The Blue and the Gray*, 83.

6. David Donald, *Lincoln* (New York: Simon & Schuster, 1995), 298.

7. *OR*, 2:588–90; italics in original.

8. James M. McPherson, *Battle Cry of Freedom: The Civil War Era* (New York: Oxford University Press, 1988), 286.

9. *OR*, 2:607.

10. Martin A. Haynes, *A History of the Second Regiment, New Hampshire Volunteer Infantry, in the War of the Rebellion* (Lakeport, NH: [n.p], 1896), 15;Thomas M. Aldrich, *The History of Battery A, First Regiment Rhode Island Light Artillery in the War to Preserve the Union, 1861–1865* (Providence, RI: Snow and Farnham, 1904), 6.

11. Scott, ed., *Forgotten Valor*, 255.

12. Harsh, *Confederate Tide Rising*, 64–66.

13. Mark Grimsley, *The Hard Hand of War: Union Military Policy toward Southern Civilians, 1861–1865* (Cambridge: Cambridge University Press, 1995), 30.

14. Townsend, *Anecdotes of the Civil War*, 55–56.

15. Blair to Lincoln, May 16, 1861, Robert Todd Lincoln Collection of the Abraham Lincoln Papers, Manuscript Division, Library of Congress, Washington, DC, reel 22/vol. 46.

16. Don E. Fehrenbacher, "Lincoln's Wartime Leadership: The First Hundred Days," *Journal of the Abraham Lincoln Association* 9 (1987): 15.

17. *OR*, 2:653.

PART TWO

THE CAMPAIGN

CHAPTER FOUR

THE GENERALS PREPARE

NOTHING IN IRVIN MCDOWELL'S 27-year career in the U.S. Army had prepared him for the task of commanding an army of 35,000 men. An Ohio native, McDowell had graduated twenty-third of forty-five in the West Point class of 1838, and afterward studied briefly at French military schools before returning to the academy to teach tactics. He went on to earn brevet promotions for his performance in the Mexican War and spent the rest of the antebellum period engaged in relatively mundane staff assignments. When the Civil War began, he was an obscure but highly regarded officer on Commanding General Scott's staff who first found himself assigned the task of overseeing the activities of militia volunteers in Washington. Despite his inexperience and personal quirks, McDowell would prove to have been a surprisingly good choice for army command, as events would reveal him to be a capable organizer and not without skill as a strategist.

The new Federal commander was a complex man. He was, as the celebrated British journalist William Howard Russell described him, "square and powerfully built but with rather a stout and clumsy figure and limbs, a good head covered with close-cut thick dark hair, small light blue eyes, short nose, large cheeks and jaw, relieved by an iron grey tuft somewhat of the French type." Although energetic and mentally sharp, with a manner Russell found "frank, simple, and agreeable," McDowell could also be aloof, was generally humorless, possessed a thinly veiled contempt for newspaper correspondents (whom he sarcastically suggested "should wear a white uniform to indicate the purity of their character"), and was decidedly uncharismatic. He spurned tobacco and alcohol but was a prodigious eater, capable of consuming an entire watermelon at one sitting. Twenty years' service in the regular army and his experiences in the Mexican

War had also inculcated in him a preference for West Point–trained officers, a deep disdain for political generals and "rather an unfavorable opinion" of the volunteer soldiers in his army, with whom he never really made an effort to cultivate a personal bond. Although he had a high regard for the South's West Point–trained officers, such as Joseph Johnston, Robert E. Lee, and, especially, his former classmate Pierre G. T. Beauregard, for the rebel army McDowell had nothing but contempt. Their volunteers, he assured Russell, "entered the field full of exultation and boastings," but simply lacked the discipline to make good soldiers.[1]

A number of factors explain McDowell's sudden promotion from brevet major to brigadier general in the regular army assigned to command the Department of Northeastern Virginia, even though he had never commanded a significant body of men in the field before. First, McDowell was still in uniform when the war began, unlike many other highly regarded potential Northern commanders still young enough to command troops in the field such as Ambrose E. Burnside, George B. McClellan, and William T. Sherman. McDowell's work in organizing forces around Washington during the winter of 1860–61 also helped, for it reinforced the high opinion Scott had of him and impressed President Lincoln.

Perhaps the most important factor, however, was McDowell's Ohio pedigree. Secretary of War Simon Cameron's lack of energy and preoccupation with the spoils of office in the spring of 1861 created a power vacuum at the War Department that Treasury Secretary and former Ohio governor Salmon P. Chase was all too happy to fill. In no small part due to Chase's determination that officers from the Buckeye State be at the top of the list when high commissions were handed out, the Union's two most important field command assignments in the spring of 1861, McDowell's in Virginia and McClellan's west of the Appalachians, went to Ohioans.

General Scott evidently had little influence on these appointments. Nonetheless, he greeted the latter appointment with much approval, as he had long had a warm personal relationship with the McClellan family and considered McClellan one of the true stars of the antebellum army. McDowell's assignment to command Federal troops on the Virginia side of the Potomac received a different reception from the general-in-chief. Scott liked McDowell and viewed him as a fine officer but feared his rapid promotion and appointment would offend Colonel Joseph K. Mansfield, the much more senior commander of the Department of Washington for whom the commanding general had a great deal of respect and liked personally. Thus, almost as soon as it was made, an "exceedingly displeased" Scott urged McDowell to decline his new assignment. This McDowell refused to do, as he did not believe it was proper "for me to make a personal request not to take the command which I had been ordered upon."[2]

McDowell would be poorly served by the government that employed him. All recognized that the task of organizing, training, and undertaking offensive operations with thousands of raw volunteer soldiers against a well-led enemy army in the time demanded by the government would not be an easy one. Yet the Lincoln administration made little effort to provide McDowell, or any of its new generals, with what they considered the most important resource of all: an adequate number of trained staff officers. After watching McDowell go about his business, one Washington observer remarked with dismay: "I saw him do things of detail which in any, even half-way organized army, belong to the specialty of a chief of the staff. . . . It seems that genuine staff duties are something altogether unknown to the military senility of the army."[3]

The government could not even provide McDowell with a decent map of the region in which he was expected to operate. As a consequence, he would begin the campaign with only a general knowledge of where the main roads in northern Virginia over which his army would march were located; their quality and the nature of the terrain from a military standpoint would be for all intents and purposes a mystery. To make matters worse, out of an expectation that the war would be a short one, the government declined to accept any volunteer cavalry regiments and demonstrated a notable lack of interest in developing an efficient mounted army. This left McDowell without "a cavalry officer capable of conducting a reconnaissance." Indeed, he had so little faith in the cavalry he did have that he predicted to Russell that if he did send some units out to inspect the country, "they would fall into some trap."[4]

Despite justifiable concerns about the tools given him, the attitude of his military superiors in Washington, and the immensity of the task before him, McDowell crossed the Potomac on May 28 to assume command formally of the Department of Northeastern Virginia. He then went to work organizing the regiments he found on the Virginia side of the Potomac into three brigades. To command them, he selected regular army colonels Samuel P. Heintzelman, Charles P. Stone, and David Hunter, all of whom had previously outranked him. McDowell and his subordinates then began constructing defensive works and training their raw troops. By July 1 several more brigades had been organized and were placed under the command of Daniel Tyler, Robert C. Schenck, William T. Sherman, William B. Franklin, Orlando B. Willcox, and Andrew Porter. All but Schenck were highly regarded graduates of West Point.

As he scrambled to organize and drill his troops during his first weeks in command, McDowell also, in response to "rumors of outrages committed by volunteers," made a point of letting it be known that he wanted his men to remember they were agents of conciliation as well as of war. "We are not," he believed, "theoretically speaking, at war with the State of Virginia, and we are not, here, in an enemy's country." Thus McDowell suggested it would be appropriate to follow Scott's example in Mexico by creating military commissions to punish those who violated the property or persons of civilians in occupied territory where "ordinary courts and officers of the State . . . are not in exercise of their functions." On June 2 he publicly laid out the procedures by which civilians were to be compensated for appropriation of their property for use by the army. Twelve days later, McDowell issued orders letting it be known that any attempt to arrest or trespass on the property of any resident of northern Virginia not "in arms against the United States" would not be tolerated and that any soldier caught doing so would immediately be punished. In line with his own policy, when he appropriated the Custis-Lee mansion on the Arlington heights for his headquarters, McDowell made a point of tenting on the grounds rather than in the house itself and assured the wife of Robert E. Lee that he had "the most sincere sympathy for your distress."[5]

Any hopes that Scott, McDowell, or any other military man might have had that the Lincoln administration might give them the time they deemed necessary to prepare their raw troops adequately were dashed less than a week after McDowell's appointment. On June 3 the War Department asked McDowell to provide "an estimate of the number and composition of a column to be pushed towards Manassas Junction, and perhaps the gap, say in four or five days." McDowell responded the following day by saying that he believed a force of 12,000 infantry, two batteries of regular artillery, and six to eight companies of cavalry with one heavy field battery, with 5,000 infantry in reserve, would be adequate for the task. McDowell's answer also betrayed a sense that he considered his raw forces far from ready for an actual fight. To compensate for this, he suggested the administration make up in quantity what it lacked in quality by raising more troops. "As we have such numbers pressing," he asked, "might it not be well to overwhelm and conquer as much by the show of force as by the use of it?"[6]

Although the Confederates had posted forces considerably in advance of the place, it was Manassas Junction that attracted the attention of military strategists in both the North and South in the spring of 1861. There two railroads, the Manassas Gap and the Orange and Alexandria, connected thirty miles southwest of Washington, DC. The O & A ran from the port town of Alexandria in a southeasterly direction. Because of the size of the armies the Lincoln government was raising, it was necessary for logistical reasons to operate along either a river or a railroad, for they provided the only means for supplying an army of 20,000 to 30,000 men. Consequently, the O & A would inevitably be the line of advance for a Union army marching southward from Washington. The Manassas Gap Railroad was vital because it connected the Shenandoah Valley, another natural line of advance into Virginia the Confederacy had to defend, with the O & A at Manassas Junction. Possession of the junction made it possible for the South to divide its inferior military resources in northern Virginia between the Valley and the O & A with the means of concentrating its forces wherever the threat was greater—provided the Confederates were given time to do so.

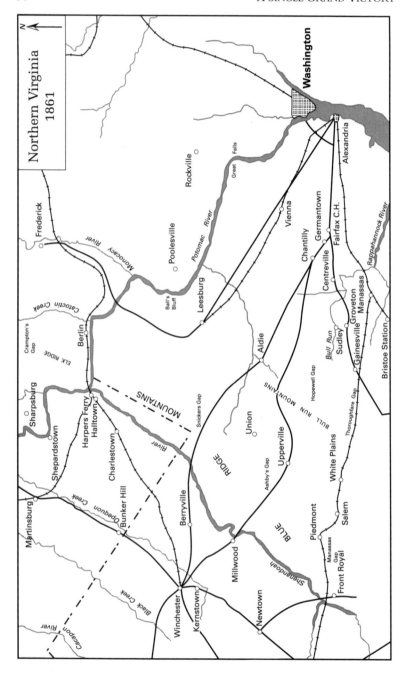

Preventing the Confederates from performing this maneuver to thwart a Federal offensive against Manassas was the task Washington assigned to Major General Robert Patterson. In 1861 only Winfield Scott possessed more experience than Patterson in leading large numbers of men in the field. A native of Ireland who at the age of six in 1798, had moved to Pennsylvania with his family, Patterson had not attended West Point, but managed to win a commission in the Pennsylvania militia during the War of 1812. He had performed well during that conflict, leading men in the field before most of the men who would attain high command during the Civil War were even born, and by the end of that war he had achieved the rank of colonel. He then returned to Pennsylvania and became a wealthy merchant, a prominent member of the state's Democratic Party, and a major general in its militia. Thanks to President James K. Polk, who insisted on surrounding Scott and other Whig generals with Democratic subordinates, Patterson returned to the service during the Mexican War with the rank of major general. Despite their political differences, Patterson served the commanding general well as a division commander during his triumphant campaign against Mexico City.

After Fort Sumter, Scott secured a major general's commission for his former subordinate and assigned as his first task the reopening of the lines of transportation between Washington and the North after the Baltimore riots. This assignment, however, was too much for Patterson, whose vacillation and indecision led Massachusetts militia general Benjamin F. Butler to seize control of Baltimore on his own initiative. Scott then sent Patterson to Chambersburg, Pennsylvania, to muster in troops and, with the aid of regular army officers stationed at nearby Carlisle Barracks, organize a force for an advance southward to seize control of Hagerstown, Maryland. Once this had been accomplished, Patterson was then to cross the Potomac into Virginia to reclaim Harpers Ferry and menace the Shenandoah Valley in such a way as to prevent Confederate troops there from being sent to Manassas.

Patterson arrived at Chambersburg on June 3 and four days later began his advance on Hagerstown. Five companies of cavalry, a battalion from the First U.S. Artillery, a battalion from the Eighth U.S. Infantry, and three Pennsylvania regiments, all under the command of an outstanding regular army colonel by the name of George H. Thomas, led the advance, followed by a brigade of four Pennsylvania regiments. Patterson remained behind at Chambersburg to coordinate the occupation of Hagerstown with the advance over the Baltimore and Ohio Railroad of an Indiana regiment under the command of Colonel Lew Wallace from McClellan's command at Grafton, Virginia, to Cumberland, Maryland. To support Patterson's operations, Scott sent him a highly regarded regiment of Rhode Island troops under the command of Colonel Ambrose Burnside, with its battery, from Washington, and two regular army units from Carlisle Barracks. He also arranged for a 2,500-man force under Colonel Charles P. Stone to advance from Rockville toward the Potomac to threaten a crossing near Leesburg, Virginia. To Patterson's plan to continue his advance, cross the Potomac near Williamsport, Maryland, turn the enemy out of Harpers Ferry, and then advance on Winchester, Scott gave his full approval. Yet at the same time, the commanding general also urged caution. "We must," he told Patterson, "sustain no reverse . . . a check or a drawn battle would be a victory to the enemy, filling his heart with joy, his ranks with men. . . . Attempt nothing without a clear prospect of success."[7]

~~ The importance of Manassas Junction, the Shenandoah Valley, the railroad that linked them, and how they would shape Federal operations did not escape the attention of Southern military leaders. Even before Confederate authorities had assumed control of military affairs in the Old Dominion and Virginia voters had had a chance to ratify the state convention's decision for secession, Richmond began deploying troops in northern Virginia with an eye to guarding the Valley and Manassas.

The first step toward securing the former, in the eyes of Virginia's governor, John Letcher, who had only converted to the secession cause after Fort Sumter, was to seize control of Harpers Ferry, the site of the Federal arsenal made famous by John Brown's October 1859 raid and the northernmost point in the Confederacy (not counting the Unionist counties of western Virginia), at the conjunction of the Shenandoah and Potomac Rivers. This was accomplished with little difficulty on April 18 by a militia force under the command of 60-year-old Kenton Harper, a Pennsylvania native who held a brigadier general's commission in the Virginia state militia and also happened to be the mayor of Staunton, Virginia. Harper's command, however, was not able to move quickly enough to prevent Lieutenant Roger Jones, commander of the small Federal contingent guarding the place, from setting fire to the arsenal and destroying nearly 20,000 small arms. The conflagration was so spectacular that to members of a militia unit several miles away, "each rock and tree on the Loudon [sic] and Maryland Heights were distinctly visible."[8]

After its seizure, Harpers Ferry became a gathering place for hundreds of enthusiastic Virginia volunteers. Command of the place fell upon Harper and three other militia generals who, one observer later recalled, "surrounded themselves with a numerous staff. . . . Every fair afternoon the official display in Harper's Ferry of 'fuss and feathers' would have done no discredit to the Champs Elysees." Cooking was done by black servants and some training took place, but it was not especially vigorous. Few of the officers would or could take a very strict attitude toward discipline, as democracy ruled in the militia units with soldiers unwilling to defer to any authority "beyond the will of the majority of the company."[9] The most significant activities involved harassing trains of the Baltimore and Ohio Railroad that passed by Harpers Ferry on their way to Washington.

The holiday atmosphere at Harpers Ferry was short-lived, however. On April 27, Major General Robert E. Lee, commander of Virginia's armed forces, decided a firm, professional hand was needed there. His choice for the command was Colonel Thomas Jonathan Jackson, a hard-driving, eccentric former professor at the Virginia Military Institute. To facilitate Lee's efforts to place trained professional officers in charge, the state convention passed an ordinance vacating every rank in the state militia above captain and authorizing the governor to fill the vacancies.

Jackson arrived at Harpers Ferry late in the afternoon of April 29 and immediately plunged into his duties. Although the soldiers at Harpers Ferry who had been his cadets at VMI were quick to welcome their old instructor, others were not so sure about this simple fellow who quietly went about his business clad in a well-worn, unadorned uniform. "The Old Dominion must be sadly deficient in military men, if this is the best she can do," one newspaper correspondent complained after his first encounter with Jackson. "He is nothing like a commanding officer. There is a painful want in him of the pride, pomp and circumstance of glorious war."[10]

Jackson, however, knew his business and went about it, one man later wrote, "as exact in the performance of his duties as a mathematical proposition." Within a few days of his arrival, a complete transformation had taken place at Harpers Ferry. The "feather bed and corn-stalk" militia generals and their large staffs were dismissed (although Harper would eventually receive a colonel's commission and command of a regiment), order and discipline improved, and the 2,500 eager, young would-be soldiers began receiving instruction under Jackson's stern, professional eye. Not all the men welcomed the twelve hours of daily drill instituted by the new regime and its insistence upon subordination to military authority. At company meetings indignation was expressed and protests were lodged against the measures adopted by their new taskmaster. Jackson ignored their complaints and within a couple of days, one soldier recalled later, "few had a good word to throw at the new man."[11]

At the other end of the Manassas Gap Railroad, along what was known as the "Potomac" or "Alexandria" line in northeastern Virginia, Governor Letcher initially assigned direction of affairs to brigadier general of militia Philip St. George Cocke. An 1831 West Point graduate who had become a successful planter after leaving the army in 1834, Cocke assumed command on April 23. With the assistance of General Lee, who forwarded troops to him as quickly as he could, Cocke immediately went to work building up his new command. Beginning in the first week of May, even though he still had fewer than 1,000 men, Cocke began focusing his efforts, again at Lee's direction, on establishing and fortifying a strong position at Manassas Junction.

On May 21, however, Cocke, as a consequence of Virginia's effort to streamline their officer corps and the transfer of Virginia troops to Confederate service, was demoted to the rank of colonel and was superseded by Brigadier General Milledge Bonham. A South Carolinian, Bonham had seen service during the Seminole and Mexican Wars and had risen to the rank of major general in the South Carolina militia before the Civil War. A lawyer and politician by profession, who was serving in the U.S. Congress when the Palmetto State seceded, Bonham's political connections (he was a particularly close associate of South Carolina Governor Francis W. Pickens) and participation in the operations against Fort Sumter in April helped him overcome his lack of a West Point pedigree and secure a brigadier generalship in the Confederate army.

When Bonham arrived at Cocke's headquarters to assume command on May 23, he found Confederate outposts advanced almost to the Potomac, which was much farther forward than he was comfortable with. The very next day, after Union forces crossed the Potomac to seize Alexandria and the Arlington heights upon which General Lee's home rested, Bonham ordered his advance units to pull back to Fairfax Court House and put his men to work building on Cocke's efforts to strengthen the defenses around Manassas.

A little more than a week after his arrival, Bonham's men received their first test, albeit a minor one. On May 31 a detachment of fifty Federal cavalry under Lieutenant Charles Thompkins fought a skirmish at Fairfax Court House with a Confederate force under the command of Lieutenant Colonel Richard Ewell. It was a small-scale encounter, in which the Confederates sent the Federals fleeing back to Alexandria, but it was notable for producing the first Confederate officer casualty, Captain John Q. Marr of the Warrenton Rifles. And although no Union officer was willing to concede publicly that the rebels had gotten the better of them in the fight, it reinforced the high command's inclination to be very cautious, as McDowell confided to an associate that Thompkins's operation "was injudicious and might have turned out very badly."[12]

Another development that took place during the last week of May 1861 would have much greater consequences: the decision of President Davis, who had arrived in Richmond only a few days before, to appoint a new commander for northeastern Virginia. His name was Pierre Gustave Toutant Beauregard.

Whether or not he was in fact, as biographer T. Harry Williams proclaimed, "the most colorful of all the Confederate generals," Beauregard certainly was, for better or worse, one of the most interesting and important of the men who commanded

Southern troops during the Civil War.[13] Born in Louisiana in 1818 into one of the state's most prominent French Creole families, Beauregard entered West Point at the age of sixteen and managed to rank second in the class of 1838, twenty-one places ahead of Irvin McDowell. Assigned to the elite Army Corps of Engineers, he distinguished himself during the Mexican War, and by 1860 his status as one of the most highly respected members of the antebellum officer corps had led to his appointment as superintendent of West Point. When Louisiana seceded in January 1861, however, Beauregard was removed from his command at West Point. Within a month after leaving the military academy, he was commissioned a brigadier general in the Confederate army and, at the behest of President Davis, took command at Charleston Harbor. His successful operations against Fort Sumter in April unleashed a wave of popular enthusiasm throughout the South and made Beauregard the first Southern military hero of the war.

After a month of basking in the afterglow of his victory, Beauregard was summoned to Richmond by President Davis on May 28. He reached the capital two days later and was greeted by an enthusiastic crowd. On May 31 he met with General Lee, who had just returned from an inspection of the troops at Manassas Junction, and Davis at the Spotswood Hotel. After Lee described the situation in northern Virginia, it was decided that Manassas was the place for Beauregard, who departed the following day. He reached Manassas late in the afternoon of June 1 and assumed command from Bonham.

Although at first quite anxious and pessimistic about his new command due to the small number of troops at his disposal, Beauregard immediately went to work building up his forces and establishing a personal bond with the men under his command. He worked long hours, rode up and down the lines, conducted innumerable inspections, oversaw the construction of fortifications around Manassas, and made a practice of walking through the camps and talking with his men. Morale quickly rose among the troops, as did Beauregard's confidence in them and his situation. By the middle of June, sufficient reinforcements had arrived to induce the general to seriously contemplate taking the offensive.

In addition to organizing and preparing his forces for action, Beauregard also decided during his first weeks in command to issue an ill-conceived proclamation that would strengthen the hand of those in the North who demanded immediate action by reinforcing the perception that the South needed a good rapping. On June 5 he advised the people of northern Virginia that they faced invasion from a "reckless and unprincipled tyrant" who would pay no heed to the rules of chivalrous and civilized warfare. "Abraham Lincoln," he warned, "regardless of all moral, legal, and constitutional restraints, has thrown his abolition hosts among you who are murdering and imprisoning . . . committing other acts of violence and outrage too shocking and revolting to humanity to be enumerated." The cause of the Confederacy he proclaimed to be the cause of constitutional liberty, self-government, civilization, and "humanity itself." In contrast, the enemy, casting aside "all rules of civilized warfare," Beauregard advised, would "proclaim by their acts, if not on their banners, that their war cry is 'Beauty and booty.' "[14]

Not surprisingly, Northerners responded with disgust to Beauregard's insults. The *New York Times* contrasted Beauregard's proclamation with one issued a few weeks earlier by General McClellan. The *Times* vigorously praised McClellan's, which pledged to respect the rights and property of Southerners, as "calm, dignified, elegant . . . indulging in no asperities, no vulgarities of epitaph" and indicative of the moral superiority of the Union cause. Beauregard's use of the "stale and exploded falsehood of 'booty and beauty,' " on the other hand, the *Times* argued, was simply evidence of "the mere wantonness of treason."[15]

As Beauregard was putting together his forces at Manassas and antagonizing the North, General Joseph E. Johnston was at work in the Shenandoah Valley. "Of medium stature but of most extraordinary strength, vigor & quickness," Confederate artillerist E. Porter Alexander would write after the war, "I think Gen. Jos. E. Johnston was more the soldier in looks, carriage & manner than any of our other generals." [16] It was more than appearance, however, that led Southerners to place a great deal of faith in Johnston in 1861, even though he had never before commanded more than a few hundred men in the field. He was the highest-ranking officer in the antebellum army to tender his sword to the Davis administration. A native Virginian, he had graduated in the same West Point class as Robert E. Lee and served with distinction in the Black Hawk, Seminole, and Mexican Wars. By 1861 these accomplishments, political connections, and an insatiable (and somewhat unseemly) hunger for promotion had helped him become the first graduate of West Point to achieve the rank of brigadier general. However, this rank was attained by leaving a line command, the lieutenant colonelcy of the First Cavalry Regiment, to join the quartermaster's office, which meant that if he wished to return to a field command, he could do so only at his previous rank of lieutenant colonel.

When the Virginia convention voted to secede in April 1861, the 54-year-old Johnston accepted the "hard necessity" of resigning his commission and, thanks to the efforts of his former West Point classmate Lee, secured an appointment as a major general in Virginia's armed forces.[17] Then, however, the state convention, deciding that only Lee should hold the rank of major general, rescinded Johnston's commission and offered him a brigadier generalcy. Always exceedingly touchy as to the matter of rank, and believing that, having held a general's commission before the war, he was entitled to at least equal rank with Lee, who had only achieved the rank of colonel in the U.S. Army, Johnston bitterly declined. Fortunately (and somewhat ironically considering that a dispute over rank would play a major role in Johnston's and the president's coming to despise each other), Jefferson Davis stepped in and offered Lee and Johnston commissions as brigadier generals in the Confederate army. His ego assuaged, Johnston accepted the appointment and headed off to Montgomery to meet with Davis, from whom he received his assignment to take command in the Shenandoah Valley on May 15.

Upon arriving at Harpers Ferry nine days later, Johnston assumed command and, in cooperation with Colonel Jackson, whom he had superseded, went to work drilling, organizing, and training his troops. Despite Jackson's labors, the Virginia men were not yet soldiers, and Johnston was appalled by what he found. When told by a member of the Second Virginia that the unit was one he could rely on in a fight, Johnston contemptuously replied, "I would not give a company of regulars for the whole regiment."[18]

In addition to maintaining a rigorous training regimen, Johnston also conducted several reconnaissances of his position during his first week in command and quickly determined that Harpers Ferry could not be defended successfully if General Patterson utilized his forces with any degree of skill. When Johnston complained to Richmond that "I regard Harper's [sic] Ferry as untenable by us . . . against a strong enemy" and asked for authority to fall back up the Valley, Davis and Lee let him know that they did not share his apprehension.[19] They did, however, advise Johnston that if he deemed it a military necessity, they would not prevent him from retreating.

On June 13, after learning that Patterson had advanced to Hagerstown, Maryland, with a force rumored to be three times larger than his own, Johnston ordered his small army to evacuate Harpers Ferry and other posts along the upper Potomac River. Two days later, Johnston withdrew in the direction of Winchester, which he considered the true gateway to the Shenandoah Valley. He then posted his 7,000 men in a strong position near Bunker Hill, which was about midway between Winchester and Martinsburg. Shortly thereafter, Patterson's forces marched into Harpers Ferry and claimed the town.

Curiously enough, at the same time that Davis was attempting to manage a retreat-minded Johnston, he found himself dealing with a general in northeastern Virginia whose ambition to "make the most enterprising, warlike use of the interior lines we possessed . . . and thus conquer an early peace by a few well-delivered blows" was so great that it often overcame his otherwise good military sense.[20] Without any knowledge of what Johnston was doing or the situation in the Shenandoah Valley, on June 12, Beauregard proposed that troops from the Valley be sent to Manassas so that they could cooperate in an attempt to retake Alexandria and the heights opposite Washington at Arlington. Davis promptly rejected the plan. Undeterred, Beauregard continued formulating plans for taking the offensive and on July 13 submitted yet another proposal to Richmond. Once again, he called for Johnston to bring his forces to Manassas so that they could participate in a battle to crush McDowell's army. Once this had been accomplished, Beauregard suggested that Johnston's army could then return to the Valley. After defeating Patterson (the possibility that the raw Southern armies might at some point achieve less than a decisive victory evidently was not something

Beauregard allowed himself to consider), Johnston would then cross the Potomac into Maryland and march on Washington, while Beauregard and his army attacked it from Arlington.

Although, as future events would demonstrate, Davis and Lee were by no means averse to seizing the strategic initiative by taking the offensive, they again rejected Beauregard's fantastic and unrealistic scheme. On July 16 the staff officer whom Beauregard had dispatched to Richmond to present his plan returned to Manassas with the verdict. This rejection in no way diminished Beauregard's eagerness to take the offensive. By the sixteenth, however, the strategic initiative had passed to the Federals. McDowell was on his way to Manassas.

NOTES

1. Russell, *My Diary North and South*, 232–33, 250.
2. U.S. Congress, *Report of the Joint Committee on the Conduct of the War*, 3 vols. (Washington, DC: Government Printing Office, 1863), 2:37. (Hereafter cited as *JCCW*.)
3. Adam Gurowski, *Diary, from March 4, 1861 to November 12, 1862* (Boston: Lee and Shepard, 1862), 61.
4. Russell, *My Diary North and South*, 236, 251.
5. *OR*, 2:654–55, 659; 51, part 1:400.
6. Ibid., 2:662, 664–65.
7. Ibid., 2:671.
8. Dennis Frye, *2nd Virginia Infantry* (Lynchburg, VA: H. E. Howard, 1984), 4.
9. John D. Imboden, "Jackson at Harper's Ferry in 1861," in *Battles and Leaders of the Civil War*, edited by Johnson and Buel, 1:118; Frye, *2nd Virginia*, 5.
10. James I. Robertson, *Stonewall Jackson: The Man, the Soldier, the Legend* (New York: Macmillan, 1997), 224.
11. D[aniel] B. Conrad, "History of the First Battle of Manassas and the Organization of the Stonewall Brigade," in *Southern Historical Society Papers*, edited by J. William Jones et al., 52 vols. (Millwood, NY: Kraus Reprint Co., 1977 [1891]), 19:83; Frye, *2nd Virginia*, 6.
12. Strong, *Diary of the Civil War*, 154.
13. T. Harry Williams, *P. G. T. Beauregard: Napoleon in Gray* (Baton Rouge: Louisiana State University Press, 1957), 1.
14. *OR*, 2:907.
15. *New York Times*, June 30, 1861.
16. Gary W. Gallagher, ed., *Fighting for the Confederacy: The Personal Recollections of General Edward Porter Alexander* (Chapel Hill: University of North Carolina Press, 1989), 48.

17. Craig L. Symonds, *Joseph E. Johnston: A Civil War Biography* (New York: W. W. Norton, 1992), 96.

18. Frye, *2nd Virginia*, 8.

19. *OR*, 2:881.

20. [Pierre] G. T. Beauregard, "The First Battle of Bull Run," in *Battles and Leaders of the Civil War*, edited by Johnson and Buel, 1:198.

CHAPTER FIVE

THE UNION ON THE MARCH

THE LAST WEEKS of spring and the first weeks of summer in 1861 saw Federal forces on the offensive in several theaters. These operations, relatively minor in comparison to later clashes in the war, nonetheless made a significant impression upon the nation at the time, and some would have a considerable long-range impact on the course of the war. These offensives did not flow from a single will in Washington, but from commanders independently responding to developments on their immediate front.

In western Virginia, General George B. McClellan pushed Ohio troops, preceded by a regiment nominally made up of Virginia Unionists, into that loyalist region of the Old Dominion on the same day that Union forces seized the Arlington heights and Alexandria. Moving swiftly along the tracks of the Baltimore and Ohio Railroad, Union forces under Brigadier General Benjamin F. Kelly seized the strategic rail town of Grafton with little difficulty. Then, during the first week of June, Kelly and Colonel Ebenezer Dumont pushed forward from Grafton toward the small village of Philippi. On June 3 they managed to surprise the rebel forces stationed at Philippi under the command of Colonel George Porterfield. After a few shots, the Confederates retreated with such haste that gleeful Northerners quickly dubbed the affair the "Philippi Races."

To redeem the situation in western Virginia, Richmond dispatched Brigadier General Robert Garnett, a well-respected former commandant of cadets at West Point whom one man later described as "military discipline idealized and personified," to the region.[1] Upon his arrival in western Virginia, Garnett decided to establish strong positions at Laurel Hill and Rich Mountain to thwart further Union penetration into the Old Dominion. Garnett managed to finish deploying his command just as McClellan reached western Virginia and took direct command in the field. Upon his arrival from Cincinnati in late June, McClellan conceived a plan that called for a portion of his command under Brigadier General Thomas Morris to make a demonstration at Laurel Hill, while he personally led the bulk of his command against Rich Mountain. McClellan, thanks largely to the efforts of Brigadier General William S. Rosecrans, managed to score decisive victories at the battles of Rich Mountain on July 10 and Corrick's Ford three days later. These accomplishments made McClellan, who crowed to Washington after his victories that "our success is complete and secession is killed in this country," a hero in the North and ended Southern hopes of saving Unionist western Virginia for the Confederacy.[2]

As McClellan was at work, several hundred miles away in Missouri, the Union cause was likewise achieving success. By mid-June 1861 an energetic and relentless brigadier general by the name of Nathaniel Lyon, with the assistance of Congressman Francis P. Blair Jr. and his family connections in Washington, had seized control of the situation in that divided state. Despite deep— and well-founded—misgivings about the loyalty of the state's governor Claiborne Fox Jackson and the commander of the State Guard Sterling Price, Blair and Lyon consented to a meeting on June 11 at the Planters' House in St. Louis to see if a peaceful solution could be reached. When Jackson and Price refused to submit to Lyon's demand that they disband the State Guard and submit unconditionally to the authority of the Federal government, the general ended the meeting and immediately launched a campaign to crush them. "Better, far better," Lyon told Price and Jackson, "that the blood of every man, woman, and child within the limits of the State should flow, than that she should defy the federal government. This means war."[3]

After transporting his men up the Missouri River on steamboats to seize the state capital at Jefferson City, Lyon smashed a contingent of the State Guard on June 18 at Boonville. Jackson's and Price's men retreated southward from the battlefield with such haste that the battle became known as the "Grand Steeplechase." By mid-July, Lyon had driven Jackson's and Price's forces out of all but the southwestern corner of Missouri, which would eventually enable the Lincoln administration to install a loyal government under Hamilton Gamble. To add insult to injury for the South, reports quickly circulated of Price's being stricken with a severe gastrointestinal ailment during the campaign, which one Unionist paper immortalized in verse:

"Follow me, lads," the General cried,
"I'll bet you'll smell gunpowder."
They followed, and, they say, enjoyed
An odor somewhat louder.[4]

In eastern Virginia, Federal offensives did not produce such positive results for the Union cause. In early June, General Benjamin F. Butler, whose exploits in Maryland had induced Washington to transfer him to command at Fort Monroe at the tip of the peninsula formed by the York and James Rivers, decided to push a force up the peninsula with the intention of destroying a Confederate camp at Big Bethel. Unfortunately, Butler's efforts, as they would so often during the war, resulted in a humiliating defeat for the Union. On June 10 his men launched an assault on a small Confederate force under Colonel Daniel Harvey Hill at Big Bethel that was repulsed with embarrassing ease.

Then, one week after the Big Bethel fiasco, Union forces near Washington suffered a setback. On June 17, McDowell decided to place 700 men under Brigadier General Robert C. Schenck on a Loudoun and Hampshire Railroad train to conduct a reconnaissance toward Vienna, a small village a few miles north of Fairfax Court House. When Schenck's men reached Vienna, they were greeted by what one man described as "raking masked batteries" and several hundred rebel troops under the command of Colonel Maxcy Gregg.[5] Caught totally by surprise and abandoned by their engineer, panic seized Schenck's men and they were forced to ignominiously retreat to their camps.

Big Bethel and Vienna were minor setbacks for the Union and in the long run were of much less importance than McClellan's and Lyon's successes. With the public mind fixated on eastern Virginia, however, those defeats loomed much larger in the minds of the people in both North and South than did the Federal triumphs in Missouri and the mountains of western Virginia. McClellan's, Lyon's, Butler's, and Schenck's operations were certainly of interest and McClellan's and Lyon's of real significance, but no one in July 1861 believed they had the potential to end the war. It was McDowell's operations upon which all eyes were fixed. It was at Manassas, all agreed, that the decisive battle of the war would take place.

～◯ General Scott, however, still wanted nothing to do with an attack on Manassas, regardless of what the public, press, or President Lincoln wanted. Nonetheless, he recognized that something had to be done to satisfy the public desire for a tangible accomplishment. Thus, in mid-June, Scott, still wishing to avoid a major showdown battle in Virginia, decided to push Patterson's modest operations to secure the upper Potomac rather than McDowell's. To this end, on June 20 he asked Patterson to submit a plan of operations "to sweep the enemy from Leesburg towards Alexandria."[6] To support this operation, Patterson would have the assistance of Colonel Charles P. Stone, who had been placed in command of the Union forces covering the crossings of the Potomac below Leesburg. Scott also decided it would be a good idea to have McDowell push a force toward Leesburg from the direction of Alexandria. Thus, Scott thought, McDowell's showcase command would be doing something and, it was to be hoped, quieting those becoming anxious over its perceived inactivity, but still not launching the sort of full-scale offensive against Manassas he sought to avoid.

McDowell, however, disliked the plan, not because he was especially eager to undertake an advance just to satisfy public impatience (he, like Scott, was concerned about the rawness of his army), but because he did not think he had adequate wagon transportation to support an overland march toward Leesburg. More important, he feared that as he advanced on Leesburg, the left flank of his column would be perilously vulnerable to attack by Confederate forces at Manassas, Fairfax Court House, Germantown, Centreville, and Fairfax Station, which McDowell estimated all together at "23,000 to 25,000 infantry and about 2000 cavalry and a supply of well-provided artillery." Consequently, he warned that an advance in the direction of Leesburg beyond Vienna would not be prudent.[7]

Almost as soon as he had finished this report, McDowell received verbal instructions from Scott to estimate the size of Beauregard's command and draw up a plan for attacking it. McDowell responded by proposing an advance from Alexandria and Arlington with Manassas Junction as its objective. The Confederate forces, he believed, consisted of 23,000 infantry, 1,500 cavalry, and 500 artillery. He advised, however, that this force would undoubtedly be augmented as soon as the Federal army began its advance, which would be impossible to conceal. If Patterson in the Shenandoah and Butler at Fort Monroe managed to keep the forces in their front engaged, however, he thought the Confederates would not be able to send more than 10,000 reinforcements to Beauregard.

Assuming a Confederate force of 35,000 in all, McDowell proposed marching with a 40,000-man army composed of 30,000 advancing in three columns and 10,000 as a reserve. One column would march to Vienna and from there to a point between the Confederate posts at Fairfax Court House and Centreville to cut the former off, while another advanced directly against Fairfax along the Little River Turnpike. A third column would move along the Orange and Alexandria Railroad, repairing the road as it advanced. After uniting these three columns north of Bull Run, McDowell then proposed attacking the main Confederate position at Manassas by "turning it, if possible, so as to cut off communications by rail with the South."[8]

This plan was not, McDowell quickly learned, a mere academic exercise. On June 29, President Lincoln called him, Scott, and several other officers to a meeting in order to present the plan to the cabinet. After hearing McDowell describe his sound and well-thought out proposal, only General Mansfield had any suggestions to make, and none were of any consequence. Thus, Lincoln approved McDowell's plan and instructed him to execute it as soon as practicable. Scott protested and once again spoke up for his Anaconda. He told the cabinet that, McDowell later recalled, "he was never in favor of going over into Virginia. He did not believe in a little war by piecemeal. . . . He was in favor of moving down the Mississippi river with 80,000 men. . . . We were to go down, take all the positions we could find and garrison them, fight a battle at New Orleans and win it, and thus end the war."[9]

McDowell advised the cabinet that he "did not think well of that plan." He also let it be known, however, that he had serious qualms about carrying out his own proposal. In order for the plan to work, Confederate forces in the Shenandoah would have to be kept from reinforcing Beauregard. That appeared to McDowell to be less than a sure thing. Scott promised that Patterson would do his job. McDowell also protested that his raw army was not ready for the field; it needed more time for preparation. Lincoln, however, it quickly became clear, would settle for nothing less than an immediate advance. When Scott, realizing that this was the case, suggested McDowell could begin his advance in a week, July 8 was set for the beginning of the offensive against Manassas. McDowell continued to protest, but to no avail. "The answer was," he later complained, "you are green, it is true; but they are green also; you are all green alike."[10]

Preparatory for its advance, McDowell decided to organize his army into five divisions. The First Division was assigned to Brigadier General Daniel Tyler. Tyler had graduated from West Point nineteen years before McDowell and as a junior officer had spent over a year in France studying at the French Artillery School at Metz. The excellent reports of his experiences that he submitted to the War Department were published and earned him a reputation as an expert on ordnance. Tyler left the army in 1834—and as a result did not serve in the Mexican War—to become a prominent businessman in Connecticut. Appointed brigadier general of Connecticut volunteers after Fort Sumter, he was first assigned a brigade and then a division in McDowell's army. The four brigades in his division were commanded by Robert Schenck, a political general from Ohio, and three West Point graduates: Erasmus Keyes, William T. Sherman, and Israel B. Richardson.

Tyler would be a conspicuously troublesome subordinate for McDowell. He clearly resented being placed under the command of a much younger man and went into the campaign with a great deal more confidence in his own judgment and abilities than in McDowell's, whom he would later describe as "an expensive ornament to the military service [whose] courtier-like services in the salon have immeasurably exceeded his military services in the field." Moreover, the jealous Tyler believed to the end of his days that the entire campaign, which he had misgivings about from the start, was, contrary to all evidence, "gotten up by

McDowell and his friends, and was intended to make him the hero of a short war."[11]

McDowell's Second Division was led by Colonel David Hunter, and was composed of two brigades under the command of Colonels Ambrose Burnside and Andrew Porter, both of whom were West Pointers of some ability. Hunter, like Tyler, had graduated from West Point several years—sixteen to be exact—before McDowell had. Unlike Tyler, however, the 59-year-old Hunter was still in the army when the Civil War began. Yet, despite his having served over thirty years, he had only achieved the rank of major by 1860, and there was little to recommend him for a high command. He did, however, assiduously cultivate a highly congenial relationship with President Lincoln that paved his way to promotion to brigadier general and appointment as a brigade, and then division, commander.

Hunter's starting out at such a high rank would prove to have long-term consequences for the Union cause. Division command was a level or two beyond the former paymaster's capabilities, and Hunter did not possess the ability to recognize his limitations or learn on the job. Moreover, like many officers, he was highly sensitive to the matter of rank and, even after his limitations were clearly exposed, he would refuse to accept any assignment he deemed beneath his stature. Thus, after the Bull Run Campaign, by dint of his seniority, the Lincoln administration would give Hunter important commands in Kansas, along the Georgia and South Carolina coast, and in the Shenandoah Valley. In all three areas, his tenure would be distinguished by political and personal controversy and performances as a field commander that ranged from mediocre to horrible.

McDowell's Third Division was commanded by a tough old regular by the name of Samuel P. Heintzelman. Like Tyler and Hunter, Heintzelman had finished the program at West Point over a decade before McDowell had. Unlike Tyler and Hunter, after graduating from the military academy in 1826, Heintzelman had actually gained experience leading men in combat, serving with distinction in the Mexican War and in conflicts with the Native Americans in the southwest. By the time the Civil War began, Heintzelman had, after thirty-five years in the army, finally achieved the rank of lieutenant colonel and impressed one of his brigade commanders as "a hardy, fearless, energetic character" who possessed "a frank way of expressing the exact truth whether it hurt or not . . . which our undisciplined levies then especially needed."[12] Although there is some evidence that the promotion of younger men with fewer years in the service, such as McDowell and McClellan, above him rankled Heintzelman, he would be a loyal subordinate. And even though he was clearly a cut above Hunter in terms of competence, his performance as a division and corps commander during the Civil War would be solid rather than spectacular, and he would be shelved by the end of 1862. The three brigades McDowell assigned to his division were commanded by Colonels William B. Franklin, Orlando B. Willcox, and Oliver Otis Howard. All three were well-regarded West Point–educated men destined for bigger things.

McDowell's last two divisions would play minor roles in the campaign. The small Fourth Division, whose regiments were not even brigaded, was commanded by militia general Theodore Runyon. It would serve as a reserve force during the Bull Run Campaign. McDowell's Fifth Division was commanded by Colonel Dixon S. Miles. His two brigades were commanded by Colonels Louis Blenker and Thomas A. Davies. Miles was an old regular who, in the thirty-five years since his graduation from West Point, had seen service in the Seminole and Mexican Wars and participated in a number of campaigns against Native Americans. Unfortunately, he had also developed a fondness for the bottle by 1861.

Curiosity as to what sort of army McDowell and his subordinates would be leading in the field induced William Howard Russell to commandeer a horse early on the morning of July 13 and spend the entire day riding through the camps on the Virginia side of the Potomac. What he saw shocked and appalled him. The army was hardly, he noted in his diary, the "magnificent force, well disciplined, well clad, provided with fine artillery, and with every requirement to make it effective," described in the Northern newspapers. Only gross and utter ignorance "of what an army is or should be," he concluded, could explain the reports. The officers were "unsoldierly-looking" and their inability to impose discipline on their men, who were clad in "all sorts of uniforms," Russell complained, had left "the camps dirty to excess." "I doubt," he speculated, "if any of these regiments have ever performed a brigade evolution together, or if any of these officers know what it is to deploy a brigade from column to line." He found the artillery "miserably deficient" and he did not believe there were even five fully equipped and manned batteries in the entire army. Even those five, he thought, had "the worst set of gunners and drivers which I ever beheld." The cavalry was even worse. What little there was could not stand a charge of British colonial irregulars, Russell predicted, and he was sure the first serious movement in the field would see many men expelled from their saddles by their mounts. In terms of matériel, he found the army's transport to be "tolerably good." But even here he found that "they have no carriage for reserve ammunition; the commissariat drivers are civilians under little or no control."[13]

Whatever Russell may have thought of them and whatever reservations may have lingered in the minds of their own West Point–trained commanders, McDowell's men had no lack of confidence in themselves and were eager to take the field and whip the rebels. "I for one am ready," Charles B. Haydon, a sergeant in Richardson's brigade, wrote in his diary on the eve of the campaign, "to work and give if need be all that I am worth . . . till the last secessionist is dead or subdued. . . . There are very few in the Regt. who want to see Mich. till after they have smelled the enemies' power. . . . We are as ready for fighting now as we shall ever be." When he got word of the advance, Elisha Hunt Rhodes of the Second Rhode Island remarked in his diary, "Hurrah! We are all packed and waiting to move." So eager for the field was Rhodes that when his captain tried to convince him he "was too slight built to march" and should instead remain behind to guard company property, he would have none of it. "I insisted that I would go, orders or no orders," wrote Rhodes, "and finally told my Captain that if he left me in camp I would run away and join the Regiment on the road as soon as it became dark." Rhodes was not alone in his determination not to let anything prevent him from participating in the campaign. In the Second New Hampshire, "men who had been under the surgeon's care for weeks buckled on their armor and obstinately refused to be left behind while the death blow was given the rebellion." "The soldiers composing the expedition displayed the highest emotion of joy," recalled another man, "and those who were compelled by their physical weakness to remain in the rear were affected with grief, and some shed tears." The confidence and eagerness of the army was infectious. By the time the order to advance came, even Colonel Orlando Willcox, a West Pointer, came to share it. "I feel confident of our troops and our cause," he wrote his family. "We are all alive for the grand move. . . . I have no fear for the result."[14]

NOTES

1. Gallagher, *Fighting for the Confederacy*, 48–49.
2. *OR*, 2:204.
3. Christopher Phillips, *Damned Yankee: The Life of General Nathaniel Lyon* (Columbia: University of Missouri Press, 1990), 214.
4. Ibid., 220.
5. *OR*, 2:126.
6. Ibid., 2:709, 711.
7. Ibid., 2:718–19.
8. Ibid., 2:719–21.
9. *JCCW*, 2:37.
10. Ibid., 2:37–38.
11. Daniel Tyler, "Autobiography," in *Daniel Tyler: A Memorial Volume Containing His Autobiography and War Record, Some Account of His Later Years, with Various Reminiscences and the Tributes of Friends*, edited by Donald G. Mitchell (New Haven: Tuttle, Morehouse, and Taylor, 1883), 49.
12. Oliver Otis Howard, *Autobiography of Oliver Otis Howard, Major General United States Army*, 2 vols. (New York: Baker and Taylor Company, 1907), 1:142.
13. Russell, *My Diary North and South*, 240–41.
14. Stephen W. Sears, ed., *For Country, Cause and Leader: The Civil War Journal of Charles B. Haydon* (New York: Ticknor and Fields, 1993), 40, 45–46; Robert Hunt Rhodes, ed., *All for the Union: The Civil War Diary and Letters of Elisha Hunt Rhodes* (New York: Orion Books, 1985), 23; Haynes, *History of the Second Regiment, New Hampshire*, 19; Henry N. Blake, *Three Years in the Army of the Potomac* (Boston: Lee and Shepard, 1865), 7; Scott, ed., *Forgotten Valor*, 281–83.

CHAPTER SIX

THE MARCH ON CENTREVILLE

FINALLY, ON JULY 16, eight days behind schedule, McDowell's army began its much-anticipated offensive. It would be, Northerners believed, a grand march to the field of battle where the memory of Butler's and Schenck's blunders would be wiped away. Victory would be achieved there to demonstrate that the rebellion was a balloon full of bluff and gasconade.

Fairfax Court House was McDowell's first objective. Three major roads came together there and, more important, the rebels had established an advanced post under the command of Brigadier General Milledge Bonham that consisted of one Virginia and four South Carolina regiments, four troops of cavalry, two batteries, and part of one troop of cavalry. Bonham had his horsemen continually scouting the lines of probable approach and had standing orders from Beauregard to evacuate Fairfax Court House once the enemy advanced. His men, however, like their Federal counterparts, itched for an opportunity to prove their mettle in combat. "Our men," Thomas J. Goree, a staff officer stationed at Fairfax, advised his family, "are very impatient and anxious for a fight. They don't think of a defeat." The main source of concern for the Confederates at Fairfax was the local population. Goree wrote: "There are hundreds of tories who we dread much more than the Yankees. The traitors are not native Virginians but Yankees who have settled here. And they are not a few."[1]

McDowell's plan for the march to Fairfax called for Tyler's division to take the Georgetown Turnpike and Leesburg Stone Road to Vienna on the sixteenth. Then, at daylight on the seventeenth, he was to turn southward and move "to the right or the left of Germantown," a small hamlet a mile or so west of Fairfax Court House on the Little River Turnpike. Once he reached Germantown, Tyler would be in position to prevent Bonham from

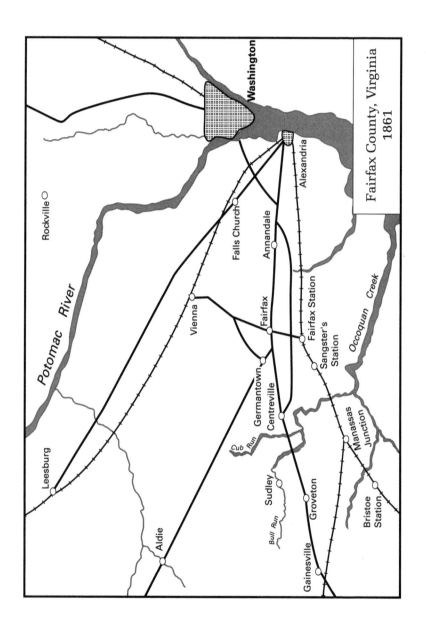

falling back to the main Confederate line at Centreville and Manassas.[2] As Tyler advanced on Fairfax from the north, Hunter's division, accompanied by McDowell, would take the Columbia Turnpike to Annandale, where the turnpike intersected the Little River Turnpike, on the sixteenth. The next day Hunter would move directly on Fairfax via the latter road. Miles would march parallel to Hunter along the Little River Turnpike to Annandale on the sixteenth and then along the Braddock Road to a point south of Fairfax on the seventeenth. If things worked out as planned, Bonham would be surrounded, with Tyler in his rear, Hunter in his front, and Miles advancing from the south. McDowell would have himself a nice little prize—not a bad way to begin the campaign.

As these advances took place, Heintzelman's division would march south of Miles. On the sixteenth, McDowell wanted Heintzelman to take the Old Fairfax Road from Alexandria as far west as Pohick Run. Then, while Tyler, Hunter, and Miles were disposing of Bonham on the seventeenth, Heintzelman would march to Fairfax and Sangster's Stations on the Orange and Alexandria Railroad. Heintzelman's movements would serve two purposes. First, he would protect the southern flank of the other three divisions should Beauregard attempt to disrupt the operation against Fairfax by attacking from Manassas. More important, if everything went as planned, Heintzelman would be in position on the eighteenth to cross Bull Run at Union Mills or the Occoquan River at Wolf Run Shoals, turn the Confederate right, and cut the O & A while Beauregard's attention was focused on Fairfax and the road from there to Bull Run via Centreville.

McDowell's plan was a good one and clearly reflected the influence of Napoleon on how Civil War generals approached strategy. Like Napoleon, McDowell chose not to keep his army concentrated on a single line of operations, but to advance along several different routes, with an eye to creating an opportunity to turn the enemy's position. Also, like Napoleon, he anticipated that, should the enemy attempt to thwart his advance by concentrating on one of the Union columns with the goal of beating it before the others could come to its assistance, that column would be "so strong and well provided that, though they may be for a time checked, they should not be overthrown" before reinforcements could come to its aid. Nonetheless, McDowell urged caution upon his subordinates. "The three following things will not be pardonable in any commander," he instructed them, "1st. To come upon a battery or breastwork without a knowledge of its position. 2d. To be surprised. 3d. To fall back. Advance guards, with vedettes well in front and flankers and vigilance, will guard against the first and second."[3]

The first day's march was neither particularly efficient or eventful, but all four of McDowell's divisions did manage to reach their designated stopping points, even though July 16, 1861, was a miserably hot and humid day in Fairfax County. Burnside's brigade of Hunter's division had the pleasure of forming for their day's march right on Pennsylvania Avenue and thus got to bask in the enthusiastic cheers of the people of Washington as they marched to the Long Bridge over the Potomac. "It was a glorious spectacle," one of McDowell's staff officers later recalled. "The various regiments were brilliantly uniformed according to the aesthetic taste of peace, and the silken banners they flung to the breeze were unsoiled and untorn." (The following day, however, William Howard Russell would note in his diary: "a great improvement in the streets of Washington, which are no longer crowded with turbulent and disorderly volunteers or by soldiers disgracing the name, who accost you in the by ways for money"— suggesting the enthusiasm of the capital for the army's departure may have been motivated by more than patriotic ardor.)[4]

As his army began its march, McDowell was stuck at the railroad station near the Capitol awaiting the arrival of two batteries. There he encountered Russell, who was just returning from a trip to Fort Monroe. The British journalist expressed surprise that the commanding general of the nation's most important field army was there tending to a matter better left to staff. McDowell responded: "Well, it is quite true, Mr. Russell, but I am obliged to look after them myself, as I have so small a staff." The general was, Russell found, in fairly good spirits, but he did not seem as confident as he had a few days before and expressed concern over how little he knew about the country he was marching his army into and the location of Beauregard's position, which he had heard was at Fairfax, but "could not get any certain knowledge of the fact." When Russell suggested he send out a reconnaissance,

McDowell dismissed the suggestion out of hand: "I have not an officer on whom I could depend for the work." The next day, an exasperated Russell noted in his diary that even "the worst-served English general has always a young fellow or two about him who can fly across country, draw a rough sketch map, ride like a foxhunter, and find something out about the enemy." In the United States, Russell lamented, he looked for "the types of these in vain."[5]

Ignorant of the problems their commanding general was experiencing, the men of McDowell's army were in excellent spirits when they began their march. As they stepped onto the soil of the Old Dominion near Fort Runyon, the largest of the forts constructed by Union engineers to protect the capital, the regimental band of the Second New Hampshire "struck up 'Dixie' with might and main, while the soldiers made the air resound with their marching songs and cheers." After passing Fort Runyon, Hunter's men continued their march west on the Columbia Turnpike until they reached Annandale between 10:00 and 11:00 P.M. and went into bivouac. It had been a fairly modest march— McDowell had set relatively conservative marching orders for his raw troops. Nonetheless, it had proved to be too much for many of Hunter's men. "The heat and suffocating dust," one man later recalled, "soon began to tell upon the men, not yet hardened for such a march, and many were obliged to fall out of the ranks."[6]

Upon reaching Annandale, Hunter's men stacked their arms and went to work making themselves comfortable despite a lack of tents. The men of the Second Rhode Island made their camp in a large meadow and did not let McDowell's instructions to leave Southern property alone stand in the way of making their camp as pleasant as possible. "Rail fences were plenty," wrote Elisha Hunt Rhodes in his diary, "we soon had fires burning and coffee cooking. . . . I enjoyed the evening sitting by the fire and speculating on what might happen on the morrow." "It was a beautiful starlight night," recalled a man in a Rhode Island battery encamped nearby, "with the exception of a few long faces, everybody seemed cheerful. . . . It was a grand sight to look at the camp-fires as far as the eye could reach."[7]

Meanwhile, Tyler's command, which began its march one hour after Burnside's, advanced toward Vienna. The march went fairly smoothly. As with the rest of the army, trees felled by the rebels to obstruct their progress proved to be the most vexing problem, although the large contingent of Maine lumberjacks in Erasmus Keyes's brigade made clearing the roads less time-consuming than it could have been. The efficiency of the Yankee axemen greatly impressed their Confederate opponents. One South Carolina soldier who had helped create the obstructions recalled later: "For miles out, in all directions, wherever the road led through wooded lands, large trees, chestnut, hickory, oak, and pine were cut . . . creating a perfect abatis across the road—so much so as to cause our troops . . . to think it almost an impossibility for such obstructions to be cleared away in many days; whereas, in fact the pioneer corps of the Federal army [would clear] it away as fast as the army marched."[8]

Although the Federals encountered no significant armed resistance, there was enough sporadic fire from rebel pickets to remind the green troops that this was war and inspire caution. Nonetheless, the men were in good spirits and even found time to debate what they would do after they whipped the rebels. (And no one doubted they would.) A proposal to take a train down to Richmond, hang Jefferson Davis, and then return home to the cheers of their neighbors received a highly positive response.

By nightfall, most of Tyler's men had reached Vienna. The only rebel force posted at Vienna was a small contingent of men who were busy drilling when Tyler's skirmishers first arrived and fled when they caught sight of the Federal column marching their way. Vienna was a village Colonel Sherman, echoing the sentiments of his men, proclaimed "hardly entitled to the name." Still it proved to be a place of no little curiosity to the Federals as it was, one noted in his diary, "where the Ohio men under Col. [Schenck] ran into the masked battery. . . . We saw the spot and where the trees were cut upon by the balls."[9]

The memory of what had happened to Schenck's command a few weeks before would cast a powerful shadow on the minds of McDowell's men and do much to induce a cautious mind-set throughout the Federal army. The bungled reconnaissance to Vienna, although a minor affair, had attracted a great deal of attention throughout the North. Hungry for news of any kind of action, Northern newspapers immediately published Schenck's report of the battle. Schenck's complaint that his command had been ambushed by "raking masked batteries" attracted much attention, provoked much conversation, and aroused the imaginations of the raw troops gathered in the camps around Washington. Before long, Union soldiers from McDowell down to the lowliest private had become convinced that the perfidious rebels, recognizing that they could not win a fair, stand-up fight, had planted these deadly masked batteries all over northern Virginia, creating, in the words of one of the few skeptics, "a subterranean artillery, which is to explode on every step, under the foot of our army." The specter of those masked batteries made such an impression upon McDowell that, at the outset of the campaign, he had proclaimed moving "upon a battery or breastwork without knowledge of its position" the number one "unpardonable" mistake any officer could make, lest his unsuspecting column suffer the same fate as had Schenck's.[10]

As with Hunter's column, McDowell's order against molesting Southern property did little to restrain Tyler's troops. Several men of the Seventeenth Michigan of Richardson's brigade fell upon a country store (which they quickly determined was "a secession grocery") and tore the place "all to pieces and carried off everything there was in it." While passing a farm, Private Alpheus T. Budlong of the Second Wisconsin decided he would rather have fresh mutton for dinner instead of the salt pork he carried in his haversack. Unfortunately, Colonel Sherman caught him as he ran by with a quarter slung over his shoulder. Unmoved by the soldier's protest, "I was hungry, and it was rebel mutton, anyhow," Sherman confiscated the meat.[11]

As in Hunter's command, the sights and sounds of the first night in the field became impressed indelibly upon the minds of the men. "Soon after midnight," wrote one Wisconsin man years later, "I awoke with a strange sensation. . . . There was the moon at the zenith in full splendor. Of the 12,000 soldiers, apparently not another soul was awake. The silence was impressive. What thoughts flitted through the boy's mind out there on the sacred soil of old Virginia, a thousand miles from home, surrounded by scenes and circumstances so new and strange."[12]

Farther to the south, Heintzelman's three brigades also managed to reach their assigned destination on the sixteenth at Pohick

Run, although not without some difficulties. The road south of the Orange and Alexandria Railroad over which they had to march passed through swamps and thick woods and was, in the words of one man, "narrow and miserable . . . one of the chief features of the barbarism of Virginia." The lead regiment, the Fifth Massachusetts, encountered few enemy troops but "everywhere could be seen traces of the late presence of the enemy who had fled hastily," in the form of trees felled by the rebels to obstruct the march. Franklin, however, detailed fifty axemen from the Fifth Massachusetts and fifty from the First Minnesota who success-fully cleared the roads and cut new paths through the dense woods on both sides of the road to facilitate the march. Occa-sionally, the skirmishers out in front would engage the rear guard of retreating enemy outposts. This was enough to make the march for the lead regiments "quite exciting," but did little to hamper the division's advance to Pohick Run.[13]

The need to clear the road, however, meant that there were frequent halts, which became more numerous the farther the di-vision advanced. Before sunset, one man later recalled, "The men sustained the fatigues of their first march . . . in an excellent man-ner; and there were few cases of utter exhaustion or straggling." After sunset, however, halts became more frequent and the tired men grew increasingly frustrated. "The column for seven hours advanced, at irregular intervals of time, five, twenty, or one hun-dred feet," wrote one man in Franklin's brigade. "Delays of a few seconds or minutes were uncertain in their duration. . . . As soon as they had broken ranks, and prepared to rest after a sudden stop, they would be commanded to 'fall in'; and another pause frequently occurred before the moving mass had traveled the length of a company. The troops, expecting to start at once, some-times stood in their places half of an hour before the march was resumed."[14]

The most serious obstacle Heintzelman's troops encountered proved to be Accotink Creek. When Colonel Howard reached the creek at the head of his brigade, he found a bridge over the creek consisting of two logs and several men removing their shoes and socks in order to avoid slipping off the bridge as they crossed over it single file, a process which meant that, in Howard's words, "each brigade before mine had taken full two hours to pass a stream not more than twenty yards wide and the water nowhere above their knees." Howard ordered his brigade to ignore the bridge and simply march across the ford. It was a decision that provoked much grumbling among the men but one Howard never regretted. "They surely," he later reasoned, "would not have been so fresh and happy the next morning if they had been three hours later than they were getting into camp."[15]

McDowell had purposely issued modest marching orders for the sixteenth, in part because of the rawness of his command, but also because the plan for July 17 brought the very real prospect of combat and he wanted the men as fresh as possible. This was the day the Federal army was to seize Fairfax Court House. McDowell's plan called for Hunter to advance directly on Fairfax Court House from Annandale via the Little River Turnpike, while Miles marched west along the old Braddock Road to the intersection of the road connecting Fairfax Court House with Fairfax Station on the O & A Railroad. Miles would then turn north and advance on the Court House from the south. As Hunter and Miles were menacing Fairfax Court House from the east and south, Tyler was to move his division south from Vienna and "intercept the enemy's communication between Fairfax Court-House and Centreville." Heintzelman would advance his lead brigade from Pohick Run to Sangster's Station on the O & A, and, if he deemed it necessary, send the other two brigades to Fairfax Station to support Miles. If it was not necessary, the entire division would concentrate at Sangster's.[16]

Early on the seventeenth, McDowell's men were roused from their sleep and directed to get in line for their march. Despite the relatively modest march of the previous day, most of the men awoke feeling stiff, sore, and possessed by a general sense of exhaustion. Nonetheless, their officers managed to get the men moving out at a fairly decent hour toward their respective objectives for the day. With the excitement of the first day's march behind them, however, discipline, which was not good to begin with, began to deteriorate. Part of the problem was that many of the men simply tried to carry too much. One member of the battalion of regulars later recalled seeing a man desperately trying to keep up with his command while carrying "besides the regulation knapsack, haversack, canteen, blanket and rifle

. . . an assorted cargo of 'a little of everything.'" "Lord Jee!" the
man shouted as he hustled past the regulars, "I wish I was a
mule!"[17]

"I never saw black berries more plenty," wrote one man. "We
stopped and ate what we wanted and then moved on. . . . This
march partook more of the character of a pleasant ramble than
that of an armed force looking for an enemy." Episodes like this
were common throughout the army and infuriated its commander. "They would not keep in the ranks, order as much as
you pleased," McDowell later complained. "They stopped every
moment to pick blackberries or to get water." To Colonel Sherman,
"the march demonstrated little save the general laxity of discipline; for all my personal efforts I could not prevent the men from
straggling for water, blackberries, or anything on the way they
fancied."[18]

Despite the deterioration of discipline in his army, by mid-
morning on July 17, McDowell's plan was being implemented.
Tyler's division was cautiously approaching Germantown from
the north, as Hunter's command, with Burnside's brigade in the
lead, moved forward from Annandale and Miles advanced along
Braddock Road.

Colonel Keyes's brigade led the 7-mile march of Tyler's command from Vienna and did so at a respectable pace until approximately 9:00 A.M., when, after passing the Flint Hill School House
two miles north of Fairfax, they encountered a Confederate gun
emplacement. After a brief consultation with Tyler, Keyes pushed
his men forward with great caution, lest he fall victim to "raking
masked batteries." This gave the rebel gunners time to abandon
their position. The march then resumed, obstructed again by felled
trees and occasional fire from Confederate snipers. The latter
became such an annoyance at one point that Keyes brought
up artillery to shell a small dwelling from which shots had been
fired.

After clearing away these annoyances, Keyes finally managed
to reach the outskirts of Germantown at around noon. Bonham
was still in position, but, alerted to the Federal advance from
Vienna and the presence of a large Union force moving toward
him from the east, was already preparing to abandon Fairfax
Court House. "Their approach was from two sides," recalled one

of Bonham's staff officers, "and when I saw them it almost seemed as if there were 500,000."[19] When the Confederate entrenchments near Germantown came into view, Keyes deployed the Second Maine and Second Connecticut in line of battle, supported by artillery, and ordered them forward. The sight of Keyes's command and a few rounds from the Federal guns convinced Bonham that it was finally time to go, and orders went out to his command to retreat to Centreville

By daylight on the eighteenth, Bonham's men were safely behind Bull Run and had taken up a position at Mitchell's Ford after what proved to be an exhausting retreat. "Marching along a narrow, dusty road, at almost a double-quick," one man later recalled, "the dust and heat of the sun was almost suffocating." Although Bonham had successfully extricated his men from McDowell's trap, his handling of the retreat induced one staff officer to proclaim him "*totally* unfit for a military leader." "Everything was done very hurriedly," the officer complained, "and a considerable amount of property was left behind." (General McDowell, in fact, reported to Washington on the evening of July 17: "The enemy's flight was so precipitate that he left in our hands a quantity of flour, fresh beef, intrenching tools, hospital furniture, and baggage.") To his men, "Gen. Bonham all the time appeared very much flurried. After moving his troops around and making some demonstrations as if for a fight, he ordered a retreat, which ought to have been done before the enemy was so close. . . . Our retreat no doubt appeared more like a rout than a retreat in good order."[20]

While Keyes's brigade and the rest of Tyler's division took possession of Germantown, a few miles to the east Hunter's division moved into Fairfax Court House after having encountered "no worse obstruction . . . than a few trees" and passing through abandoned Confederate earthworks east of the village during their march from Annandale. When the men of Burnside's brigade entered Fairfax, they found the Confederates had set fire to several of the buildings and left a secession flag flying above the courthouse. Exultant over their conquest and possessed of "a clearly defined impression that a serious blow had been dealt the rebellion," two men from the Second Rhode Island, Sergeant James Taggart and Corporal Andrew McMahon, rushed into the building to tear it down. McMahon reached the top of the cupola first "and had the satisfaction of detaching the symbol of the rebellion," which he then threw from the roof to the delight of his comrades. "The men were very much excited over the capture of Fairfax," one man recalled. "We thought if we met with no more opposition than we had thus far encountered the life of a soldier must indeed be very fine. 'On to Richmond!' was the cry."[21]

Ignoring the fact that they were engaged in an effort to persuade Southerners that their interests would be secure under the Federal government, once they gained control of Fairfax and Germantown, Union soldiers began looting both villages. "It seemed as if the men from every regiment tried to see who could do the most foolish thing," recalled a member of Hunter's division. "Men who in home and camp life were quiet and unassuming, seemed possessed with the desire to destroy everything that came within their reach." "The soldiers," Private William C. Lusk of Tyler's division wrote his family after the day was over, "were ransacking the houses for food, destroying and burning what they could not use themselves." Lusk, however, comforted himself with the thought that "Germantown is but a poor place though and $200 would probably cover the damage done to it."[22]

Looting also took place farther to the south. As directed by McDowell, Heintzelman sent his first brigade under Franklin, followed by Howard's, directly to Sangster's Station. Although the last of his troops had not gotten into camp until just an hour before, Heintzelman roused his command at 4:00 A.M. and soon had them marching with what some considered excessive caution toward Sangster's Station. "Hardly a musket shot was fired," one marcher wrote later, "but our commanders were fearful of masked batteries, and proceeded as timidly as old maids eating shad in the dark."[23] After a slow, tiring 12-mile march, Franklin's vanguard managed to reach the station at around 3:00 P.M., too late to engage the small party of South Carolina troops from Brigadier General Richard Ewell's brigade that had set fire to the two railroad bridges over Pope's Run between Sangster's Station and Bull Run during the retreat from Fairfax Station. "Deprived of bodily vigor" by the previous day's march and the intense heat of the seventeenth, "hundreds of men were obliged to leave the ranks" temporarily during the march, although most managed to find their way to Sangster's Station by the end of the day. It was a matter of no little delight to Heintzelman's weary men when they arrived at Sangster's to find a freshly mowed field near the railroad where the retreating rebels had conveniently abandoned their tents. That night, one Massachusetts man later recalled, "camping simply meant rolling oneself in his blanket and lying down to such dreams as sleep might afford."[24]

Those soldiers who did not immediately take advantage of the opportunity to rest began foraging. Within an hour, they had seized several pigs and about one hundred and fifty sheep. News of what his men had done just as quickly reached Colonel Franklin, who was as zealous a proponent of conciliation as there was in the army. He responded by immediately issuing orders to his officers that they were to shoot any man caught slaughtering any of the captured animals. The orders were ignored and, combined with the efforts of some officers to enforce McDowell's general orders regarding Southern property, stirred considerable resentment among the men in the ranks. That night they disregarded Franklin's directive, "stealthily cooked in the night what they had slaughtered and concealed," and grumbled about their officers.[25]

In addition to sending Franklin to Sangster's Station, Heintzelman, exercising the discretion granted him by the commanding officer, had Willcox march his brigade north toward Fairfax Station to locate Miles's left. Before they reached Fairfax Station, Willcox's men heard gunfire and rushed forward, only to encounter some of Miles's men hunting turkeys. Upon reaching Fairfax Station around noon, Willcox managed to capture eleven prisoners and a rebel flag. He then moved forward to Fairfax Court House, but found it already occupied and countermarched his men back to Fairfax Station, where they encamped for the night.

McDowell, who was much more sensitive to the political implications of his army's conduct, was infuriated when he arrived at Fairfax Court House and found his men looting and pillaging. The following day he responded to the incident by issuing an angry order to his troops stating: "It is with the deepest mortification [that] the general commanding finds it necessary to reiterate his orders for the preservation of the property of the inhabitants. Hardly had we arrived at this place when, to the horror of every right-minded person, several homes were broken open and others were in flames by some of those who, it has been the boast of the loyal, came here to protect the oppressed and free the country from the domination of a hated party." To prevent such a recurrence, McDowell directed each regiment to appoint a provost marshal and 10-man police force whose "special and sole duty it shall be to preserve the property from depredation and arrest all wrong-doers." Although it provoked a great deal of grumbling, there were men who welcomed McDowell's action. The order, William Lusk informed his family on the nineteenth, enabled him "to march forward with a lighter heart, for it was not pleasant to be connected with thieves."[26]

Hoping to convert his men from vandals back into soldiers and frustrated that the rebels had escaped his well-laid trap, McDowell also responded to the scene at Fairfax and Germantown by ordering Tyler, whom he blamed for the failure to bag Bonham, to put his men on the road to Centreville in pursuit of the fleeing rebels. Unfortunately, looting and two days of marching had left the division exhausted. Tyler was able to march only a few miles on the Warrenton Turnpike toward Centreville before the sun set on July 17. That evening McDowell called Tyler to headquarters and instructed him to continue his advance on the turnpike the following day, seize Centreville, and then "observe well the roads to Bull Run and to Warrenton . . . [to] keep up the impression that we are moving on Manassas."[27]

After his meeting with Tyler, McDowell rode over to Sangster's Station. There he met with Heintzelman "to make arrangements to turn the enemy's right and intercept his communications with the South," while Tyler distracted him from the direction of Centreville.[28] After talking with Heintzelman and conducting a personal reconnaissance of the area, however, McDowell decided the terrain was too wooded and the roads too narrow and irregular to carry out his plan of crossing Bull Run at Wolf Run Shoals in force, turning Beauregard's right, and cutting the railroad south of Manassas. Consequently, he directed Heintzelman to march his division to Centreville, whence McDowell decided he would look for opportunities to operate against the Confederate left.

Back in Washington, the movements of McDowell's army were being followed closely by General Scott, whose headquarters William Howard Russell visited on the seventeenth. What Russell saw underwhelmed him. "I look around me for a staff and look in vain," he noted. "I see no system, no order, no knowledge, no dash!" What he did find were "a few plodding old pedants" and "some ignorant young and not very active men, who loiter about the headquarter halls, and strut up the street with brass spurs on their heels . . . as if they were soldiers." One of Scott's aides, Colonel George Cullum, briefly took Russell aside to show him some maps and explain the situation in the Valley and at Manassas. The briefing did little to diminish the journalist's skepticism about the operation and the army that was carrying it out. After leaving headquarters, Russell proceeded down Pennsylvania Avenue to Willard's Hotel. There he encountered several drunken officers who provided him with "the most exaggerated accounts of desperate fighting" and assured him that General Scott was about to take the field personally. The experience severely tried Russell's ability to be objective about the events and men he was witnessing. "It is not fair to ridicule either officers or men of this army," he wrote in his diary that night, "and if they were not so inflated by their own pestilent vanity, no one would dream of doing so; but the excessive bragging and boasting . . . tax patience and forbearance overmuch."[29]

∽ "The enemy has assailed my outposts in heavy force," P. G. T. Beauregard wrote President Davis on July 17. "I have fallen back on the line of Bull Run. . . . If his force is overwhelming I shall retire to the Rappahannock. . . . Send any re-enforcements at the earliest possible instant and by every possible means."[30]

The Federal advance came as no surprise to Beauregard. He had a network of female spies operating throughout northern Virginia, and even in Washington, who rushed to his outposts to inform him the moment McDowell's advance began. Although the exploits of these femmes fatales make for fine romance, their importance should not be overrated. Every male in Fairfax County would have had to have been blind, deaf, and dumb not to know that McDowell and his Yankee army had begun their advance.

That did not, however, change the fact that Beauregard's army lacked the means to deal adequately with the Federal advance. On the seventeenth, he managed to get his outposts back behind Bull Run successfully, but more was needed. Richmond recognized this as well, and even though word had just reached the capital of disastrous defeats at Rich Mountain and Corrick's Ford in western Virginia, as soon as Beauregard's message arrived announcing the need for reinforcements, President Davis did not hesitate. Orders immediately went out to Johnston stating: "Beauregard is attacked. To strike the enemy a decisive blow a junction of all your effective force will be needed. If practicable, make the movement."[31]

The first question was, could Johnston make the movement? Preventing him from doing so was the task General Scott confidently assured his subordinates and President Lincoln that General Patterson would perform. Indeed, Scott refused to consider the possibility that Patterson might fail in his mission, as General Tyler learned when, during a private meeting on July 13, he challenged the commanding general's confident assurance that McDowell would succeed due to his greater numbers. "Suppose Jo. Johnston should reinforce Beauregard," Tyler asked, "what result should you expect then, General?" "Patterson," Scott sternly advised Tyler, "will take care of Jo. Johnston."[32]

After crossing the Potomac to occupy Harpers Ferry following Johnston's retreat from the town in mid-June, Patterson had, at the direction of General Scott, sent Burnside's regiment of Rhode Island troops and all of his regular army units of infantry and cavalry to Washington. It was the presence of the regulars that in Patterson's mind had induced Johnston to retreat to Winchester. Now that they were gone, he feared the rebels would cross the Potomac at Williamsport and cut off Harpers Ferry. Patterson's anxiety was shared by Senator John Sherman, who had gone up to Hagerstown to investigate the situation and had become so alarmed at the decision to call the regulars to Washington that he felt compelled to file a protest with Secretary of War Simon Cameron that had no effect. Consequently, when rumors reached him that Johnston was planning such a move and that the size of his force "could not have been less than 14,000 men" (both of which rumors were inaccurate), Patterson ordered his forces to recross the Potomac on June 18.[33]

When the rumors about Johnston's advance proved false, although reports still grossly exaggerated the strength of Confederate forces along the Upper Potomac, Patterson began recrossing the river on July 2. Patterson's crossing provoked a sharp skirmish at Falling Waters with Colonel Jackson's command, which Johnston had pushed to Martinsburg along with Colonel James Ewell Brown Stuart's cavalry to watch the enemy. After the skirmish, Jackson and Stuart fell back to a position at Darkesville three miles north of Winchester. There, on July 3, Jackson encountered Johnston and advised him of the situation. Believing Patterson needed to be confronted but that the Federal force was much larger than his own, Johnston had brought the rest of his army forward from Winchester to Darkesville.

Johnston, however, was highly pessimistic about the ability of his raw troops to conduct offensive operations and decided merely to post his command in a strong position at Darkesville overlooking a branch of Opequon Creek. There he hoped he could entice Patterson into attacking and achieve a defensive victory. Patterson, however, refused to follow Johnston's script. Instead, he decided to bring up supplies from his base at Hagerstown, Maryland, and consolidate his position at Martinsburg. A disappointed Johnston ordered his men to fall back to their camps around Winchester on July 7.

After successfully crossing the Potomac and arriving at Martinsburg, Patterson advised Washington that he hoped to advance "to Winchester to drive the enemy from that place, if any remain."[34] But, like Johnston, Patterson did not have a great deal of faith in the ability of his command to conduct offensive operations. The enlistments of his 3-month troops were set to expire in the near future, and even though Washington promised to forward several regiments to the Upper Potomac during the first two weeks of July, they were sure to be so raw that Patterson could have little confidence in them. To make matters worse, rumors reached Patterson that Johnston had 26,000 men at Darkesville.

Nonetheless, Scott demanded that Patterson do something and to press the case, dispatched General Charles Sandford "with two of his most efficient regiments" to the Upper Potomac on July 7. Two days later, well aware that Scott and McDowell were counting on his keeping Johnston from joining Beauregard, Patterson decided to call his field commanders and staff together for a council of war. There his quartermasters offered a gloomy assessment of the army's logistical situation, and his engineers expressed grave anxiety over its position. "Our whole line," one of the latter, Captain John Newton, complained, "is a false one. We have no business here except for the purpose of making a demonstration. [Johnston] threatens us. We should be in a position to threaten him. We should go to Charlestown, Harpers Ferry, Shepardstown, and flank him."[35] The council reinforced Patterson's inclination toward caution. Consequently, he decided to await the arrival of Sandford and more regiments before he did anything.

Finally, on July 15, at the urging of General Scott, Patterson decided to push south toward Winchester. Finding Johnston had abandoned his position at Darkesville and retreated back to Winchester, Patterson pushed his command south to Bunker Hill, five miles north of Winchester. There he halted and issued orders for a reconnaissance of Johnston's position on the sixteenth, which Patterson knew coincided with the beginning of McDowell's advance.

The Federal reconnaissances on the sixteenth and seventeenth were cautious and ineffectual. They were enough, however, to raise hopes in the Confederate camp for a much-desired battle. "The boys seemed eager," one man in the Thirty-third Virginia recorded in his diary, "to give the abominable wretches a warm reception."[36]

There would be no battle with Patterson, however. Johnston easily deduced the Federal commander had no intention of attacking Winchester and was merely trying to keep him away from Manassas. His suspicions were confirmed when telegrams arrived from Richmond and Manassas just after midnight reporting that McDowell's advance had begun and that he was to go to Beauregard's assistance if he deemed it practicable. Johnston did not hesitate to deem such a move practicable. Shortly before midnight on the seventeenth, he called his brigade commanders to his headquarters and informed them that they would march to Manassas the next day.

In all, the "Army of the Shenandoah" that Johnston was leading to the assistance of Beauregard's "Army of the Potomac" at Manassas was composed of approximately 10,600 troops organized into five infantry brigades and one regiment of cavalry, the First Virginia, commanded by Colonel Stuart. Jackson, clad in his old blue army uniform, which had been adorned by the single star of a brigadier general since mid-June, commanded Johnston's all-Virginia First Brigade. Colonel Francis S. Bartow, a handsome politician from Georgia who lacked any formal military training, commanded the Second Brigade. The Third Brigade was led by Brigadier General Bernard E. Bee of South Carolina, an 1834 graduate of West Point who had seen service in the Mexican War. Colonel Arnold Elzey, a Maryland native and West Point graduate who had served in both the Mexican and Seminole Wars and commanded a Federal arsenal in Georgia when that state seceded, led the Fourth Brigade. The Fifth Brigade, organized only a week before the move to Manassas commenced, was commanded by Brigadier General Edmund Kirby Smith, a young and able West Pointer from Florida who would go on to play a major role in the Confederate war effort.

To make sure Patterson did not realize what he was doing, Johnston directed Stuart to take his cavalry north before dawn to establish a screen and report on the Federal army's activities. By 9:00 A.M. on July 18, when Stuart reported all was still in the Federal camps, Johnston was ready to go. The orders to march to Manassas were enthusiastically received by Johnston's men. "There is no man living of all that army," one man later wrote, "who can ever forget the thrill of 'Berserker rage' which took possession of us all when the news was understood. . . . Every man sprang to his place, and in an incredibly short time we were rapidly moving through the dusty streets of old Winchester."[37]

Leading the way from Winchester to Manassas would be Jackson's brigade. Jackson, as was his wont, drove his men hard. Their hot, dusty march took them first up the Valley to Millwood, where they crossed the Shenandoah River. Fording the river was, one member of a brigade that followed Jackson wrote in his diary, "by no means a pleasant task, as many of the men were footsore and the bed of the stream exceedingly rocky." After passing through Ashby's Gap in the Blue Ridge, Jackson's men arrived at Paris at approximately 2:00 A.M. and caught a few hours of sleep while, according to legend, Jackson himself stood watch before marching the last few miles to Piedmont Station on the Manassas Gap Railroad. There they received an enthusiastic greeting from the local populace. "Citizens for miles around came flocking to see us, bringing eatables of all kinds," one participant later recalled. "We had a regular picnic; plenty to eat, lemonade to drink, and beautiful young ladies to chat with." After breakfasting and waiting for cars to arrive at the station for two hours, at 8:00 A.M. on July 19, Jackson's men finally boarded the train, "bade the ladies a long farewell," and began a painfully slow eight-hour, 34-mile train trip to Manassas packed "like so many pins and needles" into cars pulled by the single locomotive operating on the line.[38]

In the meantime, the man who was supposed to be preventing all this, Patterson, was ineffectually maneuvering north of Winchester. Although convinced that reports that Johnston's force at Winchester now numbered 42,000 were correct and gravely concerned about the number of units in his command scheduled to be mustered out in a few days, after occupying Bunker Hill, Patterson nonetheless pushed a force forward toward Winchester on July 16. However, upon encountering and pushing back Stuart's cavalry screen, his demonstration force halted and Patterson decided not to continue on to Winchester the following day. Instead, concerned that the terms of service for eighteen regiments of Pennsylvania troops were set to expire within a week and that their departure meant that "any active operations toward Winchester cannot be thought of until they are replaced by three years' men," at midnight he ordered his men to withdraw toward Charlestown to be closer to Harpers Ferry.[39]

Even after a message arrived from Scott in Washington reminding him that he was expected to press the Confederates at Winchester hard and that the week remaining in the enlistments of his troops was still "enough to win victories," Patterson remained determined to fall back. "I have certainly been expecting you to beat the enemy," wrote Scott, "or, at least, [to have] occupied him by threats and demonstrations. . . . Has he not stolen a march and sent reenforcements toward Manassas Junction?" "The enemy," Patterson assured Scott, "has stolen no march upon me. I have kept him actively employed."[40] Of course, that evening Jackson's men were in fact on the march to Piedmont Station.

For this performance, Patterson would lose his command and his reputation. But there were mitigating circumstances to be taken into account. The first, of course was the matter of the enlistments of Patterson's Pennsylvania regiments. Those troops made up the bulk of his command, their enlistments were up, and nothing could persuade them to stay on beyond the ninety days they had signed up for. Second, Patterson was convinced that, regardless of Scott's expressed anxiety, there was now no way Johnston could reach Beauregard in time to prevent his defeat by McDowell. In this, Patterson was not altogether wrong. The battle of Bull Run would indeed be decided by the timely arrival of Johnston's army—but it was a very close call. Had McDowell's marches and maneuvers against Beauregard gone on schedule or been better executed, there would not have been time for Johnston's men to reach the battlefield.

By the time the sun went down on July 19, Jackson was at Manassas, and Bartow's Second Brigade was en route. The former would arrive at approximately 8:00 A.M. the next morning. Shortly after dawn on the twentieth, Bee's command, accompanied by Johnston, began boarding trains. At approximately noon, Johnston reached Manassas and headed to Beauregard's headquarters. The concentration was slowly, but surely, under way. Would McDowell give them the time to complete it? Or would there be a decisive fight before it was done? The fate of the Confederacy hung in the balance.

NOTES

1. Thomas W. Cutrer, ed., *Longstreet's Aide: The Civil War Letters of Major Thomas J. Goree* (Charlottesville: University Press of Virginia, 1995), 21.
2. *OR*, 2:303–4.
3. Ibid., 2:305.

4. James B. Fry, "McDowell's Advance to Bull Run," in *Battles and Leaders of the Civil War*, edited by Johnson and Buel, 1:176; Russell, *My Diary North and South*, 252.

5. Russell, *My Diary North and South*, 250–51.

6. Haynes, *A History of the Second Regiment, New Hampshire Volunteer Infantry*, 20.

7. Rhodes, ed., *All for the Union*, 24; Aldrich, *The History of Battery A*, 14–15.

8. Wheeler, *A Rising Thunder*, 306.

9. Simpson and Berlin, *Sherman's Civil War: Selected Correspondence*, 120; Sears, ed., *For Country, Cause and Leader*, 51.

10. Gurowski, *Diary*, 1:58; *OR*, 2:305.

11. Sears, ed., *For Country, Cause and Leader*, 51; Thomas S. Allen, "The Second Wisconsin at the First Battle of Bull Run," in George H. Otis, *The Second Wisconsin Infantry*, edited by Alan D. Gaff (Dayton, OH: Press of Morningside Bookshop, 1984), 221.

12. H. B. Jackson, "From Washington to Bull Run and Back Again," in Otis, *Second Wisconsin Infantry*, 233.

13. Blake, *Three Years in the Army of the Potomac*, 8; Roe, *Fifth Regiment Massachusetts Infantry in Its Three Tours of Duty*, 65; Edwin S. Barrett, *What I Saw at Bull Run* (Boston: Beacon Press, 1886), 12.

14. Blake, *Three Years in the Army of the Potomac*, 8–9.

15. Howard, *Autobiography*, 2:148.

16. *OR*, 2:304.

17. Dangerfield Parker, "Personal Reminiscences: The Battalion of Regular Infantry at the First Battle of Bull Run," *War Papers Read before the Commandery of the District of Columbia Military Order of the Loyal Legion of the United States*, 4 vols. (Wilmington, DE: Broadfoot Publishing Co., 1993 [1897–1903]), 2:207.

18. Rhodes, ed., *All for the Union*, 24; idem, "The First Campaign of the Second Rhode Island Infantry," *Personal Narratives of Events in the War of the Rebellion, Being Papers Read before the Rhode Island Soldiers and Sailors Historical Society*, 10 vols. (Providence, RI: Sidney S. Rider, 1878–79), 1:11; *JCCW*, 2:39; William T. Sherman, *Memoirs of General W. T. Sherman*, 2 vols. (New York: Charles L. Webster, 1875), 1:198.

19. Cutrer, ed., *Longstreet's Aide*, 25.

20. James I. Robertson, *18th Virginia Infantry* (Lynchburg, VA: H. E. Howard, 1984), 4; *OR*, 2:305; Cutrer, ed., *Longstreet's Aide*, 25.

21. Haynes, *History of the Second Regiment, New Hampshire Volunteer Infantry*, 21; Augustus Woodbury, *The Second Rhode Island Regiment: A Narrative of Military Operations in Which the Regiment Was Engaged from the Beginning to the End of the War for the Union* (Providence, RI: Valpey, Angell and Company, 1875), 29; Aldrich, *History of Battery A*, 16.

22. Aldrich, *History of Battery A*, 15–16; William Chittenden Lusk, ed., *War Letters of William Thompson Lusk* (New York: [n.p.], 1911), 52.

23. Harold Adams Small, ed., *The Road to Richmond: The Civil War Memoirs of Maj. Abner R. Small of the 16th Maine Vols., With His Diary as a Prisoner of War* (Berkeley: University of California Press, 1959), 18.

24. Blake, *Three Years in the Army of the Potomac*, 10; Roe, *Fifth Massachusetts Volunteers*, 66.

25. Blake, *Three Years in the Army of the Potomac*, 11.

26. *OR*, 2:743–44; Lusk, ed., *War Letters*, 53.

27. *OR*, 2:305–6, 312.

28. Ibid., 2:307–8.

29. Russell, *My Diary North and South*, 251–52.

30. *OR*, 2:439–40.

31. Ibid., 2:478, 981.

32. Tyler, "Autobiography," 49.

33. *OR*, 2:702–4.

34. Ibid., 2:158.

35. Ibid., 2:161, 164.

36. Lowell Reidenbaugh, *33rd Virginia Infantry* (Lynchburg, VA: H. E. Howard, 1987), 5.

37. Conrad, "History of the First Battle of Manassas and the Organization of the Stonewall Brigade," 19:86.

38. John G. Barrett, ed., *Yankee Rebel: The Civil War Journal of Edmund DeWitt Patterson* (Chapel Hill: University of North Carolina Press, 1966), 7; John O. Casler, *Four Years in the Stonewall Brigade* (Girard, KS: Appeal Publishing Company, 1906), 22; Conrad, "History of the First Battle of Manassas and the Organization of the Stonewall Brigade," 19:87.

39. *OR*, 2:167.

40. Ibid., 2:168.

CHAPTER SEVEN

BLACKBURN'S FORD

ACTUALLY, BY THE TIME Jackson's brigade boarded the railroad cars at Piedmont Station, there had already been a fight along Bull Run. It caused a great deal of excitement, but was not the big, climactic battle everyone anticipated. In the predawn hours of July 18, McDowell ordered Tyler to advance from his position a few miles south of Fairfax Court House along the Warrenton Turnpike toward Centreville, seize the village, and then await the rest of the army. Tyler was not—and the orders McDowell issued before he went off to Sangster's Station to consult with Heintzelman were explicit on this—to "bring on an engagement," but merely to "keep up the impression that we are moving on Manassas."[1]

At 7:00 A.M., Tyler's men were on the road to Centreville. They reached the village two hours later and found extensive fortifications that Tyler later described as "the meanest, most miserable works ever got up by military men," but no rebel troops. Upon his arrival, Tyler directed one of his cavalry commanders to "bring to my headquarters any respectable looking citizens that he might find" and sent a report to McDowell asking for instructions.[2] Within a half-hour, six local residents had been rounded up. They informed Tyler that the rebels had evacuated Centreville the previous night and were now behind Bull Run. Tyler, concerned about the lack of water in Centreville to slake the thirst of his troops and not having received a response from McDowell to his earlier message, decided to push Colonel Israel B. Richardson's brigade south to reconnoiter the ground between Centreville and Bull Run. By 10:30 A.M., Richardson had rounded up two companies of infantry and some cavalry, and, accompanied by Tyler, was on the road to Blackburn's and Mitchell's Fords.

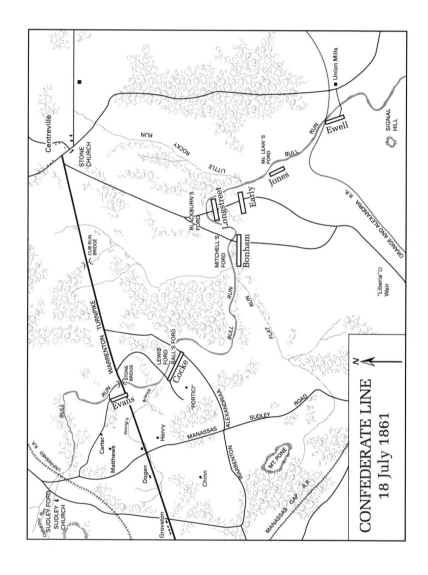

CONFEDERATE LINE
18 July 1861

Tyler and Richardson found no substantial Confederate forces between Centreville and Bull Run and soon found a point from which they could see General Bonham's brigade in a strong position covering Mitchell's Ford. They could also see that the terrain between their position and Bull Run commanded the other side of Blackburn's Ford. Tyler and Richardson were then joined by Major John G. Barnard, the army's chief engineer, who reminded them that McDowell did not want to do battle here, but also advised them that he did not see how a demonstration could do any harm.

Tyler and Richardson eagerly decided a demonstration was indeed in order. From his command post at the Butler farm, Tyler directed Richardson to bring the rest of his command forward as rapidly as possible and sent orders to Colonel Sherman to have his brigade ready to move if necessary. He then called for Captain Romeyn B. Ayres to bring forward his two 20-pound rifled cannon and directed the forces under Captain Robert Brethschneider, already with him, to deploy as skirmishers. Once Ayres and his gunners were in position and had unlimbered, they opened fire in an effort to induce the rebels to reveal their position at Blackburn's.

The forces guarding the ford that Tyler so badly wanted to find out about belonged to the brigade commanded by Brigadier General James Longstreet. Destined to become Robert E. Lee's "Old War Horse" and one of the war's most controversial generals, Longstreet was a native Georgian who had graduated from West Point in 1842 and performed well as a combat commander in the Mexican War. He had opposed secession, but nonetheless resigned his commission as a major in the U.S. Army after Fort Sumter. On July 1, 1861, he was appointed a brigadier general in the Confederate army and sent to Manassas. There General Beauregard placed him in command of a 1,400-man brigade, composed of the First, Eleventh, and Seventeenth Virginia Infantry Regiments with the task of guarding Blackburn's Ford.

Longstreet found his position on the south (right) bank of Bull Run to be anything but a good one. At the apex of a great bend in the stream, it was dominated by a 15-foot bluff on the other side, which was covered with tangled overgrowth. Recognizing immediately the advantage of taking a position on the north side of the stream, when his command arrived at the ford, Longstreet decided to post his regiments there and set his men to clearing it of trees. When Beauregard found out about this, however, he put a stop to the efforts of Longstreet's men and instructed their commander that "the advanced position of the brigade would mar his general plan and ordered the line to be taken along the river bank of the south side."[3]

Longstreet complied and redeployed his men. On the morning of July 18, he had Colonel Montgomery D. Corse's Seventeenth Virginia posted to the left and Colonel P. T. Moore's First Virginia to the right of the of the road connecting Centreville and Manassas that crossed at the ford. Colonel Samuel Garland's Eleventh Virginia was placed to Corse's left, where they were to serve as a link with Bonham's command guarding Mitchell's Ford. Serving as a reserve for Longstreet's command, as well as for the rest of the brigades guarding Bull Run, was a brigade under Colonel Jubal A. Early posted near the home of Wilmer McLean about a mile to the rear of Blackburn's Ford, which Beauregard was using as his headquarters.

Longstreet learned of Tyler's advance at around 11:30 A.M. from the pickets he had stationed on the north side of Bull Run. He then placed his two pieces of artillery "in convenient position," but, with a healthy respect for the power of Federal artillery and the nature of the ground on the opposite side of Bull Run, also directed his cannoneers "to retire the moment it was ascertained that our pieces were commanded by those of the enemy." It took only one shot from Ayres's Federal guns to induce Longstreet to give the order to his gunners to retire "till a fairer opportunity was offered them."[4]

To the great frustration of Tyler and Richardson, however, Longstreet and Bonham managed to keep their infantry under control. A half-hour of lobbing shells across Bull Run brought Tyler "no positive information as to the infantry force at Blackburn's Ford." Thus, he decided to quickly advance Richardson's entire brigade toward the ford. Barnard and Captain James B. Fry of McDowell's staff, who had just arrived from Fairfax, vehemently protested to Tyler that he was violating the commanding general's desire not to bring on an engagement "on the straight road to Manassas, at one of the strongest crossings on Bull Run." Tyler, however, was unmoved by their arguments and sure of his own judgment, as Barnard put it, "that the enemy would run wherever menaced by serious attack." By noon he had Richardson's men moving forward toward the stream to engage the rebels.[5]

Leading the Federal advance on the left side of the road to Blackburn's Ford, were three companies from Colonel Robert Cowdin's First Massachusetts Infantry under the immediate command of Lieutenant Colonel George Wells. Some of Longstreet's Virginians panicked at the first volley fired by Wells's men and started to break and run. The sight of Longstreet with a cigar in his mouth and a saber in his hand, riding "amid a perfect shower of balls" and determined to give those who ran "the sword and my horse's heels," however, managed to persuade the men there would be "as much danger in their rear as in front."[6] They returned to the firing line and poured a volley into Wells's ranks. Wells responded by impetuously ordering his gray-clad men to charge. Longstreet's men coolly greeted them with volleys from their muskets, which halted the Federal advance and compelled Wells to take a position on the ridge overlooking Bull Run. From the crest of the ridge, Wells's men continued exchanging fire with the rebels for almost an hour.

Tyler then decided to send Ayres and his two cannon forward, supported by two companies of cavalry under Captain A. G. Brackett. Richardson then suggested that the rest of his brigade be allowed to push forward so it could be in position in case the opportunity for a successful attack on the Confederate position at the ford presented itself. Unable to judge how many Confederates actually were at the ford and eager to prove his ability in independent command, Tyler approved Richardson's proposal. Richardson then formed his brigade with Colonel Ezra Walrath's Twelfth New York on the far left with Ayres's guns to his right. To the right of Ayres was Codwin's First Massachusetts, with Major Adolphus W. Williams's Second Michigan next to it, and Colonel Daniel McConnell's Third Michigan on the Federal right.

As Richardson was getting his command into line and preparing to advance toward the ford, Ayres brought his two guns into position and fired a shot of canister across the creek. Longstreet's men responded with a furious volley that stunned Tyler.

"It appeared to me," he later recalled, "that there were 5,000 muskets fired at once."[7] This convinced Tyler that the ford was too heavily defended to attack with much prospect of success and that he should end the fight. Worse for the Federals, the Confederates quickly and effectively targeted Ayres's guns. One was crippled when its horses and six members of the crew fell either dead or wounded. Ayres then ordered the other gun withdrawn, along with Brackett's cavalry. Ayres was eventually able to retrieve the other gun, but there would be no artillery support for Richardson's regiments, who had already began to advance, with Tyler powerless to stop them.

Walrath's New Yorkers pushed forward into the woods to the left of the road leading to the ford. As they approached the banks of Bull Run they were greeted with a thunderous volley from across the stream fired by the First Virginia Infantry. Although unsupported by artillery, Walrath's men stood their ground and exchanged fire with the enemy on the other side of Bull Run for approximately twenty minutes, during which time, wrote one observer, "There was one continuous roar of musketry."[8] Then, one of Walrath's companies began to fall back, which the rest of the regiment interpreted as a general order. As they all fell back, panic set in among the green New Yorkers. Shouting, "We are all cut to pieces!" to the units they encountered as they fell back, their retreat quickly degenerated into a rout that neither Walrath nor Richardson could stop.[9]

After repulsing the Twelfth New York, Longstreet ordered some of his frontline troops to cross Bull Run and called for help from Early, who had already dispatched Colonel Harry T. Hays's Seventh Louisiana to Blackburn's Ford. The disintegration and flight of Walrath's men exposed the left flank of the First Massachusetts and the Second Michigan, and they came under a punishing fire from the front and flank from the two companies that Longstreet managed to get across the stream. Yet neither the disintegration of his left nor the beleaguered condition of the First Massachusetts and Second Michigan diminished Richardson's desire to push across Bull Run. Tyler, however, had had enough. When he rode up to see what was going on, Richardson requested permission to push his three regiments farther forward. He was sure, he told Tyler, that with Sherman's and Ayres's help, he could "clear out those fellows from the bottom in two hours."[10] Tyler, however, desiring to wrap up the affair himself, declined Richardson's request and ordered him to withdraw his forces.

Richardson began his withdrawal just as Early's men were arriving on the field. Their movement to the front had not been an easy one, as it was made in clear view of Richardson's forces on the opposite side of Bull Run. "Quite a brisk fire of musketry" from the Federals was all it took to throw Lieutenant Colonel Lewis B. Williams Jr.'s raw Seventh Virginia "into some confusion and caus[ed] it to begin firing without orders, while there were some of our troops in front of it."[11] The firing caused much distress for Longstreet, who had no desire to see his men killed by friendly fire. His first impulse was to ride in front of Early's line to tell the men to stop. That this was not a good idea did not cross Longstreet's mind until he found himself staring down the barrels of Early's muskets. To avoid being shot himself, he "found it necessary to dismount" and throw himself upon the ground "till the loads were discharged."[12] Fortunately for Longstreet and his men, Early quickly managed to restore order in his command. He then placed Hays's men to the left of Blackburn's Ford, relieving Corse's Virginians, advanced the Seventh Virginia to the support of the First Virginia on Hays's right, and brought up two artillery pieces.

The experience of taking fire from the rear, however, had a chilling effect on Longstreet's men on the opposite side of Bull Run. After crossing the stream, Longstreet's first instinct was to launch a counterattack against Richardson's men. The Federals, however, still held the high ground and, despite having their flank exposed by the retreat of the Twelfth New York, were able to put up a pretty stiff fight as they withdrew. The combined effects of "encountering the enemy in front, and receiving fire from our friends in rear," Longstreet later recalled, "were not reassuring."[13] Deciding nothing more could be done, he called back his advanced units to the right bank of Bull Run and let Tyler and Richardson retire relatively unmolested.

Although both sides had withdrawn their infantry, neither Tyler nor Longstreet was ready to stop the fight completely. For about another hour the combatants continued to fire their artillery at one another without much harm on either side. That did not make the situation any easier on the nerves of the thirsty men at the front who were experiencing their first taste of combat on what was a very hot day. "We . . . laid down on ground a little lower than the batteries," wrote one member of the Second Michigan. "The balls mostly passed abt 4 feet over our heads. One struck a man in Co. H abt 20 ft. from me shattering his arm and turning him over endwise."[14]

Perhaps the most significant casualty of the artillery duel was General Beauregard's dinner, which was ruined when a Union shell crashed into the McLean house just as he was sitting down to eat. "The interruption so annoyed him," Longstreet later recalled, "that he sent us four 6-pound and three rifle guns . . . to return fire and avenge the loss of his dinner."[15]

As this was going on, Colonel Sherman's brigade came up to cover Richardson's retreat and support Ayers's battery. There they remained until after the artillery duel ended at around 4:00 P.M. "The cannonading was quite brisk," Sherman reported to his brother the following day, "but the shots mostly passed over us, the Batteries were simply firing at each other." He also reported: "Gen. McDowell arrived during the cannonading and I think he did not like it."[16]

Sherman was correct. However much the loss of his dinner may have bothered Beauregard, it in no way matched the level of annoyance McDowell felt when he arrived at Centreville after his visit to Sangster's Station and found out what Tyler had done. He was angry because his order to avoid an engagement had not been obeyed, and he sensed that the unauthorized fight "had a bad effect upon our men."[17] Nonetheless, he decided not to rebuke his subordinate directly at the time.

Of more pressing importance to McDowell that evening, now that he knew his plan to turn the Confederate right was impracticable, was the task of getting his army concentrated at Centreville and provisioned. In his orders for July 19, McDowell instructed his division commanders to wait where they were for supplies to come up. If supply trains did not arrive in a timely manner, they were to "procure beef from the inhabitants." Then, once provisioned with at least two days' cooked rations, Heintzelman was to march from Sangster's Station to Little Rocky Run on the road to Centreville, where they would encamp. Miles would go to Centreville, while Tyler moved west of Centreville on the Warrenton Turnpike and Hunter advanced "as near as Centreville as he can get water."[18]

Casualties on both sides in the fight at Blackburn's Ford were relatively light. Longstreet calculated his losses at sixty-three killed and wounded; Richardson reported only eighty-three men killed, wounded, or missing. Still, both sides interpreted the fight as a Confederate victory, and the fiasco at Blackburn's Ford was the third straight embarrassment for the Union forces in Virginia.

NOTES

1. *OR*, 2:312.
2. *JCCW*, 2:205; Tyler, "Autobiography," 51.
3. James Longstreet, *From Manassas to Appomattox: Memoirs of the Civil War in America* (Philadelphia: J. B. Lippincott, 1895), 35.
4. *OR*, 2:461; Longstreet, *From Manassas to Appomattox*, 38.
5. Tyler, "Autobiography," 53; *JCCW*, 2:163; John B. Barnard, *The C.S.A. and the Battle of Bull Run* (New York: D. Van Nostrand, 1862), 49.
6. Cutrer, ed., *Longstreet's Aide*, 26; Longstreet, *From Manassas to Appomattox*, 39.
7. *JCCW*, 2:200.
8. Cutrer, ed., *Longstreet's Aide*, 26.
9. Allen, "The Second Wisconsin at the First Battle of Bull Run," in *Second Wisconsin Infantry*, 223.
10. Tyler, "Autobiography," 54.
11. *OR*, 2:464; Jubal A. Early, *Narrative of the War between the States*, with notes by R. H. Early and an introduction by Gary W. Gallagher (New York: Da Capo Press, 1989 [1912]), 8.
12. Longstreet, *From Manassas to Appomattox*, 39.
13. Ibid., 40.
14. Sears, ed., *For Country, Cause, and Leader*, 53.
15. Ibid., 40.
16. Simpson and Berlin, eds., *Sherman's Civil War*, 120–21.
17. *JCCW*, 2:39.
18. *OR*, 2:307–8.

PART THREE

THE BATTLE

CHAPTER EIGHT

"THE PLAN OF THE INTENDED BATTLE . . . WAS A GOOD ONE"

ALTHOUGH THE EVENTS at Blackburn's Ford had been an embarrassment for the Federals and had significantly boosted morale among Beauregard's Southerners, they had by no means decided the campaign. General McDowell still enjoyed a significant numerical advantage over his Confederate counterpart and had every intention of capitalizing on it. The question was how to do so. Obviously, the direct road from Centreville to Manassas via Blackburn's Ford was strongly guarded. Tyler's blundering, lamentable as it was, had at least made that clear. And in any event, McDowell had no intention of making a direct assault on the Confederate line with his green troops. Instead, he hoped to find a way to flank his opponent, just as Winfield Scott had fifteen years earlier at Cerro Gordo during the Mexican War. From his visit to Sangster's Station and conversations with Colonel Heintzelman he had concluded that the terrain around the Confederate right was "unfit for the operations of a large army," so turning the Confederate left was the only available option.[1] To carry out this operation, McDowell ordered Heintzelman and the rest of his division commanders to concentrate at Centreville. There the men would rest, refit, and await the orders from General McDowell that would send them into battle along Bull Run.

McDowell first had to find out exactly where Beauregard's flank was and whether there was a practical means of crossing the stream to turn it. For the answers to these questions he turned to his chief engineer Major John Gross Barnard. From his maps, Barnard was able to locate several possible crossings upstream from Blackburn's Ford. By far the best was the Stone Bridge where the Warrenton Turnpike crossed Bull Run. But it would be foolish to hope that Beauregard was incompetent enough not to have posted strong forces there. And, in fact, reports soon came in indicating that not only were considerable artillery and infantry posted there, as well as at the fords between Blackburn's and the turnpike, but that the Confederates had also mined the bridge.

Much more promising was a crossing two miles north of the bridge known as Sudley Ford. It was too far upstream for Beauregard, if he was also to defend adequately the crossing of the O & A near Union Mills, to hold in strength without stretching his line too thin and was clearly usable (the Manassas–Sudley Road crossed the stream there). Barnard immediately decided that Sudley Ford would admirably serve his commander's objectives. The only question was how to get thousands of men to the crossing. Although there were reports of a road leading from the Warrenton Turnpike west of Cub Run to Sudley Ford and another reportedly usable ford between Sudley and the Stone Bridge, they were not on any of Barnard's maps. Obviously, before he could recommend Sudley Ford to his chief, Barnard would have to confirm these reports. Thus, on the morning of July 19, Barnard, accompanied by a company of cavalry, Rhode Island governor William Sprague, and Captain David Woodbury, set out on a reconnaissance west of Cub Run to find a road to Sudley Ford.

Barnard and his companions quickly found the reported road, which turned north just west of Cub Run near an old blacksmith shop. They followed the road north a short distance until they encountered Confederate cavalry patrols. Not wishing to alert the enemy to their intentions, Barnard decided not "to pursue the reconnaissance farther." "We had," he later asserted, "seen enough to be convinced of the perfect practicability of the route."[2] Later that night, however, he authorized Woodbury to conduct another reconnaissance along the road. Woodbury's expedition also encountered Confederate patrols. Not wishing to arouse suspicion, Woodbury turned back without fully scouting the route to Sudley. Despite the incompleteness of these expeditions, Barnard confidently assured McDowell on July 20 that Sudley Ford offered a convenient route around the Confederate left.

With Barnard's report in hand, McDowell drew up his battle plans and at 8:00 P.M. called his division and brigade commanders to headquarters, spread out a map on the ground, and explained their assignments for the following morning. Tyler would march three of his brigades west along the Warrenton Turnpike from Centreville toward the Stone Bridge, followed by David Hunter's 3-brigade division and Samuel Heintzelman's division of four brigades. Tyler would make a demonstration at the bridge so that Beauregard would think the main attack would come there, while Heintzelman's and Hunter's divisions, approximately 13,000 men in all, turned north and marched toward the Bull Run crossings. At 7:00 A.M., Hunter would cross at Sudley and Heintzelman at Poplar Ford. They would link up on the other side of Bull Run and march south along the Manassas–Sudley Road to crush Beauregard's left and rear and, "if possible, destroy the railroad leading from Manassas to the Valley of Virginia." To distract the Confederates further and cover the Federal left and rear, Richardson's brigade of Tyler's division, supported by Dixon Miles's division, would operate in front of Mitchell's and Blackburn's Fords. One brigade commander later recalled coming out of the meeting with the impression that "the plan of the intended battle, from all I could learn of the field and the position of the enemy, was a good one. I noticed no want of confidence in our commander."[3]

It was indeed a good plan. Its success, however, like McDowell's entire campaign, depended upon whether or not Robert Patterson's army in the Valley could prevent Johnston from reinforcing Beauregard. Unfortunately for McDowell, Patterson failed, and on July 19 units from Johnston's army had begun boarding railroad cars bound for Manassas. As Barnard conducted his reconnaissances, the Federals at Centreville (but not Barnard who was deaf) could hear the sound of trains arriving at Manassas Junction. After two days of hearing trains, Tyler felt compelled to warn McDowell: "I am sure as that there is a God in Heaven, you will have to fight Jo. Johnson's [sic] Army at Manassas tomorrow."[4]

McDowell, however, would not let himself believe that Patterson had failed to keep Johnston in the Shenandoah Valley, even when creditable reports began circulating that the trains were in fact carrying Johnston's troops. After all, General Scott had guaranteed Patterson would do his job, and, besides, all kinds of rumors had been making the rounds. In any event, General

McDowell knew that regardless of whomever or whatever those trains were carrying, canceling his offensive was simply not an option at this point. Washington expected a battle; the enlistments of his 90-day regiments were fast expiring (indeed, two regiments had departed that day); and in the only fighting that had yet occurred, the action at Blackburn's Ford, the rebels had clearly gotten the better of it. To pull back now and assume the strategic defensive could be interpreted only as a defeat that would have a devastating effect on morale in the North and the South. He had no choice but to carry out the offensive he had planned.

Beauregard similarly hoped to take the offensive. After Blackburn's Ford and the news that Johnston would be sent to his aid, Beauregard experienced a rush of confidence and conceived a new plan for disposing of McDowell. Instead of sending all his forces to Manassas, Beauregard suggested to Johnston that he send part or all of his army north to pass through the Bull Run Mountains at Aldie. Then, while Beauregard's forces at Manassas attacked McDowell's front across Bull Run, Johnston's men would "press forward by way of Aldie, north-west of Manassas, and fall upon McDowell's right-rear."[5]

Johnston, however, rejected Beauregard's plan almost as soon as he received it and instead pushed his entire force to Manassas Junction. Arriving at the junction himself around noon on the twentieth, Johnston proceeded immediately to Beauregard's headquarters. Although it was clear even before Johnston's arrival that no forces would be pushed to Aldie, Beauregard let Johnston know that he still had no intention of passively awaiting McDowell's attack. Johnston himself was anxious that Patterson, once he realized the Confederates had given him the slip, would immediately go to McDowell's aid. Thus, he shared Beauregard's desire for immediate action. After describing the terrain, McDowell's location at Centreville, the fight at Blackburn's Ford, and the disposition of his forces along Bull Run, Beauregard proposed an attack on Centreville. Johnston decided to "rely upon [Beauregard's] knowledge" of the ground "and of the enemy's positions" and, although senior in rank, left the planning of an offensive to the hero of Fort Sumter.[6]

When Beauregard finished working out his attack plan early on the morning of July 21, 1861, his and Johnston's forces were positioned in an 8-mile line behind Bull Run that began at Union Mills Ford on the right. There, guarding the crossing of the O & A over Bull Run, was Brigadier General Richard S. Ewell's brigade. Upstream from Ewell, Bull Run made a sharp bend where three good crossings were located close together. It was here that Beauregard had concentrated the strength of his army. Brigadier General David R. Jones's brigade guarded McLean's Ford, and James Longstreet's, now with Thomas J. Jackson's brigade in support, was still posted at Blackburn's Ford. Milledge Bonham's command, with Brigadier General Barnard Bee and Colonel Francis Bartow's brigades in support, watched Mitchell's Ford. In addition to these forces, the reserve brigade commanded by Brigadier General Jubal Early was in a position approximately equidistant from McLean's, Blackburn's, and Mitchell's Fords. Just upstream from Bonham, Colonel Philip St. George Cocke's brigade covered Ball's Ford. Defending the Confederate far left three miles upstream from Cocke, was Colonel Nathan G. Evans, commanding only a regiment and a battalion—1,100 men in all— at the Stone Bridge where the Warrenton Turnpike crossed the stream.[7]

Beauregard planned to have Longstreet, supported by Jackson, Jones, and Ewell, cross Bull Run and advance to the east of Centreville in order to cut the Federal line of retreat to Washington, while Bonham, Bartow, and Cocke advanced directly on and assaulted the Federal position at Centreville. Although he agreed with Beauregard on the need to take the offensive along Bull Run, Johnston, who was by nature cautious and defensive-minded, could not help but be concerned about the weakness of the Confederate left. Thus, in a decision that would have a great impact on the events of July 21, he directed that Bee's and Jackson's brigades not participate in the offensive, but instead go to the support of Evans and Cocke on the left. Indeed, Johnston so impressed upon Beauregard the need to guard the left that the Creole general assigned Wade Hampton's Legion, which had just arrived from Richmond that morning, to the left as well. With these modifications implemented, Beauregard anxiously awaited

daylight and the opening of the grand offensive that he anticipated would send the Yankees fleeing back to Washington and
secure the new-born Confederacy its independence.

Unfortunately for Beauregard's plan, by the time he had developed it, McDowell's army was already on the move to turn
the Confederate left. Fortunately for the Confederacy, McDowell's
movements would not follow the timetable that the Federal commander had set.

At 2:00 A.M., Tyler, as directed, roused his men in their slumbering camps around Centreville and within a half-hour had them
on the march along the Warrenton Turnpike toward the bridge.
That maneuver, however, was about all that would go as planned
for the Union this early morning. For the march to the Stone
Bridge, Tyler placed Schenck's brigade in the lead, followed by
Sherman and Keyes. With five companies from the First and Second Ohio out in front on either side of the turnpike as skirmishers, Schenck and his men, haunted by the memory of the "masked
batteries" at Vienna, moved through the pitch-black night at gla-
cial speed, taking nearly an hour to cover the half-mile to Cub
Run, where they expected to meet resistance or at least find the
bridge destroyed. To their great relief they found no rebels at the
stream and the structure itself intact. The flimsiness of the bridge,
however, induced McDowell to direct his engineers to reinforce
the structure to ensure its being strong enough to carry the army's
wagons and heavy artillery, including the 3-ton Parrott rifled artillery piece, commanded by Lieutenant Peter C. Hains, attached
to Schenck's command. Not until 5:30 A.M. did Schenck and
Sherman finally get all their men across Cub Run, which allowed
Hunter and Heintzelman to begin their march to the road that
would take them to their crossing points.

The pace of Schenck's advance to the Stone Bridge improved
very little once he was across Cub Run, much to the dismay of
the units behind him. After encountering east of the bridge some
Confederate pickets, who fired a few shots and then fell back
across the run, Schenck ordered his men into line south of the
turnpike. Sherman, coming up behind Schenck, then deployed
north of the road in the midst of what one soldier later described
as "a grand old forest which, with its friendly foliage, sheltered
us from the scorching rays of the July sun."[8] They next moved

forward to the crest of the ridge overlooking the creek and pushed forward skirmishers who drove the few rebel pickets who remained east of Bull Run back across the creek. Tyler then deployed his artillery and at approximately 6 A.M. turned to Lieutenant Hains and directed him to fire his 30-pounder Parrott three times to signal the beginning of the demonstration at the Stone Bridge. Hains took aim at a large white house that he deduced a high-ranking officer would naturally have chosen as his headquarters and fired the first shot of the battle of Bull Run. (The house, ironically enough, actually belonged to a Unionist named Alexander Van Pelt.) According to McDowell's plan, the sound of this gun would tell the flanking column at Sudley Ford the demonstration was under way.

Hains's assumption that the Van Pelt house on the other side of Bull Run was occupied by someone of importance was correct. That morning it was serving as headquarters for Colonel Nathan "Shanks" Evans, commander of Confederate forces guarding the Confederate left at the Stone Bridge. Few men on either side would do more to shape the course of the battle at Bull Run than would this rough, profane, hard-drinking (he rarely went anywhere unaccompanied by a 1-gallon drum of whiskey he called his "barrelita"), and hard-fighting 1848 graduate of West Point.

A veteran of several minor skirmishes with the Native Americans as an officer in the U.S. Dragoons before the war, Evans was unfazed when Hains's 30-pound shot slammed into his headquarters. The small force of skirmishers he had deployed east of Bull Run late on the twentieth had given him plenty of advance warning of Tyler's progress along the turnpike. By the time Schenck's men reached the bridge and began their demonstration at 6:00 A.M., Evans had deployed his command in line behind the crest of Van Pelt Hill and placed a company on either side of the bridge as skirmishers. Recognizing the weakness of his command, which consisted only of Colonel J. E. B. Sloan's Fourth South Carolina, Major Roberdeau Wheat's First Louisiana Battalion, two guns, and two troops of cavalry, Evans shrewdly decided not to rise to the Federal bait and, by positioning all but the skirmishers along the creek on Van Pelt Hill, kept them out of the sight of Schenck's and Sherman's commands.

When fire from Hains's Parrott gun and the 4-gun battery of Captain J. Howard Carlisle failed to provoke Evans into tipping his hand, Tyler decided to push infantry forward to reinforce the impression that the Federals were actually planning to cross Bull Run at the bridge. He ordered Schenck to push three regiments forward toward the bridge to test the Confederate defenses along the creek. Schenck complied and, in doing so, induced Evans to send four companies from Sloan's regiment and one from Wheat's battalion down Van Pelt Hill to the west bank of the creek. Sloan's and Wheat's men immediately commenced skirmishing with the Federals on the other side of Bull Run. Tyler had done his job. With most of his command committed to the fight at the bridge, by 7:00 A.M., Evans was in no condition to resist the flanking force that, according to McDowell's plans, had already crossed Sudley Ford and was at that moment advancing south in overwhelming force down the Manassas–Sudley Road.

Fortunately for Evans, but unfortunately for McDowell, not only was the Federal flanking column still on the east side of Bull Run at 7:00 A.M., it was nowhere near Sudley Ford. After finally turning north onto the road Barnard had certified as suitable for the flanking movement, Hunter's lead brigade under Colonel Ambrose Burnside found McDowell's engineer had been badly mistaken. Instead of a road suitable for the passage of infantry and artillery, Burnside found only a narrow cart path through thick woods and dense underbrush. To clear the road, Burnside ordered that shovels and axes be brought forward and assigned twenty-five men of the Second New Hampshire the task of hacking away the trees and underbrush, which transformed the march of the rest of his brigade and the four behind him into a frustrating stop-and-go affair. "What a toilsome march it was through the woods," one soldier recalled later. "What wearisome work in clearing away the fallen trees, which . . . obstructed our path!" Another wrote: "Although the wood through which we now marched furnished here and there some protection from the fierce rays of the sun, . . . its very denseness shut out the breeze and made the heat almost unbearable."[9]

As if this were not bad enough, Burnside then encountered a fork in the road and, on the advice of a guide assigned by Hunter, turned right instead of left, a decision that extended the march to the ford by more than 3 miles. The route also led the men past a small log house, out of which emerged a woman that one Union soldier later described as "a very dirty and frowzy personage," who could not resist the urge to taunt the Yankee invaders. There were, she told them, "Confederates enough ahead to whip [you] all out," and her "old man" was among them. Several years later, one of the targets of her barbs would remark laconically, "Despite her disreputable appearance, it must be conceded that she had a fine military judgement."[10]

Not until approximately 9:30 A.M.—three hours behind schedule—did Burnside's hot, tired, and thirsty men reach Sudley Ford. "In two minutes," wrote one man, "the stream was a perfect mudpuddle; everybody rushed into it knee-deep to get water."[11] As their men took advantage of their arrival at the ford to rest their tired legs and slake their thirst, Burnside and Hunter dispatched Colonel William Averell and Captain Amiel Whipple forward to reconnoiter down the Sudley Road. Mounting their horses, they ascended the ridge overlooking Sudley Ford, rode past the small Methodist church where parishioners were engaged in their regular Sunday services, and followed the Sudley Road south past pasture as well as woods of blackjack and white oak and thick underbrush that bordered the road until they reached some high ground on its left side. There, to their great dismay, they saw a formidable force of Confederate infantry coming up. Soon, Averell and Whipple were back at Sudley Ford relaying the bad news to Hunter and Burnside: The delay in getting to the ford meant that they would have to fight their way to Manassas.

Hunter and Burnside immediately responded. Within minutes, Colonel John Slocum's Second Rhode Island Infantry was on the road moving south, accompanied by the young Rhode Island governor, William Sprague, who was serving as a volunteer aide to Burnside, a battery of six guns commanded by Captain William Reynolds, and Colonels Hunter and Burnside. Just then, General McDowell arrived at Sudley and, already suspecting that his plan to reach the rebel rear undetected had gone awry, urged Burnside forward.

Few officers who served at First Bull Run would play as significant a role in the Civil War as would the affable brigade commander whose Rhode Island brigade was spearheading the Federal advance south from Sudley Ford. A native of Indiana who had been an apprentice tailor before receiving an appointment to West Point, Ambrose Burnside managed to graduate from the military academy in 1847, but not before earning a reputation as one of the more incorrigible cadets of his class. He then spent a relatively undistinguished decade in the army before resigning his commission and moving to Rhode Island to manufacture a superb carbine of his own design. Through no fault of Burnside's, the business failed, and he was eventually compelled to appeal to his old army friend George B. McClellan for work with the Illinois Central Railroad. Despite his business difficulties, during his days in Rhode Island Burnside had attracted a great deal of positive attention from men of wealth and influence in the state, and, after Fort Sumter, he was chosen to command the first regiment organized by the state. After reaching Washington, he was promoted to brigade commander. Physically impressive, with a distinctive moustache and sideburns (hence "Burnside cut"), intelligent, and personally courageous, Burnside impressed a lot of people, including President Abraham Lincoln, and led them instinctively to expect great things of him. As his performance at Bull Run would demonstrate, those expectations were not completely unjustified. There were, however, as Burnside himself knew and modestly admitted, limits to his talents. Tragically for Burnside and his countrymen, those limits would not be evident until after they had resulted in a spectacular disaster for Union arms at Fredericksburg in December 1862.

With half of the unit deployed out front as skirmishers, Burnside pushed the Second Rhode Island forward. The men advanced south at "double quick time yelling like so many devils" for about a mile until a rise in the terrain, upon which the home of Edgar Matthews came into sight. There they were, wrote one Union soldier, "saluted with a volley of musketry, which, however, was fired so high that all the bullets went over our heads. . . . My first sensation was one of astonishment at the peculiar whir of the bullets . . . the Regiment immediately laid down without waiting for orders."[12]

The rebel muskets on Matthews Hill, from which those bullets had come, belonged to skirmishers thrown in front of the

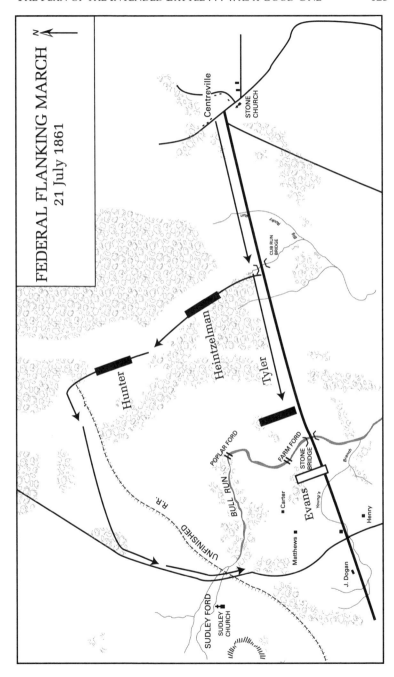

FEDERAL FLANKING MARCH
21 July 1861

N

Centreville

STONE CHURCH

Bull Run

Rocky

CUB RUN BRIDGE

Big Rocky

Heintzelman

Hunter

Tyler

POPLAR FORD

FARM FORD

STONE BRIDGE

Branch

Young's

Carter

Evans

Henry

BULL RUN

R.R.

UNFINISHED

Matthews

J. Dogan

SUDLEY FORD

SUDLEY CHURCH

brigade commanded by "Shanks" Evans that Tyler was supposed to be keeping occupied at the Stone Bridge. As previously mentioned, at 7:00 A.M., Tyler was indeed accomplishing his mission. By advancing Schenck to the banks of the creek south of the bridge, he induced Evans to commit the bulk of his command to the creek and rendered him incapable of reacting to the Federal flanking movement. The ruse, however, could only last so long, and by 8:00 A.M., seeing no sign that the Federals were increasing their presence in his front or making anything in the way of preparations to actually cross the creek, Evans had begun to suspect that he was seeing only a demonstration designed to keep him distracted from events occurring elsewhere.

Two developments then confirmed his suspicions. First, reports arrived from the small band of pickets he had stationed near Sudley Church of a large Federal force approaching the ford. Next a message arrived at the signal station Evans had established on Van Pelt Hill. Captain E. Porter Alexander, commander of the Confederate station at Wilcoxen's Hill on the Confederate right near Union Mills, had witnessed sunlight glinting off metal north of the Warrenton Turnpike and, upon closer inspection, detected brass cannon and a large body of infantry moving north. He realized that he was witnessing a large Federal force marching north to cross Bull Run and turn the Confederate left. Alexander then fired off a message to Van Pelt Hill warning Evans to "look out for your left, you are flanked."[13]

Evans reacted boldly and decisively. Leaving behind just four companies of Sloan's Fourth South Carolina along Bull Run to deter Tyler, Evans rounded up the remaining 900 troops of his 1,100-man brigade and concentrated them along Van Pelt Hill. He then advised Colonel Cocke at Ball's Ford that he had decided to diminish "my position at the bridge" and was advancing to attack the enemy.[14] With Wheat's battalion of Louisianans in the lead, Evans ordered his command past the once-grand estate of Landon Carter known as "Pittsylvania" and on to Matthews Hill. There he deployed his command on the southern slope of the hill with Sloan's South Carolinians positioned just east of the Sudley Road and Wheat's Louisianans to their right. Matthews Hill, located less than a mile south of Sudley Ford, was the best spot between the ford and the Warrenton Turnpike from which to resist a Federal advance from the north, as it offered a clear field of fire toward the north. But with only 900 men, Evans could not hope to hold his position against General McDowell's 13,000-man flanking force without significant help.

Fortunately for Evans, help was already on the way. Just as Evans finished placing his men on Matthews Hill, the brigades of Barnard Bee and Francis Bartow arrived on Henry Hill a mile to the south. Ordered by Beauregard that morning, at the behest of Johnston, to move from his position at Mitchell's Ford, where he was initially supposed to participate in the Confederate offensive against Centreville, to the support of Evans, Bee had just about reached the Stone Bridge when he learned of the Federal crossing at Sudley. He responded to the crisis by leading the Fourth Alabama to Henry Hill and then rode back to the vicinity of Portici, the mansion belonging to a Francis W. Lewis, located near Ball's Ford. There he found the 4-gun Staunton Artillery and persuaded their commander, Captain John D. Imboden, to follow him back to Henry Hill. Soon after their arrival, they were joined by Colonel Bartow's brigade. With a clear view of the fighting that had just commenced only one mile to the north on Matthews Hill, Bee could not contain his excitement. "Here is the battlefield," he ecstatically shouted to Imboden, "and we are in for it!"[15]

NOTES

1. *OR*, 2:330.
2. Ibid., 2:331.
3. Ibid., 2:326; Erasmus D. Keyes, *Fifty Years' Observation of Men and Events Civil and Military* (New York: Charles Scribner's Sons, 1884), 432.
4. Tyler, "Autobiography," 56–57.
5. [Pierre] Beauregard, "The First Battle of Bull Run," in *Battles and Leaders of the Civil War*, edited by Johnson and Buel, 1:200.
6. *OR*, 2:473
7. Ibid., 2:440–41, 473.
8. Michael E. Stevens, ed., *As If It Were Glory: Robert Beecham's Civil War from the Iron Brigade to the Black Regiments* (Madison, WI: Madison House Publishers, 1998), 6.
9. Woodbury, *Second Rhode Island Regiment: A Narrative of Military Operations*, 31; Parker, "Personal Reminiscences," 2:210.
10. Haynes, *A History of the Second Regiment, New Hampshire Volunteer Infantry*, 23–24.

11. Aldrich, *History of Battery A*, 19.

12. Rhodes, ed., *All for the Union*, 32, 26.

13. Gallagher, ed., *Fighting for the Confederacy*, 50.

14. *OR*, 2:559.

15. John D. Imboden, "Incidents of the First Bull Run," in *Battles and Leaders of the Civil War*, edited by Johnson and Buel, 1:232.

CHAPTER NINE

DEVILS MINGLE ON
MATTHEWS HILL

ALTHOUGH GREEN AS GRASS, the five companies from the Second
Rhode Islanders that composed Colonel Burnside's skirmish line
responded to the first volley from Colonel Evans's pickets by
halting and coolly returning the favor. At the direction of Hunter,
who in his excitement forgot that as a division commander he
had other responsibilities besides directing skirmishers, they continued their push forward and drove the rebel skirmishers back
to the main rebel line on Matthews Hill. Burnside and Slocum
then directed the rest of the Second Rhode Island to get back on
their feet and deploy into line east of the Sudley Road.

After completing their deployment, Colonel Slocum ordered
his men forward across the field and up the slope leading to the
Confederate position. Evans's infantry, supported by two guns
from the Lynchburg Artillery commanded by Captain George S.
Davidson, immediately opened fire on Slocum's advancing troops.
Their fire blunted the Federal advance, and a vicious little firefight
commenced along a 300-yard front between Wheat's and Sloan's
Louisianans and South Carolinians and Slocum's Rhode Islanders with neither side gaining an advantage. Then the six James
Rifles of Captain William Reynolds's battery rolled into position
on an elevation between the Sudley Road and Slocum's right. "It
was," Private Thomas Aldrich of Reynolds's command later recalled, "a startling sight as the battery reached the hill to see men
shooting at us less than two hundred yards away. How they ever
let us get on the top of the hill is more than I can imagine."[1]

From there they pounded Evans's line. Neither side, however, managed to gain much of an advantage as casualties piled
up on both sides. "The balls came in thick as hail," one of Wheat's

men described it later. "Grape, bomb and canister would sweep our ranks every minute."[2] On the Federal side, Colonel Slocum and Major Sullivan Ballou of the Second Rhode Island both fell mortally wounded. Then Hunter suffered a severe, but not fatal wound, on his face and neck. Weakened by loss of blood, he encountered his junior brigade commander as he headed to the rear and told him: "Burnside, I leave the matter in your hands. Slocum and his Regiment went in handsomely, and drove the scoundrels."[3]

Hunter had not performed well in his capacity as division commander directing Federal operations on Matthews Hill. Despite having a substantial advantage in numbers and artillery, he had not been able to overcome Evans's defenses. Only one of Burnside's regiments had actually been engaged on Matthews Hill, while three others stood useless on the other side of the Sudley Road. This was due to Hunter's incomprehensible decision that assistance for the Second Rhode Island should come from Colonel Andrew Porter's brigade, not Burnside's other regiments, which Porter's men would have actually had to pass through to reach the scene of the fighting on Matthews Hill. Hunter also evidently made no effort to find the Confederate flanks, which were in fact quite vulnerable. Had he not bothered himself with such a minor detail as the operations of his skirmishers during the initial stages of the fighting (and to be fair he was hardly the only brigade or division commander on this day whose preoccupation with minutiae would lead them to lose sight of the broader tactical picture), he might have done a better job of planning the battle and quickly dispatched Evans's small command. As it was, when control over the fight for Matthews Hill passed into the more competent hands of Burnside and Porter, valuable time had been wasted.

Fortunately for the Federals, the loss of their division commander fazed neither Burnside nor Porter one bit, and both men moved quickly to press Federal operations on Matthews Hill. Freed from Hunter's order to hold back his other regiments, Burnside ordered Colonel Henry P. Martin's Seventy-first New York and Colonel Gilman Marston's Second New Hampshire forward to Matthews Hill. Marston's men for some reason decided not to cross the Sudley Road, but instead moved south to the west of the road. If that was not bad enough, Martin's men were so green that orders to advance only threw them into confusion. An exasperated Burnside then rode over to his rear regiment, the First Rhode Island, which he had once commanded and was now led by Major Joseph P. Balch, and personally led it across the Sudley Road and into position on the left of the Second Rhode Island.

Burnside's quickness in seizing authority served the Federal cause well, for Balch's command arrived on the field at a highly propitious moment. Frustrated with the stalemated battle and acutely aware of the strength the Federals were marshaling in front of them (however badly it was being applied), by 10:30 A.M., Evans and Wheat had decided a spoiling attack was necessary. Sensing a slackening in the Second Rhode Island's fire, Evans turned to Wheat and ordered him to charge his battalion. Brandishing bowie knives (some even went so far as to throw away their firearms during the assault) and emitting such a yell that they would henceforth be known as the "Tigers," the Louisianans surged forward toward Reynolds's guns. They managed to get within twenty yards of them before the First Rhode Island arrived into line and opened a ferocious fire into their ranks that shattered their advance.

Among those to fall was Major Wheat, who was hit by a Federal ball that entered under his armpit, went through his chest, and exited on the other side of his body. Wheat would, to the surprise of many, including the doctor who first reached him, recover from his wound. When told by a surgeon that his wound was fatal, Wheat replied, "I don't feel like dying yet." The doctor then informed him, "There is no instance on record of recovery from such a wound." To this Wheat replied, "Well, then, I will put my case on record."[4]

Despite the resolution of their wounded leader, the fire of Burnside's Rhode Islanders devastated the Louisianans. Soon they were in full retreat and would not halt their flight until they found cover on John Dogan's farm all the way on the other side of the Sudley Road, leaving Sloan's undersized regiment alone east of the road to face both of Burnside's regiments.

With his command in dire straits, Evans rode off in search of help. He soon found General Bee, who had posted his infantry on Henry Hill and placed Captain John Imboden's guns in front of the widow Judith Henry's house, where they overlooked the valley between Matthews and Henry Hills and had a clear view of the fighting on the latter. Still convinced that, as he had earlier told Imboden, the fight would be at Henry Hill, Bee's first response to Evans's request for help was to propose that Evans pull back to Henry Hill. Evans, however, somehow persuaded Bee to set aside his own judgment and to fight on Matthews Hill. Bee then rode back to Henry Hill, where he found his men and Bartow's enduring long-range artillery fire from the Federals on Matthews Hill, which had brought an end to a hunt for apples on Mrs. Henry's trees and was making life very uncomfortable for the men. One soldier later recalled thinking during the ordeal that he "was in the presence of death," and, "this is unfair, someone is to blame for getting us all killed. I didn't come out here to fight this way; I wish the earth would crack open and let me drop in."

Upon his arrival on Henry Hill, Bee first rode over to Colonel Egbert Jones's Fourth Alabama Regiment and shouted, "Up, Alabamians!"[5] Jones's men sprang to their feet and, with Bee personally leading them forward, headed north to rescue Evans's command on Matthews Hill. There Bee placed them to the right of Sloan's South Carolinians, where they immediately joined the fight with Burnside's men. Bee saw at once that one regiment would not be enough to hold Matthews Hill for any length of time and sent orders back to Henry Hill to his other regimental commanders and Bartow to bring their commands to Matthews Hill. Without hesitation, Bee's and Bartow's men marched north down Henry Hill, into the valley through which ran the Warrenton Turnpike and a stream known as Young's Branch, past the Stone House at the intersection of the turnpike and the Sudley Road, and then up Buck Hill. There they found Bee, who used Colonel W. C. Falkner's Second Mississippi to fill a gap between Sloan's and Jones's regiments and Colonel Lucius J. Gartrell's Seventh Georgia and Lieutenant Colonel W. M. Gardner's Eighth Georgia of Bartow's brigade to extend the Confederate right into a thicket beyond the Federal left. Altogether, Bee's efforts brought the total number of rebels engaged on Matthews Hill to 2,800.

If Bee and Evans had hoped to do more with these troops than simply buy time for their high command to respond to the crisis, the actions of Burnside and Porter ensured that the Federal advantage in numbers would translate into victory on Matthews Hill. First, Burnside managed to untangle Martin's regiment of New Yorkers on the west side of the road, just as Bee's and Bartow's men were arriving, and get them, accompanied by two howitzers, into the fight on the right of the increasingly weary Second Rhode Island. With the arrival of the New Yorkers and Bee's forces, the fight on Matthews Hill reached a fever pitch as North and South poured artillery and musket fire into one anothers' ranks, with men on both sides performing much better than anyone could have expected from such green troops. "Such fighting never was done," one of Wheat's men later recalled. "It did not seem as though men were fighting, it was devils mingling in the conflict, cursing, yelling, cutting, shrieking."[6] With the fight stalemated and Bartow's Georgians starting to inflict severe punishment on his left flank units, Burnside decided the time had come to unleash the division's ace in the hole: the battalion of regulars commanded by Major George Sykes that was attached to Porter's brigade.

Unfettered as he was earlier by Hunter, Porter at that time was marching his command southward west of the Sudley Road with an eye to occupying Dogan Ridge to the south. If he could get his infantry and artillery into position there, he would turn the Confederate right and make Evans and Bee's position on Matthews Hill untenable. Just as he was getting his brigade into position on Dogan Ridge, however, Porter was greeted by the sight of an extremely agitated Ambrose Burnside riding up and shouting: "For God's sake let me have the Regulars. My men are all being cut to pieces."[7]

Now that he had flanked the Confederates, Porter was at first reluctant to grant Burnside his request. On top of his other blunders that morning, Hunter had created a potentially confused command situation by telling Burnside, "I leave the matter in your hands," when in fact Porter was senior brigade commander. Burnside, however, had decided not to interpret Hunter's statement to mean that he, not Porter, commanded the division, but to assume that only he had control of the fight for Matthews Hill. Fortunately, just as Burnside was requesting assistance, Captain Whipple of Hunter's staff rode up and clarified the command situation by directing Porter to take charge of the division. Finally, Burnside's argument that if the regulars were not used on Matthews Hill, the Confederates there would beat his brigade and then cut off and destroy Porter's command on Dogan Ridge induced Porter to send Sykes to Burnside's aid.

After receiving his orders from Porter, Sykes turned to his men and, one soldier later recalled, "gave us to understand that there would probably be some work for us to do."[8] Urged forward personally by Sykes and Burnside, the regulars crossed the Sudley Road and passed all the way behind the Federal battle line on Matthews Hill. Their arrival provided a much-needed boost to the morale of Burnside's men, and they were cheered lustily by their comrades. Upon reaching the far left flank, they deployed into line, turned to the right, and began firing at the Confederates. Although the accuracy and discipline of the regulars' fire belied their awesome reputation, their arrival marked the beginning of the end for the Confederates on Matthews Hill.

Not only were Evans's, Bee's, and Bartow's commands on the firing line strained almost to the breaking point on their front as more and more Federal troops arrived on the field, but the Yankees were also maneuvering into positions from which they could threaten both Confederate flanks. Shortly after 11:00 A.M. the first regiment from Heintzelman's division, Colonel Willis A. Gorham's First Minnesota of Colonel William B. Franklin's brigade, reached the field and went into position to the left of Sykes's battalion, extending the Federal line to a point beyond the flank of Bartow's Georgians on the Confederate right. Meanwhile, to the west of the Sudley Road beyond the Confederate left, Porter had maneuvered the bulk of his 3,700-man brigade, which included the six guns of Captain Charles Griffin's Company D, First U.S. Artillery, into position on Dogan Ridge. As if this situation were not bad enough, a new threat was arriving on the field from the east in the form of a fresh brigade under the command of Colonel William T. Sherman.

When McDowell had arrived at Sudley Ford earlier that morning and found that his plan for crossing Bull Run there had fallen way behind schedule, he decided that Tyler needed to do more than simply demonstrate against the Stone Bridge. Thus, he dis-

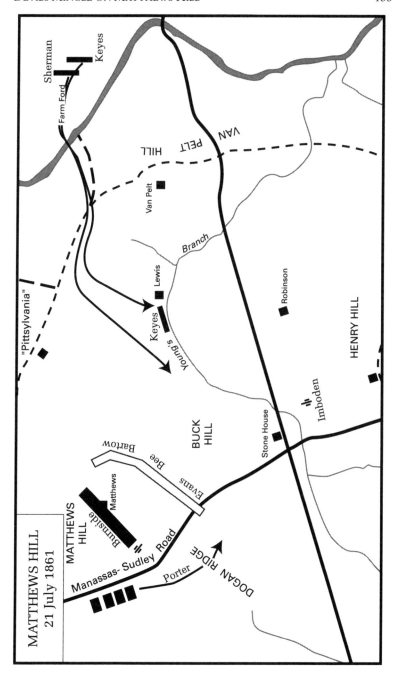

MATTHEWS HILL
21 July 1861

MATTHEWS
HILL

Sherman

Keyes

Farm Ford

VAN PELT HILL

Van Pelt

Branch

Lewis

Keyes

Young's

"Pittsylvania"

Robinson

HENRY HILL

Imboden

Stone House

BUCK HILL

Bee Barlow

Evans

Matthews

Burnside

Manassas-Sudley Road

Porter

DOGAN RIDGE

patched a staff officer back to the Warrenton Turnpike with orders to Tyler to "press forward his attack."[9]

At around 11:00 A.M., as the battle for Matthews Hill raged, McDowell's orderly found Tyler, who had failed to detect Evans's shift of his forces away from his front and was still supervising a now pointless demonstration in front of the Stone Bridge. Tyler interpreted McDowell's order as a directive to cross Bull Run. Still concerned about reports that the bridge was mined, Tyler decided against ordering Schenck across, but instead directed Sherman to cross the stream north of the bridge, followed by Colonel Erasmus D. Keyes's brigade. Some of Keyes's men had spent the morning enjoying the contents of some unguarded hives of honey they had located as they awaited the beginning of the morning's march. Although delighted to partake of the honey, some of the men expressed concern that the bees "had gone to sting the Rebellion to death and cheat us out of a cocksure victory."[10]

Fortunately, Sherman had not spent the morning whiling away the hours enjoying the shade of the forest. Almost from the moment skirmishing had begun along Bull Run, Sherman had been reconnoitering the stream in front of his position north of the bridge in search of a convenient ford should a crossing prove necessary. Fortunately, the enemy proved most helpful. "About 9 o'clock I was well down to the River—with some skirmishe[r]s," he wrote his wife a week after the battle, "and observed two men on horseback ride along a hill, descend, cross the stream, and ride out towards us—[one] had a gun in his hand which he waved over his head, and called out to us, 'You D_____d black abolitionists, come on & c.' "[11]

Of all the men who fought at Bull Run, none would rise to greater heights during the Civil War than the red-headed Ohioan who commanded Tyler's third brigade. The foster son and son-in-law of Thomas Ewing Sr., one of the nation's most prominent Whig senators, Sherman had graduated from West Point in 1840 and spent an undistinguished thirteen years in the army before, seduced by the seemingly boundless opportunities the booming national economy offered, he resigned his commission. As a businessman, however, Sherman was a complete and utter failure. Fortunately, with the help of some old army acquaintances (including, interestingly, P. G. T. Beauregard), he managed to secure the post of superintendent of the Louisiana Military Academy, a position he held until the state seceded in January 1861. Although he derived much satisfaction from his work in Louisiana and was highly sympathetic to the cultural and political outlook of Southerners (the horseman who accused him of being a "D_____d abolitionist" could not have been more off the mark), there was no doubt that Sherman would serve the Union cause after Fort Sumter or that, due to the influence of his family, especially his brother John, a Republican senator from Ohio, he would return to the service at a respectable rank. He was first commissioned colonel of the newly organized Thirteenth U.S. Infantry in May 1861, but then, instead of being sent north "to enlist the men and instruct them, as expected," he found himself ordered to Washington, where he was shortly given command of the brigade he would lead at Bull Run.[12]

Sherman brought to the task of commanding men a number of highly admirable qualities. He was by all accounts a man of boundless energy and high intelligence who possessed considerable personal courage. Yet although highly regarded by his fellow junior officers in the antebellum army, a lifetime of failure had left Sherman highly insecure and lacking in self-confidence by 1861. These traits, when combined with his vivid imagination and a tendency to play favorites among his subordinates, would cause Sherman much trouble, both personal and professional, when he found himself placed in positions of independent responsibility after Bull Run. Sherman also had considerable talent as a strategist, although his abilities as a tactician left much to be desired, a deficiency that in the next four years would cost the Union thousands of unnecessary casualties on the battlefields of Tennessee, Mississippi, and Georgia.

What McDowell needed from Sherman along the banks of Bull Run, however, was energy, and that Sherman possessed in spades. When instructed by Tyler to cross the stream, Sherman immediately directed his men to toss off their blankets and haversacks and march at the double-quick toward the unguarded crossing, known locally as Farm Ford, that the Confederate horsemen had been so kind to locate for him. After a rapid march under a sun "pouring down its fiercest rays," Sherman's men reached the ford and waded through the stream's "exceedingly refreshing" waist-deep water with little difficulty.[13]

For Colonel Keyes just getting to the stream was no easy task. As his brigade approached Farm Ford, a rebel battery across the stream opened fire, subjecting Keyes and his men to a brief shelling that "caused a temporary confusion and wounded several men" in the First and Second Connecticut Regiments.[14] Keyes, however, managed to restore order quickly. He next pushed his men toward Farm Ford where, after waiting five minutes for the last of Sherman's 3,400 men to reach the other side of Bull Run, they splashed across the creek.

After crossing Bull Run, Sherman and his infantry encountered no resistance as they climbed the steep bluff to the top of Van Pelt Hill (it proved to be too steep for his artillery, however, so Sherman ordered his guns not to bother crossing the stream) and cautiously pushed on toward Pittsylvania. Seeing a body of enemy troops retreating south from Matthews Hill, the lieutenant colonel of Sherman's lead regiment, the Sixty-ninth New York, attempted to arrest their retreat by attacking them. The rebels, however, put up enough of a fight to induce Sherman, who was mainly "determined to effect our junction with Hunter's division," to order his men to cease firing and proceed to Matthews Hill.[15] With their colors conspicuously displayed in order to prevent friendly fire, Sherman brought his men to the field, placed them in the rear of Porter's brigade, and sought out McDowell.

Fortunately for what was left of their battered commands, by the time the head of Sherman's column reached the field, Evans, Bee, and Bartow had come to the conclusion that they had bought all the time for Beauregard and Johnston to react to the crisis that they could. With their position now untenable and the danger of being surrounded a very real one, at approximately 11:30 A.M. the Confederate commanders gave the order for their men to retreat. Many had not needed their commanders' orders to realize withdrawal had become necessary. "As everyone about me seemed dead or wounded," one of Bartow's Georgians later wrote, "I determined to take my chances of saving myself by getting away as fast as I could."[16]

Down Matthews and Buck Hills, across the Warrenton Turnpike and Young's Branch Valley, Evans's, Bee's, and Bartow's men ran. With Federal infantry and artillery firing into their ranks, whatever order they had managed to preserve on Matthews Hill melted away as they fled pell-mell for the shelter of Henry Hill. Soon, the only thing standing between the Union army and that eminence was Captain Imboden's 4-gun battery at the north end of Henry Hill, which maintained its order and put up a bold front as it continued firing into the seemingly irresistible masses of Federal infantry gathering north of the Warrenton Turnpike and dueled with the powerful Union batteries positioned on Dogan Ridge and Matthews Hill.

Watching the scene unfold before him, McDowell was ecstatic. "Victory! Victory! We have done it!" McDowell, Heintzelman, and their staffs shouted as they rode among the men swinging their hats in the air. "They are running! The day is ours!" "How well I remember the proud bearing of McDowell," one of Sherman's men later recalled. "His every action told . . . that he then believed himself a victorious captain whose brow was wreathed with laurels of success." Despite the delays and missteps of the morning maneuvers, McDowell's flanking force had crushed the Confederate line on Matthews Hill. All that now stood between his command and the rebel rear were the disorganized rebel masses on Henry Hill, where, one Union officer assured the men, "there are not three hundred rebels."[17]

As smashing as the Federal victory on Matthews Hill was, the bravery of the men in Evans's, Bee's, and Bartow's commands had managed to buy the Confederate cause an hour and a half of precious time. It also had the fortuitous effect of snapping Beauregard and Johnston out of their offensive mind-set by forcing them to recognize that, if they did not respond to what was happening on their northern flank and set aside their original plans, the day—and indeed the whole Confederate cause—might be lost.

This was not, of course, how Beauregard had expected the battle to develop. He had assumed McDowell would attack directly along the road from Centreville to Mitchell's Ford. Such an offensive against the Confederate center, Beauregard surmised, could be as easily repulsed as had the probe toward Blackburn's Ford three days earlier. More important, it would leave McDowell vulnerable to an attack on his left and rear. To take advantage of this, the Confederate brigades at Union Mills under Ewell, McLean's Ford under Jones, Blackburn's Ford under Longstreet, and Mitchell's Ford under Bonham were to swing around the Federal left and attack Centreville. The movement was to be made en echelon, with Ewell on the far right to begin the offensive, followed in order by Jones, Longstreet, and Bonham. Initially, Beauregard was not at all displeased when word arrived at his headquarters behind Mitchell's Ford of Tyler's demonstration at the Stone Bridge. As he saw it, McDowell appeared to be playing right into his hands, albeit a bit farther north than had been anticipated, by leaving himself vulnerable to the Confederate attack that Beauregard was confident would "achieve a complete victory for my country by 12 m."[18]

Beauregard's attack orders reached both Longstreet and Jones a little after 7:00 A.M., and both crossed their troops over Bull Run. In Longstreet's case, this gave him and his men their first opportunity to see the effect of their handiwork of three days earlier. As they caught their first glimpse of the Union dead, Longstreet's men also found themselves "much exposed to the fire" of artillery attached to Richardson's brigade, which McDowell had posted on the road from Centreville to Blackburn's Ford to distract Confederate attention from the flanking force. Longstreet responded by ordering his men to lie down and take cover. Jones, however, encountered no serious physical obstacles on the other side of Bull Run. His problem was the wording of Beauregard's 7:10 A.M. order. "General Ewell," it read, "has been ordered to take the offensive upon Centreville. You will follow the movement at once by attacking him in your front."[19] Jones chose to overlook the mandate to attack his colleague and instead tried to establish contact with Ewell via a messenger. When he failed to hear anything back from Union Mills, Jones decided to cross the creek anyway at McLean's Ford. Once across, he posted his infantry and battery in a position from which it could join the attack once Ewell had started.

Jones would end up waiting for over two hours, for Ewell had not, for some reason, received the order to attack, and if the wait caused some frustration for Jones, it was nothing compared to what it was doing to Ewell. Just downstream from Jones, the bald-headed and quite eccentric Ewell paced back and forth at his headquarters near Union Mills in a manner one of his subordinates likened to that of a lion that had gotten a whiff of blood. Ewell had awakened that morning with his spirits in what one observer described as "a flutter of exultation." A great battle was to be fought that day, of that he was sure, and what greater honor could a brigade commander want than to be entrusted with the sacred task of spearheading the attack that would secure his country's independence? As the morning passed, however, Ewell's mood grew darker and darker. What had happened, he muttered to himself, to his orders? At one point, he ordered a regiment, John B. Gordon's Sixth Alabama, to cross Bull Run and conduct a reconnaissance. Gordon returned to find Ewell still snappish and frustrated. When a woman rode up to his headquarters, Ewell pointed toward the other side of the creek and told her: "Look out there, miss! Don't you see those men with blue clothes on? . . . They are going to fire, and fire quick, and fire right here. You'll get killed. You'll be a *dead damsel* in less than a minute. *Get away from here!*" When she refused to do so, Ewell turned to Gordon and remarked: "Women would make a grand brigade—if it was not for snakes and spiders! They don't mind bullets—women are not afraid of bullets; but one big black-snake would put a whole army to flight."[20]

Finally, Ewell's suspense ended when a courier he sent to Jones to find out what was going on returned with a copy of Beauregard's orders to Jones. That cleared matters up considerably. Ewell immediately ordered his brigade across Bull Run to get into position to attack the Federal rear. But almost as soon as his men had gotten across, orders arrived directing him to recross the stream. Ewell complied and had just reached his previous position when another courier came up directing him to cross Bull Run yet again. For the third time (the fourth for the Sixth Alabama), Ewell's men plunged into the creek. This time they managed to march over one mile toward Centreville before they were stopped once again by an order directing Ewell to return to the other side of Bull Run.

This final order to Ewell, which directed him to march his command to the Stone Bridge once he was back across Bull Run, reflected the fact that the Confederate high command had finally concluded that any thought of taking the offensive would have to be set aside as a consequence of the fighting on Matthews Hill and the crisis that was brewing on Henry Hill. Although missteps and delays had characterized much of the Federal effort that morning, McDowell had, in fact, seized the strategic and tactical initiative. The battlefield would be not at Centreville, but at Henry Hill. Johnston and Beauregard had no choice but to call off their offensive and hope they could get reinforcements to Henry Hill in time to stop the Federal juggernaut that had begun rolling southward from Sudley Ford that morning.

NOTES

1. Aldrich, *The History of Battery A*, 19–20.
2. Terry L. Jones, *Lee's Tigers: The Louisiana Infantry in the Army of Northern Virginia* (Baton Rouge: Louisiana State University Press, 1987), 51.
3. Woodbury, *Second Rhode Island Regiment*, 33.
4. Jones, *Lee's Tigers*, 55.
5. Hennessy, *The First Battle of Manassas*, 55.
6. Jones, *Lee's Tigers*, 52.
7. Edward K. Eckert and Nicholas J. Amato, eds., *Ten Years in the Saddle: The Memoir of William Woods Averell, 1851–1862* (San Rafael, CA: Presidio Press, 1978), 297.
8. Parker, "Personal Reminiscences," in *War Papers*, 2:211.
9. *OR*, 2:319.
10. Horatio Staples, "Reminiscences of Bull Run," *War Papers Read before the Commandery of the State of Maine, Military Order of the Loyal Legion of the United States*, 4 vols. (Portland, ME: Lefavor-Tower Company, 1908), 3:132.
11. Simpson and Berlin, eds., *Sherman's Civil War: Selected Correspondence*, 123.
12. Sherman, *Memoirs of General W. T. Sherman*, 1:194.
13. Allen, "The Second Wisconsin at the First Battle of Bull Run," in Otis, *Second Wisconsin Infantry*, 225; Stevens, ed., *As If It Were Glory*, 6.
14. Keyes, *Fifty Years' Observation*, 433.
15. *OR*, 2:369.
16. Hennessy, *First Battle of Manassas*, 60.
17. Blake, *Three Years in the Army of the Potomac*, 16; *JCCW*, 2:201.
18. *OR*, 2:487–88.
19. Ibid., 2:537.
20. John B. Gordon, *Reminiscences of the Civil War* (New York: Charles Scribner's Sons, 1903), 38–42.

CHAPTER TEN

A STONE WALL ESTABLISHED

HENRY HILL, APPROXIMATELY one and one-half miles south of Matthews Hill and six miles north of Manassas Junction, would indeed be the key to the battle. If the Federals could capture it, there would be no stopping their march southward to Manassas Junction. Johnston, Beauregard, and their subordinates would have no choice but to abandon the Bull Run line and flee southward or be cut off and forced to surrender. In either case, it would be difficult for even the most devoted champion of Confederate independence to deny that in the first major test of the manhood, martial skill, and patriotism of their respective sections, the Yankees had in fact proven themselves superior. Could the Confederacy survive if the Southern assumption of superiority over the degraded offspring of Yankeedom was exposed as a fraud?

The situation was indeed desperate for the Southern cause at 11:30 A.M. The three brigades that had been engaged on Matthews Hill and were now scurrying for safety on Henry Hill were incapable of putting up much of a fight. Nearly two hours of fighting had taken a severe toll on their ranks, and the nerves of those who still lived were shot after a pell-mell retreat that did not end until they arrived behind the crest of Henry Hill. There, around the home of James Robinson, a free black, they huddled for protection, in no condition to do any more fighting. Only Imboden's guns north of the Henry house maintained their organization and continued to put up any resistance, but if the Federals decided to make a determined attack, the rebels would be helpless before them.

To make such an advance McDowell had approximately 18,000 men at his disposal, and only one of his brigades— Burnside's—had done much serious fighting that morning. Morale could not have been higher after the smashing victory on

Matthews Hill and the sight of the much-vaunted Southern chivalry in full-blown retreat. The only dark notes sounded on the Federal side of the field came from those disappointed that they might have missed out on the grand battle.

McDowell was as aware of the situation as anyone. But instead of pushing his forces forward to finish his victory, he elected to spend the next two hours consolidating his position, content to have only his batteries on Dogan Ridge and Matthews Hill pound Henry Hill at long range. The fire was effective enough to make life very uncomfortable for the already demoralized rebel forces on the hill. Nonetheless, there were limits to what long-range artillery could do. If the rebels were to be dislodged and Henry Hill claimed for the Federals, McDowell simply had to take it physically with infantry.

McDowell's decision to halt his attack and not exploit his victory at Matthews Hill, although it was in retrospect an error of monumental proportions, was not without a rationale. First, he understandably wanted to consolidate his position, bring up all of his reinforcements, and make sure he had a firm grip on his green army before it made another major effort. Second, McDowell was well aware that his job was not simply to defeat the rebels in combat but also to reconcile them to the authority of the Union. Too many dead Southern boys, too much humiliation for the South might complicate the process of restoring Southerners once again to the authority of the Federal government. If long-range artillery could induce the rebels to give up Henry Hill without a major fight, it would reduce the number of casualties on both sides. It would also have the salutary effect of conserving the Federal infantry for the final drive toward Manassas Junction, where there would surely be resistance.

Finally, McDowell may well have lacked the physical and mental energy at 11:30 A.M. to carry out yet another offensive. Indeed, when one soldier recalled the scene on Matthews Hill, he speculated, "Many were in that state of fatigue in which it was more natural to sleep than to fight."[1] For several weeks, McDowell had been shouldering a burden without precedent in American history. Given thousands of raw troops led by officers of dubious merit, he was expected not only to transform them into an army in a few weeks but also to lead them to victory in a campaign where the stakes were no less than the survival of the Union itself. Then, once he took the field, there were frustrations over the failure to bag Bonham at Fairfax, finding his original plan of swinging around the Confederate right impracticable, and the fiasco at Blackburn's Ford. On top of all of this came the dramatic swing from stress and worry over the pace of the flanking march to the relief and euphoria induced by the victory on Matthews Hill, which may simply have been too much for his system to handle and left him depleted of energy. Although these factors make the decision not to push immediately on to Henry Hill understandable, in retrospect it is clear that McDowell's decision to halt his drive south was a terrible mistake—one of the most important made by any officer during the entire campaign.

⁓ By the time McDowell halted his troops, Johnston and Beauregard had already begun shifting troops to the left to deal with the Federal threat. Throughout the morning, both men had sat anxiously at their headquarters on Lookout Hill behind Mitchell's Ford awaiting the beginning of their offensive against Centreville. Although alerted by Captain Alexander of the Federal flanking march at the same time Evans was, neither Johnston nor Beauregard saw much cause for alarm. After all, the farther north and west the Federals advanced, the more vulnerable Centreville would be to the attack on their flank and rear that Beauregard had conceived.

By 10:30 A.M., however, both Johnston and Beauregard had cause to reassess the situation. First, the sound of the fighting to the north made it clear that McDowell may well have gotten to the Confederate flank in numbers too great for Evans, Bee, and Bartow to handle alone. Then, Beauregard's hopes that the attack on Centreville might redeem Confederate fortunes along Bull Run were dashed when messages arrived from Generals Jones and Ewell indicating that the orders for the attack had miscarried. Beauregard retained some slight hope that the attack could still take place and that nothing else would be necessary to relieve the situation to the north. Johnston, however, did not. "The battle is there," he announced to Beauregard. "I am going."[2]

Johnston's proclamation finally induced Beauregard to conclude that his grand offensive was in fact impracticable. He

A SINGLE GRAND VICTORY

immediately sent orders to Longstreet, Ewell, and Jones to abandon their plans to advance on Centreville and instead to "make a strong demonstration all along their front," while all available reserves shifted north to deal with the Federal offensive there. After Beauregard advised Johnston of his actions, which were fully approved, the two generals, with their staffs in tow, "set out at full speed for the point of conflict."[3]

The first Confederate reinforcements to arrive at Henry Hill were the 600 men of the Hampton Legion, which just that morning had arrived by train from Richmond. Commanded by Colonel Wade Hampton, one of the wealthiest slaveowners in the entire South, the Legion was a mixed South Carolina unit of infantry, artillery, and cavalry (although the cavalry would not reach the front in time to fight at Bull Run), clad in the finest uniforms and equipped with the best gear that their commander's deep pockets could provide. Greeted at Manassas Junction by orders from Beauregard to march toward the Stone Bridge to support Evans, Hampton led his South Carolinians north to Portici. There, informed by a scout of the situation on the Confederate left, Hampton directed his men to head for Henry Hill via a farm road that connected it with Portici.

Scouting ahead of his men, Hampton reached Henry Hill just in time to see Evans's, Bee's, and Bartow's commands begin to break on Matthews Hill and the Federal masses gathering north of the Warrenton Turnpike. When the rest of his command arrived, Hampton led his men into position near the Robinson house, where they came under fire from the Federal batteries on Dogan Ridge. After suffering a shower of clay created by a Union ball smashing the ground beneath him, Hampton directed his men to take cover behind the fence that bordered the lane that linked the Robinson house to the turnpike.

Just as they arrived in position, Hampton and his men found themselves confronted with an unauthorized advance by elements of Porter's brigade, now commanded by Colonel William W. Averell. First, as the Confederate position on Matthews Hill collapsed, on their left, Colonel Henry W. Slocum's Twenty-seventh New York pushed south along the Sudley Road to clear the area around the Stone House of the last remnants of Confederate infantry and decided to push to the east along the Warrenton Turnpike in order to avoid the fire from Imboden's guns on Henry Hill. Slocum's men managed to advance to within 200 yards of Hampton's line until they saw troops clad in gray with their flags furled. Confused, some officers shouted out: "Don't shoot; it is a Massachusetts regiment, or the Eighth New York." Slocum's men paused until a Confederate flag appeared, and before they could respond to the sight, the rebels "opened a terrific fire of musketry." "Ne-ne-never mind a f-f-few shells, boys, G-G-God Almighty is merciful," Slocum's lieutenant colonel, who had an unfortunate tendency to stammer when excited, assured his men. "G-G-Give it to 'em b-b-boys; God l-loves a cheerful g-g-giver."[4] Despite Slocum's best efforts, the initial Confederate volley effectively halted his regiment's advance. After a brief firefight, Slocum decided to withdraw back up Buck Hill, whence his men continued to exchange fire at long range with Hampton's.

Soon after repulsing Slocum's advance (and in the process wounding the future general in the leg), Hampton and his men were subjected to the sight of yet another Federal advance in their direction. This movement was prompted by the withdrawal of Imboden's worn-out gunners from the ridge overlooking the turnpike, to which Colonel Averell responded, without authorization from McDowell, by ordering Colonel George Lyons's Eighth New York and Colonel A. M. Wood's Fourteenth Brooklyn (technically the Fourteenth New York State Militia) to advance toward Henry Hill from Dogan Ridge. After reaching the turnpike, however, the two regiments decided to move east along the turnpike rather than advance directly up Henry Hill. Fortunately for Hampton's command, although they were forced back from an advanced position along the turnpike that they had taken during their still ongoing skirmish with Slocum's command, neither Lyons's nor Wood's men were able to do serious damage to the Legion. When the Federals got close enough to Hampton's position to exchange musket fire, Confederate artillery on Henry Hill began ripping through their ranks, destroying the cohesion of both regiments and prompting both to make a hasty retreat down the turnpike. "The eighth New York," Averell later disgustedly reported, "broke and never afterwards formed to any extent. . . . There were only two officers who afterwards displayed any courage and coolness at all."[5] Had the two regiments advanced directly up Henry Hill as he had ordered, Averell later asserted, the disaster that befell Union arms on that hill later that day might very well have been avoided.

The fire from Henry Hill that thwarted Averell's advance announced the presence of the next—and by far the most important—of the reinforcements Johnston and Beauregard would get to Henry Hill that day: the five regiments of Brigadier General Thomas J. Jackson's First Virginia Brigade. No man—not even his own commanders—would be more closely associated with this battle at Bull Run than he.

Perhaps the most eccentric figure in all American military history, Jackson was born into a family of modest means in Clarksburg, a town located in present-day West Virginia, in 1824. Somehow he managed to secure an appointment to West Point and, to the amazement of the other members of a class that would include such future Civil War notables as George B. McClellan, Dabney Maury, and George E. Pickett, managed to graduate from the academy in 1846. One of his instructors would later write of Jackson that he "observed no unusual sign or indication of genius. . . . His conduct was good, his appearance manly, and his demeanor quiet."[6] After graduation he served with distinction in the Mexican War, in which he earned two brevet promotions for gallantry. He resigned from the service in 1852 and accepted a position teaching military science at the Virginia Military Institute. There his religious zeal, dull lectures, personal eccentricities, and strictness as a disciplinarian and taskmaster won him the enmity of many cadets, who referred to him as "Old Tom Fool" and on two occasions challenged him to duels.

When Virginia seceded in 1861, Jackson was appointed a colonel and assigned by General Robert E. Lee to take command at Harpers Ferry. There, aided by several of his former students at VMI, he instituted a program of rigorous training and constant drill that gradually transformed the mobs of Southern chivalry that were assembling in the Lower Shenandoah into efficient and disciplined soldiers. On May 23, Johnston arrived to supersede Jackson and appointed the former VMI professor the commander of the First Virginia Brigade, which at Bull Run would consist of Colonel James W. Allen's Second, Colonel James F. Preston's Fourth, Colonel Kenton Harper's Fifth, Lieutenant Colonel John

Echols's Twenty-seventh, Colonel Arthur C. Cummings's Thirty-third Virginia Infantry, and the four guns of Captain William N. Pendleton's Rockbridge Artillery. After Bull Run, these 2,600 men would be better known as the "Stonewall Brigade."

Arriving at Manassas on the afternoon of July 19 as the vanguard of Johnston's Army of the Shenandoah, Jackson and his brigade were directed by Beauregard to take up a position from which they could support Bonham's and Longstreet's efforts to defend Mitchell's and Blackburn's Fords. Jackson's initial assignment on the morning of July 21 was to support Longstreet's brigade as it crossed Bull Run at McLean's Ford and advanced on Centreville. This assignment was not welcomed by his men, many of whom were "very keen for a fight," as one of them wrote later, "and while we were down on the run they were afraid it would be over before we got into it."[7]

Soon after word of the fighting at the Stone Bridge reached army headquarters, however, Beauregard and Johnston decided to shift Jackson's command to the north to support General Cocke at Ball's Ford. Having moved toward the Stone Bridge in response to Cocke's request that he take the place of Evans there, Jackson learned that Bee "was hard pressed" and decided to march to his assistance.[8] As he marched to Henry Hill via the same farm road that had carried Hampton there from Portici, Jackson encountered Bee as he and his fought-out and disorganized command were arriving from Matthews Hill. "General," Bee told Jackson, "they are driving us." To this Jackson calmly replied, "Sir, we will give them the bayonet."[9]

Shortly after his conversation with Bee, Jackson encountered another hero of that morning's fighting, Captain John Imboden, who had just managed to salvage three of the guns with which he had put up such a bold front against the Yankees that morning. Furious at having been left isolated on Henry Hill after Bee's, Bartow's, and Evans's retreats, Captain Imboden "expressed himself with some profanity, which," he later wrote, "I could see was displeasing to Jackson." Although Jackson would later admonish Imboden that "nothing can justify profanity," at that moment on Henry Hill, Jackson decided to overlook the artilleryman's language. What he could not ignore, however, was Imboden's statement that, because he only had three rounds left for a single gun, he would not be doing any more fighting, at least until he had replenished his ammunition. Jackson managed to persuade Imboden not to continue his trek back to the rear, but instead to return to Henry Hill "till the other guns get here . . . I'll support your battery," he assured Imboden when they reached a swell of ground on the southeastern edge of the hill at approximately 11:30 A.M. "Unlimber right here." Jackson then posted two guns from Captain P. B. Stanard's Thomas Artillery next to Imboden and instructed the two artillerymen to put up a bold front and, as Jackson put it, "play upon the advancing foe."[10] (It was no doubt their fire that had played such havoc with the second Federal advance along the turnpike against Hampton.)

Jackson next began deploying his arriving infantry. He first posted Preston's Fourth Virginia and Echols's Twenty-seventh Virginia directly behind Imboden and Stanard to support their guns. To the right of the guns, next to Echols, he placed Harper's Fifth Virginia; to their left, next to Preston, he posted Allen's Second Virginia, and to Allen's left, Cummings's Thirty-third Virginia. Jackson then directed all five regiments to lie down in two lines two ranks deep (because Preston's and Echols's lines overlapped, Confederate lines directly behind the guns were actually several ranks deep) on the wooded reverse slope of Henry Hill. There they would have some protection from Union artillery fire and be invisible to the Federals. At the same time, Jackson also ordered the two other pieces of Stanard's battery and the four guns of Pendleton's Rockbridge Artillery forward. When they arrived, along with four more guns from Captain E. G. Alburtis's Wise Artillery under the command of Lieutenant John Pelham, Jackson finally let Imboden depart to replenish his ammunition chests.

As Jackson was establishing his line, Johnston and Beauregard arrived on the scene. Their appearance shortly after noon on Henry Hill immediately provided a morale boost for the Confederate defenders. Seeing Jackson was handling matters with his brigade well enough, Johnston first rode over to area behind Hampton's command near the Robinson house, where the remnants of Bee's, Bartow's, and Evans's commands were attempting to recover from their morning defeat. There he encountered the Fourth Alabama, which had managed to regain some of its discipline despite having lost many officers. When informed of their situation, Johnston grasped the regimental colors and offered to lead them personally back into the fight. The regiment's color bearer, Sergeant Robert Sinclair, refused to give them to the general. "Don't take my colors from me," Sinclair protested. "Tell me where to carry them and I will place them there." Impressed with the young man's determination, Johnston released his grip on the flag and personally led the Fourth Alabama to a position where they could support both Hampton's and Jackson's commands. Soon thereafter, Johnston encountered General Bee, who with tears on his cheeks told his commander that "my command is scattered and I am alone." Unlike the stern and unbending Jackson, who had admonished him only to give the enemy the bayonet, Johnston expressed sympathy with Bee's plight. He told Bee that he did not blame him for the condition of his command and urged him not to give in to despair. "The day," Johnston assured him, "is not lost yet."[11]

For his part, Beauregard was putting his flair for the dramatic to good effect. He rode along the line giving rousing speeches, cheering his men, and displaying an air of coolness and confidence that he maintained even after a horse was killed under him by a Federal artillery shell—his spirit was infectious. Within forty-five minutes of Beauregard's and Johnston's arrival, the situation for the Confederates on Henry Hill had stabilized to the point where Beauregard decided his superior's presence was no longer needed. He rode over to Johnston and suggested that it might be better if he left the field and went to Portici to direct the forwarding of reinforcements to the battlefield. Johnston wanted the honor of conducting the battle no less than Beauregard did and at first declined the suggestion. Beauregard, however, was persistent and finally managed to persuade Johnston to accede to his request by pointing out that, as senior commander, it was his responsibility to maintain control over the broader strategic situation, which would be difficult to do if he was bogged down in the tactical details of the fight on Henry Hill.

When Johnston departed for Portici at 1:00 P.M., the combined efforts of Beauregard, Jackson, Imboden, Hampton, and Johnston had forged a formidable defensive line on Henry Hill. The battle, to be sure, was far from won, and the Union guns on Dogan Ridge were making life quite uncomfortable for Beauregard and Jackson and their men. But, with thirteen cannon backed by Jackson's brigade and the forces Beauregard continued to rally after Johnston had left, the Confederates held a northwestward-facing line that could make any advance from that direction on Henry Hill no easy task.

The Confederate right, however, was exceedingly vulnerable. Located south of the Warrenton Turnpike in the vicinity of the Robinson house, it was held by Colonel Kenton Harper's Fifth Virginia, behind whom Hampton's Legion and the brigades of Bee, Bartow, and Evans were rallying. With the exception of Harper's command, these units were in rough shape. Moreover, the flank was "in the air," unprotected by any sort of natural obstacle. If the Federals could get a force into position to take advantage of this, the potential danger to Jackson's line on Henry Hill would be grave indeed.

As Jackson completed positioning his men, just such a threat was developing. After following Sherman's brigade across Farm Ford, Keyes, at the direction of Tyler, who had accompanied his command as it crossed Bull Run, did not follow Sherman to Matthews Hill. Instead, he halted his brigade after it crossed Van Pelt Hill and posted it just north of Young's Branch. At approximately 12:30 P.M., just as Johnston and Beauregard were arriving on Henry Hill, Tyler, without giving McDowell any notice directed Keyes to form his men into a line of battle and "move so as to strike the Warrington [sic] turnpike."[12] Keyes placed Charles D. Jameson's Second Maine on the left, followed by John Spiedel's First Connecticut, and John L. Chatfield's Third Connecticut, followed by Colonel Alfred H. Terry's Second Connecticut, on the right. Keyes then marched the two lead regiments south at the double-quick toward the Warrenton Turnpike and—inadvertently—the vulnerable Confederate right.

After brushing aside a small force of cavalry that was screening Jackson's flank, Keyes's men crossed Young's Branch at the base of Henry Hill, where they were briefly subjected to "a severe fire of artillery and infantry" coming from the top of the hill.[13] After a short pause to restore order in their lines, Tyler ordered Keyes to resume the advance. The Unionists advanced approximately 100 yards up the bare slope when Keyes ordered his

two regiments to lie down, take cover under a slight rise, and load
their muskets. After this was done, Keyes ordered his men back
on their feet and directed them toward the Robinson house at the
top of the hill. "My order to charge," he later wrote, "was obeyed
with utmost prompt." The eager men from Maine and Connecticut leapt to their feet. Howling "as if two thousand demons had
been suddenly let loose from Pandemonium" and marching at
the double-quick, the two regiments surged up the slope, across
the Warrenton Turnpike, and toward the Robinson house.[14]

There they encountered the Fifth Virginia. Surprised by the
sudden and unexpected appearance of Keyes's force, Harper's
men briefly held their fire out of concern that it might be friendly.
It did not take long, however, for them to figure out it was not
and to give the Federals, wrote one member of the Second Maine,
"a hearty how'd doo' in the shape of a volley of musketry slap in
our faces." Jameson's and Chatfield's men continued moving forward through a hail of bullets, stopping occasionally to load their
muskets and give the rebels "the same kind of pills."[15] Next, the
Hampton Legion and a few men from Bee's and Evans's brigades
came up to support Harper. But the Yankees kept coming. Evans's,
Bee's, and Hampton's tired troops quickly dropped out of the
fight. Harper's command soon followed and pulled back to a
thicket of woods 100 yards from the Robinson house.

Before Keyes and Tyler lay the opportunity of a lifetime. If
they could maintain the momentum of their advance, they would
roll up Jackson's right flank and destroy the Confederate line on
Henry Hill. Then there would be nothing standing between the
Federal army and a sweeping victory that might just end the war
before too much blood had been shed and bitterness sown.

But it was not to be. As Keyes's men reached the top of the
hill, Confederate resistance stiffened. Taking advantage of the
shelter of the woods, which both Keyes and Tyler with some ex-
aggeration later characterized as "breastworks," and supported
by H. Grey Latham's Lynchburg Artillery, Harper and his men
rallied. They began pouring an intense fire into the exposed and
tired Federals who had just crested the hill. "The fire became so
hot," Keyes later wrote, "that an exposure to it of five minutes
would have annihilated my whole line."[16] Although the attack
had lost its momentum and the overpowering heat left them

crazed with thirst—one man went so far as to drink out of a puddle in which the Robinsons' pigs had been wallowing—Jameson's and Chatfield's men nonetheless continued to fight valiantly.

But, as would so often be the case for the boys in blue in this war, their exertions came to naught due to the failings of their superior officers. The timely arrival of reinforcements might well have tipped the balance of strength back to the Federals, restored their forward momentum, and led to the destruction of Jackson's flank. Unfortunately, Keyes and Tyler, unaware of the great opportunity before them, at no point during the fighting gave any thought to calling up the two reserve regiments and putting them into the fight. Nor did Tyler make any effort to contact McDowell about what was taking place. Relations between McDowell and Tyler had cooled considerably in the days before the battle. McDowell blamed Tyler for the failure to bag Bonham at Fairfax Court House and was angry at Tyler for the debacle at Blackburn's Ford. For his part, Tyler was not and never would be enthusiastic about serving under the much younger McDowell. Consequently, there was no supporting attack made elsewhere on the battlefield. Thus—and not for the last time in this war—the gallantry of Billy Yank in battle was wasted because of a lack of vision, dash, and cooperation in the high command. Unable to push farther than the Robinson house, unwilling to call up the reinforcements that were available, and worried about the punishment their men were taking, Keyes and Tyler finally decided to give up the attack. They ordered their men to fall back down Henry Hill to Young's Branch.

As the brigade rested at the bottom of Henry Hill, the members of the Second Maine could see a number of injured comrades still on the slope. Determined not to leave them behind, Jameson asked for volunteers to help him retrieve the wounded. Six men answered the call. Jameson then led them back up the hill and, despite a harassing fire from the enemy, the volunteers managed to bring back six of their wounded comrades—and two rebel prisoners as a bonus—without a loss. Two of the men who followed Jameson on this mission of mercy, Abiather J. Knowles and Henry W. Wheeler, would later be awarded the Medal of Honor for their bravery.

Once back across the turnpike, Keyes directed his regiments to move to the left. His objective was to recross the turnpike and turn the flank of the forces at the top of Henry Hill by getting between the hill and Bull Run. When he had collected his forces, Keyes marched them forward once again. Veering to the left, the brigade recrossed the Warrenton Turnpike about a half-mile west of the Stone Bridge. There they came under fire from two rebel artillery pieces at the top of Henry Hill. The aim of the gunners was not particularly good, however, and Keyes was able to reach the Confederate rear, but by the time he managed to get his men in position for another possible charge up Henry Hill, events elsewhere on that eminence had rendered such an operation pointless.

NOTES

1. Blake, *Three Years in the Army of the Potomac*, 16.
2. Gallagher, ed., *Fighting for the Confederacy*, 53; Craig L. Symonds, *Joseph E. Johnston: A Civil War Biography* (New York: W. W. Norton, 1992), 119.
3. Beauregard, "The First Battle of Bull Run," in *Battles and Leaders of the Civil War*, edited by Johnson and Buel, 1:209–10.
4. H. Seymour Hall, "A Volunteer at the First Bull Run," *War Talks in Kansas: A Series of Papers Read before the Kansas Commandery of the Military Order of the Loyal Legion of the United States* (Kansas City: Franklin Hudson Publishing Co., 1906), 155.
5. *JCCW*, 2:215.
6. Keyes, *Fifty Years' Observation*, 198.
7. Casler, *Four Years in the Stonewall Brigade*, 25.
8. *OR*, 2:481.
9. Casler, *Four Years in the Stonewall Brigade*, 26.
10. Imboden, "Incidents of the First Bull Run," 234–35, 238; *OR*, 2:481.
11. Symonds, *Joseph E. Johnston*, 119–20.
12. Tyler, "Autobiography," 60.
13. *OR*, 2:349, 353.
14. James H. Mundy, *Second to None: The Story of the Second Maine Volunteer Infantry* (Cape Elizabeth, ME: Harp Publications, 1992), 72; *OR*, 2:353; B. F. Smart to Father, July 23, 1861, Manassas National Battlefield Park Library, Manassas, VA; Davis, *Battle at Bull Run*, 233.
15. Horatio Staples, "Reminiscences of Bull Run," *War Papers*, 3:134.
16. *OR*, 2:349, 353, 553–54.

CHAPTER ELEVEN

CUT DOWN ON HENRY HILL

AS ERASMUS KEYES was making his abortive attack on the Confederate left, the eleven guns of Captain James B. Ricketts's and Captain Charles Griffin's batteries continued pounding the Confederate position on Henry Hill. The artillery duel between their guns and Jackson's was an exceedingly unequal one. The Federal guns, being rifled, were able to reach the Confederate line, while Jackson's smoothbore guns could not reach Dogan Ridge, although, as noted, they were able to cause havoc for Federal infantry in the Young's Branch Valley. Nonetheless, by 2:00 P.M., General McDowell had finally come to the conclusion that this would be insufficient if he wished to push the rebel infantry and their "annoying batteries" off the hill and clear the way for the final triumphant march to Manassas Junction.[1]

The first step toward taking Henry Hill, as McDowell saw it, was to soften up the Confederate line with artillery fire, not from Dogan Ridge, but at short range on Henry Hill itself. Thus, he turned to Major William Barry, his chief of artillery, and directed Ricketts and Griffin to take their guns across the Young's Branch Valley and up to Henry Hill. Barry rode over to Dogan Ridge to deliver the orders to Ricketts and Griffin, after which both artillerymen immediately took steps to comply and directed their men to prepare for the move. They also, however, felt compelled to express deep reservations about the move and McDowell's decision, even though he had thousands of infantrymen on hand, to send them to Henry Hill without what they felt was adequate infantry support.

Henry Hill, Griffin complained to Barry, was no place for artillery to go alone. Why not, he asked, send infantry forward first to "get into position on the hill—let the batteries (Captain Ricketts's and mine) come into position behind them, and then let them fall back"? Griffin also advised Barry that he thought a better place for the batteries would be Chinn Ridge, the "hill about 500 yards to the rear of the one to which we were then ordered." Barry, however, refused to entertain any suggestion that McDowell's orders be altered in any way. Besides, he assured Griffin, there was nothing for him and Ricketts to worry about, as orders had already been sent to the Eleventh New York to follow the batteries to Henry Hill. Griffin, with an old regular's disdain for the fancily clad Fire Zouaves, let it be known that he had no confidence that they would do the job. "Yes, they will," Barry replied, "at any rate, it is General McDowell's order to go there." This hardly assured Griffin. "I will go," he told Barry, "but mark my words, they will not support us."[2]

Ricketts likewise was unhappy to receive the order to move to Henry Hill, and saw "at a glance . . . that I was going into great peril for my horses and men." Just then Lieutenant G. W. Snyder rode up to Ricketts, who told him what he and Griffin were about to do. Snyder was dumbfounded. "You have the best position in the world," he proclaimed, "stand fast, and I will go and see General McDowell." Snyder was not gone long. He quickly found McDowell, who informed him the orders stood. Griffin, Ricketts, and Snyder were not the only ones troubled by this maneuver. After the battle, Colonel Porter confided to Griffin: "When I found you had gone a thousand yards in advance, I cannot tell you my feelings. I was afraid I had allowed you to go there upon my order."[3]

With the debate over and their commands hitched up and ready to move, Griffin and Ricketts ordered their guns down Dogan Ridge, across Young's Branch, and onto the Sudley Road, as Barry rounded up infantry support for them. Griffin's three 10-pounder Parrott guns and two 12-pounder howitzers led the march south along the Sudley Road, but thanks to a confused guide it was Ricketts who first turned his guns off the road and onto the open plateau of Henry Hill. There he had a clear view of Jackson's line just 300 yards away on the other side of the hill. Jackson's men, however, would not be the first source of trouble for Ricketts. After he had placed his six 10-pounder Parrott guns just south of the Henry house, sharpshooters inside the dwelling opened fire on the guncrews who manned them. Supremely annoyed, Ricketts "turned my guns upon the house and literally riddled it."[4]

The sharpshooters, exercising the better part of valor, immediately evacuated the house and fled to the safety of their lines almost as soon as Ricketts's men took aim. Unfortunately, they were not the only occupants of the house. The 85-year-old widow Judith Carter Henry, two of her children, and a hired black servant were all inside the house when Ricketts and his gunners rumbled into position. (An effort had been made earlier in the day to move the invalided Mrs. Henry, but it had failed amid the fighting.) When Federal ordnance began crashing into the house, all but Mrs. Henry, who could not get out of her bed, were able to find shelter under furniture and inside the fireplace. Tragically, a shell slammed through the wall to the bedroom and smashed into the bed on which the widow was lying. She was wounded in three places and thrown to the floor in a pool of her own blood. Her distraught son ran outside the house, threw himself to the ground, and, nearly oblivious to the battle raging around him, screamed, "They've killed my mother!"[5] Mrs. Henry would linger on for a few moments, but by the end of the day she would be the only civilian casualty of the Battle of Bull Run.

As Ricketts was taking care of the rebel sharpshooters, Griffin and his five guns came up from the Sudley Road. Griffin placed his guns north of the Henry house to Ricketts's left. Together they presented a front of eleven guns to face the thirteen rebel guns just over 300 yards away on the other side of the rolling, open plateau of Henry Hill. A ferocious artillery duel commenced that shook the hill and severely rattled the nerves of Jackson's prone infantry. "Oh, Lord," cried out one distraught man, "have mercy upon me! Have mercy upon me!" "Me too, Lord! Me too, Lord!" shouted another. "What love we manifested," one man later wrote of the experience, "for the soil of Virginia that day."[6]

Jackson, however, was a pillar of strength. Clad in his old blue U.S. Army coat with a handkerchief around his left hand to cover a wound caused by a spent bullet ("Only a scratch—a mere scratch" was his response when Captain Imboden saw the wound and expressed concern), he rode boldly along the lines in front of his men, alternately assuring and instructing them. "Steady, men, steady," he shouted, "all's well! all's well!"[7] Although one soldier later compared Jackson's demeanor to that of a "farmer about his farm when the seasons are good," another saw a fierce warrior beneath: "A closer glance easily penetrated his apparent tranquility and carelessness. The trust in God, and utter reliance on His will was surely there—but no apathetic calmness. The blaze of the eye . . . was unmistakable. . . . A slumbering volcano clearly burned beneath that face so calm and collected."[8]

When later asked by Captain Imboden how he managed to maintain his cool under fire, Jackson replied, "My religious belief teaches me to feel as safe in battle as in bed. God has fixed the time for my death. I do not concern myself about *that*, but to be always ready, no matter when it may overtake me. . . . That is the way all men should live, and then all would be equally brave."[9]

Meanwhile, Beauregard was doing what he could on Henry Hill. Whatever mistakes he may have made as a strategist and administrator that morning were more than made up for by the force of his personality on Henry Hill. Unlike the stoic and steady Jackson, the flamboyant Creole was a whirlwind of activity, riding up and down the lines, placing, rallying, and inspiring his troops through the power of his image and oratory. He seemed to be everywhere at once, Mars incarnate, with his sword dramatically pointed to the enemy and the fire of battle burning in his eyes. One moment he was thrilling the men of New Orleans's Washington Artillery by shouting, "Hold this position, and the day is ours. Three cheers for Louisiana!" Then, seeing a South Carolina flag on the ground, he would be pleading with the men, "Hand it to me, let me bear the Palmetto Flag." The next moment he was among Georgia troops telling them, "I salute the Eighth Georgia with my hat off! History shall never forget you."[10]

Fortunately for Jackson and Beauregard, by sending Ricketts and Griffin to Henry Hill, McDowell had made a serious tactical mistake, one that reflected his lack of experience with modern ordnance. As long as the artillery duel had been conducted at long range, the Federal artillery had held the upper hand, as their rifled guns could reach the Confederate line on Henry Hill, but were out of the range of Jackson's smoothbores. Now, on their side of Henry Hill, the Federal gunners found it difficult to get the range on the Confederate line only 300 yards away, with the result that much of their fire sailed harmlessly over the heads of Jackson's men. (To make matters worse, much of the ordnance that did reach the Confederate line failed to explode as apparently some of the Federal gunners failed to cut their fuses properly. One member of the Second Virginia later recalled "pick[ing] up many which fell to the ground with a dull sound.")[11] At the same time, the Federals were now well within the range of both Confederate artillery and infantry, whose combined fire immediately began taking a severe toll on the horses and men of their batteries. As Ricketts and Griffin had recognized when they were ordered to the hill, without infantry support, Henry Hill was an exceedingly vulnerable and unpleasant place for artillery.

Barry, however, true to his word, did make a serious and immediate effort to fulfill his promise to Griffin that he would not have to wait long for infantry support. In addition to the celebrated Fire Zouaves of Colonel W. C. Farnham's Eleventh New York from Colonel Orlando Willcox's brigade, Barry managed to round up and dispatch to the aid of his gunners Colonel A. M. Wood's Fourteenth Brooklyn and Major J. G. Reynolds's Marine Battalion from Averell's (formerly Porter's) brigade (the same Fourteenth Brooklyn whose earlier advance along the turnpike against Hampton had been brought to grief by Jackson's artillery), and Colonel Willis A. Gorham's First Minnesota from Franklin's brigade of Heintzelman's division. With Wood's Zouaves in the lead, the four units then moved south along the Sudley Road to the aid of Ricketts and Griffin. Upon reaching the field, Brigade Commander Averell placed Farnham's men directly behind Ricketts's battery on the western slope of Henry Hill, where they were concealed from the rebels on the other side of the hill. Reynolds then positioned his Marines to the left of Farnham's and Ricketts's guns, while Heintzelman personally led Gorham's Minnesotans into position well to the right of Ricketts and Farnham. (Wood's regiment, for some reason, halted its march after crossing the turnpike.)

Much like Tyler's and Keyes's earlier maneuvers on the other end of the field, Heintzelman's move unwittingly placed the Federals in a position from which they could threaten one of the Confederate flanks. As the First Minnesota and Eleventh New York advanced to the top of the western slope of Henry Hill near the woods that bordered the hill to the south, they nearly came face to face with Colonel Arthur Cummings's Thirty-third Virginia, which held Jackson's left flank. Among the first of Cummings's men to see the Federals coming was Sergeant James P. Daily, who had walked out to the brow of the hill in front of his men. After witnessing the Federal advance, he returned to his men and shouted: "Boys, there is the prettiest sight from the top of the hill you ever saw; they are coming up on the other side in four ranks, and all dressed in red."[12]

For the first, but not the last, time on this part of the field, confusion over uniforms would prove costly to the Federals. Although weeks of training under Jackson's rigorous eye had helped give Cummings's Valley men the discipline and martial bearing of soldiers, neither the state of Virginia nor the Confederate government had yet secured them a standard set of uniforms. Thus, when they arrived at Henry Hill, they were clad in diverse colors. Some wore Confederate gray, some the traditional blue of the U.S. Army (as Jackson himself did), and many simply wore their old civilian clothes. When Heintzelman first caught a glimpse of Cummings's men, he saw only men clad in "citizen's clothes" and became immediately confused as to their identity. Colonel Gorham was equally baffled and even went so far as to stop a soldier when he decided to shoot first and then ask questions. The "circumstance," Gorham later wrote, "staggered my judgment [as to] whether those in front were friends or enemies."[13]

For their part, Cummings's Virginians were no more certain of what to do than were Heintzelman or Gorham. Jackson had just directed Colonel James Ewell Brown Stuart to take his cavalry and patrol the Confederate flanks. Moreover, Johnston had ordered the first unit from Cocke's brigade to arrive at Portici for redeployment, the battalion of Virginia troops commanded by Colonel William "Extra Billy" (so known for his tendency as the former governor of Virginia to pad appropriations bills with goodies for his constituents) Smith to Henry Hill to extend the Confederate left beyond Cummings's position. Whether or not Cummings actually knew about these moves by his superiors, there was nothing to indicate that the troops that had just appeared coming up from the direction of the Sudley Road were not in fact friendly.

To settle the matter, Heintzelman rode out between the lines to inquire as to the identity of Cummings's command. When some of the Virginians (afflicted with what one of them later described as "buck fever") greeted the Union man's inquiry with a hail of bullets, Cummings directed them to stop, but to no avail. This was enough to persuade Heintzelman that the force in front of him was indeed hostile. He then turned to the Zouaves and ordered them to charge, but before they could, a volley from Cummings's muskets induced them and the First Minnesota to hit the ground instead and exchange fire from a distance. Colonel Orlando Willcox later wrote of the Zouaves' experience: "The weight of metal against us was as of ten shots to one, of every class of projectiles . . . the whole regiment was swept back as by a tornado."[14]

Within minutes, the fire of Cummings's men persuaded the men of both Union regiments to fall back. The First Minnesota and a small detachment of the Zouaves led personally by Willcox pulled back into the cover of the woods on the southern edge of Henry Hill, while the rest of the Zouaves retreated to the Sudley Road. The fire of Cummings's guns also reached the Marine battalion, which, after Farnham and Gorham had moved forward to engage Cummings, had taken up their position directly behind Ricketts's guns. Finding themselves "exposed," in the words of their commander, "to a galling fire," Reynolds's Marines, in one of the most embarrassing moments in the history of the Corps, almost immediately broke and fled back down Henry Hill.[15] The pleas of Ricketts and the other stunned officers on the field to their troops not to abandon their positions fell upon deaf ears as hundreds of Union soldiers fled to the protection of the Sudley Road. However, the road proved to be no refuge. Just as the Eleventh New York reached it, 150 mounted Confederates under the command of the dashing and energetic Colonel Stuart arrived at the road less than 100 yards south of them.

Stuart had spent much of that morning pacing nervously at headquarters, afraid that he would miss out on the great battle he could clearly hear taking place. Thus, it was a matter of great relief to the young cavalryman when an orderly from Beauregard's staff found him at around 2:00 P.M. and told him, "General Beauregard directs that you bring your command into action

at once and that you attack where the firing is hottest."[16] Ecstatic
that his moment had come, Stuart immediately had his bugler
play "Boots and Saddles" and wasted no time getting his men
moving in a column of fours toward Henry Hill. But before
Stuart's men reached what they were sure would be a field of
glory, they were forced to endure a vivid reminder that war was
not all glory and sunshine, as their path to the battlefield brought
them first to the unholy sights and sounds of a makeshift field
hospital. Many years later the macabre scene remained vivid in
the minds in one of Stuart's aides.

> Tables about breast high had been erected upon which scream-
> ing victims were having legs and arms cut off. The surgeons
> and their assistants, stripped to the waist and all bespattered
> with blood, stood around, some holding the poor fellows while
> others, armed with long bloody knives and saws, cut and sawed
> away with frightful rapidity, throwing the mangled limbs on a
> pile. . . . The prayers, the curses, the screams, the blood, the
> flies, the sickening stench of this horrible little valley were too
> much for the stomachs of the men, and all along the column,
> leaning over the pommels of their saddles, they could be seen
> in ecstasies of protest.[17]

When he finally reached the field, Stuart reported to Jackson
who instructed him "to protect his flanks, but particularly his
left." Stuart then divided his 300-man force in half. One half,
under Major Robert Swan, he ordered to guard Jackson's right
near the Robinson house. The other 150 men Stuart led personally beyond the left flank that Jackson had expressed particular
concern about to the Sudley Road.

No sooner had he arrived there than Stuart spied red-legged
troops falling back from Henry Hill. Like Cummings, he first
thought that Farnham's men were friendly (the Zouave uniform
was popular on both sides of the battlefield in 1861), and shouted
to them as loud as he could: "Don't run, boys; we are here."[18]
But, when he rode forward for a closer look, Stuart suddenly saw
a U.S. flag. This removed all doubt, and the bold dragoon ordered his men to charge.

The Zouaves at first managed to establish a firing line and
get off a "sheet of flame" that shook Stuart's men. "It was a grand
melee," one man who witnessed what happened from a treetop

wrote later. "I could see the horses rearing, sabres glistening, and revolvers flashing." But the force of the Confederate charge proved to be too much for the Federals. The Confederates slammed into their lines, getting so close that one Confederate later recalled, "I leaned down in the saddle, rammed the muzzle of [my] carbine into the stomach of my man and pulled the trigger . . . blow[ing] a hole as big as my arm clear through him."[19] After only a few minutes of resistance, the New Yorkers and Minnesotans fled into the woods on the west side of the Sudley Road. Having done all the damage he could and immensely pleased with his performance, Stuart rode back to his original position on Jackson's flank as the artillery duel continued.

As the guns roared, General Bee rode among the still-scattered remnants of his command behind the Robinson house. Spotting a familiar mass of troops, he rode over to it and began a conversation that created a nickname that would fire Southern hearts for years to come. Bee initiated it by inquiring as to the identity of the unit, to which one of their officers replied, "Why, General, don't you know your own men? This is what is left of the Fourth Alabama." After expressing consternation at this being the only part of his brigade he could find, Bee asked his men: "Will you follow me back to where the fighting is going on?" "Yes, general," one determined man replied, "we'll go wherever you lead and do whatever you say." To this, Bee responded by dramatically pointing to his left and saying the most famous words that would be uttered on any Civil War battlefield: "Yonder stands Jackson like a stone wall; let's go to his assistance."[20]

At the same time, Griffin and Ricketts remained alone on their side of Henry Hill taking tremendous punishment in their uneven duel with Jackson's line. Colonel J. H. Hobart Ward's Thirty-eighth New York of Willcox's brigade had managed to arrive behind Griffin's guns. But upon their arrival they assumed a prone position in order to avoid "a spiteful and destructive fire from the enemy's batteries" and made it clear they had no intention to move forward and engage Jackson's line.[21]

Griffin decided that a change of tactics was therefore necessary if the Federals were going to break the Confederate line. Thus, he instructed Lieutenant Charles Hazlett to continue working the three Parrott guns north of the Henry house, while he personally took the two howitzers back to the Sudley Road. Once there, he intended to turn south, swing around behind Ricketts's guns, which had taken such a beating that they were nearly disabled, and then position his two guns to Ricketts's right. From there, Griffin hoped to pulverize Jackson's left with a destructive enfilade fire.

As Griffin was maneuvering his guns, the Confederate left was being extended, thanks to the arrival of "Extra Billy" Smith's Forty-ninth Virginia Battalion on Henry Hill. Colonel Smith had begun the day by helping his brigade commander, General Cocke, guard the Bull Run crossings just downstream from Evans at the Stone Bridge. When orders came from Johnston and Beauregard to move to Henry Hill, Smith's command had been the first of Cocke's units to leave its original position and march to the battlefield. Upon his arrival, Smith immediately encountered General Beauregard, who asked, "Colonel, what can you do?" Smith replied, "Put us in position and I'll show you."[22] Beauregard then directed him to move to the left of Jackson's line and fall in there. By the time the battalion reached its designated position, Smith managed to add to his command a company from the Fourth South Carolina of Evans's brigade and two companies of the Eleventh Mississippi from Bee's brigade. When combined with his own three companies, the entire force "Extra Billy" placed on Jackson's left numbered approximately 450 men.

Smith arrived just as Griffin and his two guns had moved up a few hundred yards from the Sudley Road onto a slight rise about 200 yards from Cummings's position. At approximately 3:00 P.M., Griffin had fired two rounds from his howitzers when he observed an unidentified force moving toward his position from the woods to his right. After the force crossed a fence it stopped, and an officer, as Griffin looked on from his horse with concern and no little astonishment, "stepped out in front of the regiment, between it and my battery, and commenced making a speech." Although a number of men in this force were wearing blue uniforms, Griffin deduced that it was hostile and ordered his men to load the two guns with canister and turn them toward it. Then, just as Griffin's men were ready to rake the unidentified force with hot metal, Major Barry rode up to him and shouted: "Captain, don't fire there; those are your battery support."

Griffin shouted back: "They are Confederates; as certain as the world they are Confederates." Barry was adamant. He was sure it was a regiment Heintzelman had sent to support Griffin. "I know they are your battery support," he told Griffin. And so ended the argument. "Very well," Griffin replied as he yielded reluctantly to his superior's judgment and ordered his men to hold their fire.[23]

The unidentified force was in fact "Extra Billy" Smith's battalion, augmented by units from the Thirty-third Virginia. Once again, confusion over uniforms played a critical role, for both Smith's and Cummings's commands were irregularly clad; some in blue, some in gray, and some in civilian clothes.

After the unidentified officer finished his speech, as Griffin's bluecoats held their fire, Smith's men continued their advance until they were about 70 yards from the Federal position. Then they stopped, lowered their muskets, and, with what Smith later described as "admirable effect," fired a devastating volley at the Federal gunners. Horses and men fell to the ground in such numbers that after the battle Griffin would say of the first volley: "That was the last of us. We were all cut down." "During my subsequent experience in a score of engagements," one Union veteran later recalled when he recounted the scene, "I never saw the work of destruction more sudden or complete."[24]

With the Federal gunners reeling, Cummings shouted to his men: "Attention! Forward march! Charge bayonets! Double quick!" and pointed them in the direction of Griffin's guns. The men reacted instantly to the command. They moved forward with a rush toward Griffin's battery, which one later recalled seemed to have simply "disintegrated. It seemed every horse and man of the battery just lay down and died."[25] Cummings's men easily drove off the Federal artillerymen and jubilantly took possession of their guns in the first successful offensive action by a Confederate force this day.

Although no one knew it at the time, the Federal offensive on Henry Hill had passed its culminating point. After the capture of Griffin's guns, the question would no longer be whether the Confederates could hold the line on Henry Hill, but whether McDowell could figure out how to regain and hold on to the foothold established by Ricketts's and Griffin's batteries. And with

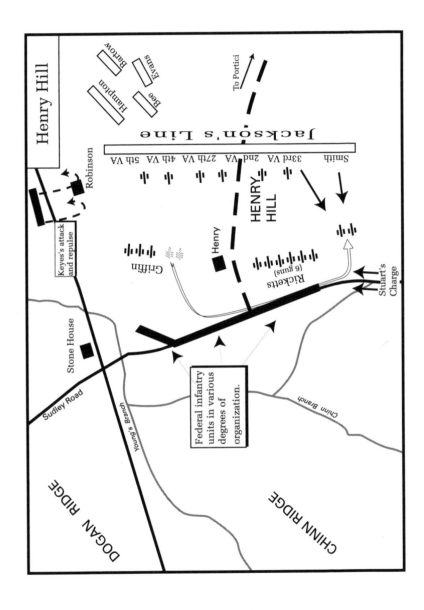

Confederate reinforcements arriving by the minute from Portici and at Manassas Junction from the Shenandoah Valley, time was everything for the Federals. For the sake of the Union cause the grand offensive simply had to achieve something more than a stalemate. In order to be victorious, the Federals had to drive the enemy from the field in a manner so decisive as to leave no doubt in the minds of Americans, North and South, as to who had triumphed. By 3:00 P.M. the chances of achieving such a victory on Henry Hill had dramatically declined. The tide of the battle had turned.

Confederate jubilation over the capture of the guns was short-lived, however, for just as Cummings's men got possession of them, they were greeted by the sight of Union infantry moving up from the Sudley Road. This was Colonel A. M. Wood's Fourteenth Brooklyn, which had finally moved up to Henry Hill and whose advance from the Sudley Road placed it in position to rake the left flank of Cummings's men, whose celebrations over the capture of Griffin's guns had totally disorganized their ranks. When the red-trousered men from New York opened fire, the effect was as devastating to Cummings's men as Smith's first volley had been to Griffin's artillerymen. The Virginians almost immediately broke and fled back to their original position, allowing Wood's men to recapture Griffin's guns, although the fact that the ground was littered with dead horses made it impossible for them to take them away to safety.

To make matters worse for the Confederates, when Colonel James Allen of the Second Virginia Regiment responded to Cummings's retreat by ordering the three companies holding his left to pull back in order to protect his rear, several of the troops interpreted the move as indicative of an order for a general withdrawal. Before he could correct this misperception, Colonel Allen was struck in the face and temporarily blinded by a limb from a pine tree that had been shattered by an artillery shell. After witnessing the disordered rout of his men and the potential disintegration of the entire Confederate left, one of Cummings's officers rode over to Jackson to report, "General, the day is going against us." Jackson, normally a man without humor, laconically replied, "If you think so, sir, you had better not say anything about it."[26]

Just as it seemed as if the Federals had gotten the upper hand, the situation suddenly changed. Instead of assuming the defensive and consolidating his newly won position, Colonel Wood decided to continue his advance against Jackson's line. The sight of the Federal advance on his disintegrating left snapped Jackson into action. He rode over to the Fourth and Twenty-seventh Virginia to steel them for the Federal charge. As Wood's men moved forward with a yell, they were greeted with a blizzard of artillery and infantry fire that broke their charge and compelled them to retreat pell-mell down to the Sudley Road.

Then, with the sort of impeccable timing that would characterize his generalship, Jackson sensed the moment had come to take the offensive. He ordered the men of the Fourth and Twenty-seventh Virginia regiments to rise to their feet and let them know the time of cowering under Federal artillery fire had come to an end. "We'll charge them now," he shouted, "and drive them to Washington!" The men sprang to their feet and surged forward toward Ricketts's battery, which was in no shape to fend them off. An hour of pounding from Jackson's artillery and infantry had left most of Ricketts's horses dead or dying and killed and wounded several of the men manning the batteries, including Ricketts himself, who had been struck in the thigh, and no amount of pleading could persuade the infantry back at the Sudley Road to help fend off the rebel attack. As if this were not enough to shake the nerves of Ricketts's men, as they moved to switch to canister, a shrill, eerie sound reached their ears. "When you charge," Jackson had admonished his men, "yell like Furies."[27] As they charged Ricketts's guns, Jackson's men followed his advice in spades, and there on Henry Hill, for the first time, was heard the "Rebel yell."

Ricketts's men managed to get off a round or two before Jackson's men were upon them. Resistance was useless. Those Federal artillerists who could fled for the safety of the Sudley Road. The rest could only hope the rebels who now claimed their guns would show mercy to the men who had manned them.

Meanwhile, to Jackson's left, Colonel Charles Fisher's Sixth North Carolina had arrived on the field. Seeing Griffin's guns where they had been earlier when Cummings had captured them, he decided to charge the position, which was still held by a few men from the Fourteenth Brooklyn. Fisher's charge easily dispersed these Federals and managed to reach the guns. Seeing that, because all the horses had been killed, removing the guns would be impracticable, Fisher then decided to push toward the Sudley Road. But then the First Minnesota, which had been holding the far Union right in the woods on the southern edge of the field ever since their earlier repulse at the hands of Cummings's command, began raking his left flank. Fisher was killed, and his men soon broke and retreated to their initial position. The Federal troops in the area then reclaimed Griffin's guns and removed them from the field.

NOTES

1. *OR*, 2:319.
2. *JCCW*, 2:169.
3. Ibid., 2:243, 172.
4. Ibid., 2:243.
5. Davis, *Battle at Bull Run*, 205.
6. Jeffry Wert, *A Brotherhood of Valor: The Common Soldiers of the Stonewall Brigade, C.S.A., and the Iron Brigade, U.S.A.* (New York: Simon & Schuster, 1999), 42; Hennessy, *First Battle of Manassas*, 79.
7. Imboden, "Incidents of the First Bull Run," 236; Robertson, *Stonewall Brigade* (Baton Rouge: Louisiana State University Press, 1963), 40.
8. Robertson, *Stonewall Jackson*, 263.
9. Imboden, "Incidents of the First Bull Run," 238.
10. Williams, *P. G. T. Beauregard*, 85.
11. Frye, *2nd Virginia Infantry*, 14.
12. Casler, *Four Years in the Stonewall Brigade*, 26.
13. *JCCW*, 2:30; *OR*, 51, part 1:21.
14. Casler, *Four Years in the Stonewall Brigade*, 27; Scott, ed., *Forgotten Valor*, 291-92.
15. *OR*, 2:392.
16. W. W. Blackford, *War Years with Jeb Stuart* (New York: Charles Scribner's Sons, 1945), 27.
17. Ibid., 28.
18. *OR*, 2:483.
19. Edwin S. Barrett, *What I Saw at Bull Run* (Boston: Beacon Press, 1886), 21; Blackford, *War Years with Jeb Stuart*, 30.
20. Jackson's receipt of his sobriquet and the circumstances under which Bee uttered his famous words have been matters of some controversy in Civil War literature. It is thoroughly and authoritatively dissected in John Hennessy's manuscript, "Jackson's 'Stone Wall': Fact or Fiction?" at the Manassas National Battlefield Park Library, Manassas, Virginia.

21. *OR*, 2:414.

22. William Smith, "Reminiscences of the First Battle of Manassas," in *Southern Historical Society Papers*, edited by J. William Jones et al., 52 vols. (Millwood, NY: Kraus Reprint Co., 1977 [1882]), 10:437.

23. *JCCW*, 2:169.

24. *OR*, 2:552; *JCCW*, 2:169; Blake, *Three Years in the Army of the Potomac*, 20.

25. Casler, *Four Years in the Stonewall Brigade*, 27; Reidenbaugh, *33rd Virginia Infantry*, 8.

26. Robertson, *Stonewall Brigade*, 41.

27. Robertson, *Stonewall Jackson*, 266.

CHAPTER TWELVE

"CROSS THE BROW OF THE HILL AND DRIVE THE ENEMY"

THE FIGHT FOR CAPTAIN RICKETTS'S battery was not over yet. McDowell still had plenty of men available and every intention of using them to recapture his lost battery on Henry Hill, to shove the Confederate defenders off the hill, and to complete his victory. The men of the Fourth and Twenty-seventh Virginia were equally determined to hold on to their position around Ricketts's guns and keep their hard-won prizes.

Fortunately for Jackson's men, the enemy provided considerable assistance to their efforts. The first significant Federal effort to recapture the guns was made by Major Alonzo F. Bidwell's First Michigan. Led personally by brigade commander Colonel Orlando Willcox, the unit's advance managed to cross the Sudley Road and reach the fence bordering it. From there they opened fire on Jackson's men. But then, because of what Willcox later described as "a blundering order," the right wing of the line fell back from the fence line.[1] The left wing of Bidwell's command managed to hold on to its position at the fence. Nonetheless, his advance effectively ended before it had really gotten started. Unable to move up the slope, the left wing fell back, and Willcox led them into the woods on the southern edge of Henry Hill.

As Willcox's attack was fizzling, two regiments from Colonel William B. Franklin's brigade arrived on the field, Colonel Samuel C. Lawrence's Fifth and Colonel George Clark's Eleventh Massachusetts, the former fueled by sandwiches provided by Senator Henry Wilson who had ridden out to Centreville to watch the battle. The regiments took up a position in the Sudley Road just west of the captured Federal battery near the Henry house. With the Fifth on the left and the Eleventh on the right, Franklin ordered them "to proceed to the vicinity of the point where Ricketts' battery was disabled to try to get back the guns." Franklin's men surged forward from the Sudley Road, "ordered to fire by company," a soldier in the Fifth Massachusetts wrote later, "and every company advancing in turn to the summit fired deliberately and then filed to the rear."[2] The two Virginia regiments that had captured Ricketts's guns had been holding their position on the western edge of Henry Hill for some time, and, although they had possessed the means necessary to overcome Willcox's fumbling offensive, they were in no condition to stop Franklin's determined advance. They put up a tough fight but were pushed back and forced to watch Ricketts's guns fall into the hands of Lawrence's and Clark's men.

By the time this had happened, however, on the other side of the field Beauregard had managed to prepare a new advance against Ricketts's position that would make Franklin's triumph a short-lived one. Sensing that a moment of crisis had come, Beauregard decided he would lead this second attack across the plateau personally. The forces he gathered for the attack were Harper's Fifth Virginia and the Hampton Legion, which had been holding the Confederate right near the Robinson house against a possible renewal of Keyes's advance. By now, however, it had become clear that Beauregard could expect no more trouble from Keyes, who had marched his men away from the Confederate right to a position between Henry Hill and Bull Run.

With Beauregard shouting to them to use the bayonet freely, the Fifth Virginia and the Legion rushed across the open plateau, with Harper's men on the left and Hampton's on the right, until Franklin's men around Ricketts's battery came into view. The Confederates then stopped and fired a devastating volley that shattered Franklin's command and led his men to retreat to the Sudley Road. Beauregard's two regiments then charged the Federal guns, which Franklin's men had made a determined, but—with all the horses wounded or killed—futile attempt to remove from the field before retreating. For the second time, Ricketts's guns fell into Confederate hands. The success of Beauregard's charge inspired other Confederate officers to push their commands forward to join the Fifth Virginia and the Legion; the Legion was now led by Captain James Conner, who had assumed command after Hampton was wounded in the charge, as they deployed to protect the guns. Among those who led their men across Henry Hill was General Bee, who decided to lead the Fourth Alabama toward Ricketts's position personally. Before he could reach the other end of the hill, however, Bee suffered a fatal wound in the abdomen.

McDowell was not done yet, however. He still had two full brigades, Sherman's and Oliver Otis Howard's, available and was determined to make the most of them. McDowell recognized, however, that the possibility of achieving a decisive success on Henry Hill itself had probably disappeared. Thus, rather than put both Howard's and Sherman's brigades into the battle for Ricketts's guns, McDowell used only Sherman's on Henry Hill. While Sherman maintained pressure on the Confederate center, Howard would march his brigade to Chinn Ridge, a hill about a quarter-mile west of the Sudley Road. If he could reach Chinn Ridge, he would be in position to turn or attack the Confederate left flank. Beauregard and Johnston would be forced either to weaken their center in order to save their flank and rear, giving Sherman the ability to break the Confederate line on Henry Hill, or to retreat in order to counter Howard's movement.

McDowell, however, was not the only one who had an eye on Chinn Ridge. At his headquarters at Portici, Johnston's thinking mirrored that of his Federal counterpart. He recognized the vulnerability of Beauregard's left on Henry Hill and was sending reinforcements forward to extend the Confederate line to the west, not only to protect its flank but also with an eye to the possibility of turning the Federal right.

As McDowell and Johnston conceived the contest to find out who had the longer reach to the west, Sherman and his brigade eagerly awaited orders north of the Warrenton Turnpike. When McDowell's orders to move toward Henry Hill finally arrived, Sherman placed Colonel I. F. Quinby's Thirteenth New York at the front of his brigade and marched the regiment south in column by divisions. He then instructed his other three regiments, Lieutenant Colonel Harry W. Peck's gray-clad Second Wisconsin, the Seventy-ninth New York commanded by Colonel James Cameron, whose brother happened to be Lincoln's secretary of war, and Colonel Michael Corcoran's Sixty-ninth New York to deploy in line of battle and follow Quinby to Henry Hill.

After crossing the Warrenton Turnpike and Young's Branch under fire, Sherman ordered Quinby to take his men up the ridge toward the Henry house. Quinby's advance had almost reached the house, when it encountered Hampton's command, which initially the New Yorkers managed to push back. Then, however, confusion over the identity of the forces in their front led them to pause long enough for the Legion to rally and put an end to Quinby's advance north of Ricketts's "severely cut up" battery. While this encounter was taking place, the rest of Sherman's brigade, after coming under fire in their advance down Buck Hill and across the Warrenton Turnpike, moved into the Sudley Road, which Sherman found "worn deep enough to afford shelter." They continued their movement south until they reached a point near Ricketts's guns, just in time to see the Marines and Zouaves break and run.[3] Sherman, however, resisted committing his men to the fight and held his entire command in the road until Major James Wadsworth of McDowell's staff rode up and directed him to order his men out of the road and have them advance up Henry Hill. Sherman then turned to Peck and instructed him to lead his gray-clad Second Wisconsin forward.

Peck's attack was a fiasco that bordered on the comic. The source of it was their gray uniforms. Almost as soon as Peck's men left the shelter of the Sudley Road to begin their assault on the Confederate position at the top of the hill, they found themselves under fire from the rear, from their own comrades who mistook them for the enemy, until Union officers managed to sort things out, stop the gunfire, and get Peck's men moving again. As they advanced on the double-quick up the hill, a small ravine compelled them to split into two separate wings. Then they caught a glimpse of a flag at the top of the hill. It was Confederate, but with all the smoke on the field and the tremendous similarity between the flags of the two nations, this identification was nearly impossible to make. Confused by the flag and shouts from an officer, "Stop firing; you are shooting your friends," a warning these particular soldiers, with the experience they had just gone through, were especially inclined to heed, the Wisconsin men slowed their advance and stopped firing. This pause gave the rebel forces at the top of the hill ample opportunity to prepare a vicious greeting for the advancing Federals. Before the Second Wisconsin could reach the crest of the hill, the Confederates above opened a devastating fire that put an end to the attack. "Our men," one Wisconsin soldier later recalled, "fell in every direction." It was, another wrote, "the most hellish shower of bullets you can imagine."[4]

The Second Wisconsin's ordeal was not over yet, however, for unless they wanted to be completely cut to pieces on the slope of Henry Hill, they had to fall back toward their comrades in the Sudley Road. Predictably, as soon as they came into view above the road, the rest of Sherman's brigade, still confused as to the identity of the gray-clad mass moving toward them, leveled their guns and fired, cutting down several more members of the Second Wisconsin before someone finally managed to identify them. Most of the Wisconsin men managed to reach the safety of the Sudley Road, but looking back on that day on Henry Hill, one of them later declared, "I cannot see how not only myself, but any of us, escaped with life."[5]

Sherman, however, was not yet finished with the Confederates on Henry Hill. He still had two relatively unbloodied regiments available and intended to make the most of them. After the repulse of Peck's men, he turned to Cameron's Seventy-ninth New York—the celebrated "Highlanders"—and instructed them "to cross the brow of the hill and drive the enemy."[6] The order came almost as a relief to some of Cameron's men in the road, "Where," one wrote, "Death began to make sad havoc in our ranks. . . . We could not see the foe, and then it was terrible to see our own boys, whose faces we knew, and whose hands we had pressed falling in Death agony."[7]

With Colonel Cameron personally leading the charge, the Highlanders leapt out of the road cut (where the Sudley Road had been so worn down by travel that a natural trench had almost been formed) and headed up the hill. They were greeted with a scorching volley that one later described as "a quick darting pestilence." In the face of this fire, Cameron and his men continued to move forward until they, too, saw what appeared to be an American flag waving over the remnants of Ricketts's battery before them. Just as had happened during Peck's advance, the

New Yorkers' advance and fire slackened just enough to give the
enemy a chance to pour into their exposed ranks "a terrible raking fire."[8] With their advance shattered and their colonel cut
down, the Highlanders retreated back down the hill to the cover
of the Sudley Road.

McDowell's conduct of the battle for Henry Hill has been
much criticized. Three decisions have especially attracted cen-
sure: his failure to ensure that the Federals put more than two
regiments at a time into the fight, his decision to send the two
batteries to the hill without infantry support, and his inability to
organize diversionary attacks elsewhere along the Confederate
position. The latter two criticisms have more merit than the first.
Clearly, not providing Ricketts and Griffin with adequate infantry support when they advanced to Henry Hill was, as several
Federal officers recognized at the time, a serious and unmistakable blunder. And although several soldiers would later attest
that McDowell's presence at the front helped bolster morale, the
Federal effort on Henry Hill would have probably been better
managed had McDowell not decided to place himself so far forward (a mistake Nathaniel Lyon would repeat a few weeks later
at Wilson's Creek). Had McDowell remained farther back, he
would have been in a better position from which to manage the
battle and gain a better grasp of the broader tactical picture. But
because he chose to lead from the front, McDowell was blissfully
unaware of the activities of Keyes's command the entire afternoon, and, after he issued the orders directing Howard to advance to Chinn Ridge and Sherman to attack Henry Hill, no effort
was made to undertake diversionary attacks against the Confederate position.

Holding McDowell responsible for the piecemeal nature of
the Federal assaults on Henry Hill, however, is less justified. To
be sure, there is no record of McDowell's making any effort to
ensure that the attacks on the western slope of Henry Hill were
made with more than two regiments at a time. Yet, it must be
noted that, once McDowell assigned the task of taking Henry Hill
to Sherman, it technically became that officer's responsibility to
coordinate the attacks of his units. Unfortunately, Sherman exercised the authority his commander delegated to him ineptly.

Sherman's failings on this day could fairly be chalked up to inexperience. Yet his performance at Bull Run reflected qualities of his generalship that would persist throughout the war. Like the good strategist he was, Sherman managed consistently to bring his troops to the right place at the right time. Once he made contact with the enemy, however, he became ineffective or worse, wasting lives in ill-planned and poorly executed assaults. This pattern would be repeated later in Mississippi at Chickasaw Bayou, in Tennessee at Chattanooga, and in Georgia at Kennesaw Mountain.

After the repulse of the Highlanders, however, Sherman still had one more regiment to throw at Henry Hill, Colonel Corcoran's Irish Sixty-ninth New York. Unlike Sherman's other regiments, Corcoran and his men would not make their attack alone. By the time Sherman had ordered the Sixty-ninth forward, Colonel J. Hobart Ward had moved his Thirty-eighth New York Infantry from its initial position in support of Griffin's guns north of the Henry house, after "finding that the enemy's artillery was telling with fearful effect upon our ranks." The New Yorkers fell back and after some maneuvering eventually came into position on Corcoran's right. There, "under the eye of the commander-in-chief, General McDowell, the men inspired by his presence," and supported by two guns from the Rhode Island battery under the command of Lieutenant J. Albert Monroe, Ward and Corcoran emerged from the road and began their assault.[9]

Harper's and Hampton's men at the top of the hill were in no condition to stop them. They had been able successfully to defend their position around Ricketts's guns against Quinby's, Peck's, and Cameron's attacks, thanks largely to the blundering and confusion that distinguished the Federal efforts. Now, exhausted, outgunned, and outnumbered, the Fifth Virginia and Legion were powerless to stop Ward and Corcoran's attack. Leading one of the companies in Corcoran's regiment was the celebrated Irish revolutionary Thomas Meagher, who shouted to his men as they advanced to "remember Ireland and Fontenoy!"[10] But before the New Yorkers even reached the top of the hill, the Confederates had broken and begun falling back across the top of Henry Hill. Ward's men immediately pushed forward toward the abandoned guns, and for the third time that day Ricketts's battery was in Federal hands.

Almost as soon as they arrived at the top of the hill, however, Ward's men looked to their right and were greeted by the sight of the First Michigan fleeing from the woods on the south side of the field. After leading his men into the woods, Willcox, under the impression that the Thirty-eighth New York would be coming to his support, rather than thrown against the Confederate center, had attempted to push forward through the woods to attack the Confederate left. Enemy resistance in the woods, however, proved to be much more than he had bargained for. As soon as the Confederates caught sight of the First Michigan, they opened a devastating fire that shattered the Union advance. Although struck in the right arm, Willcox, along with Captain William H. Withington, attempted to follow his men as they fled from the woods, until a Confederate officer, he later recalled, "charged on horseback at us thundering loud oaths, pointing his revolver and demanding our surrender."[11] Willcox and Withington surrendered.

A small Confederate force attempted to pursue the First Michigan as it retreated out of the woods. Fortunately for the Federals, by the time Willcox's men began pouring onto the open area on Henry Hill, Ward had driven off Hampton's and Harper's men and established a foothold near Ricketts's guns. When the Confederates chasing Willcox's men emerged onto the open plateau, the Thirty-eighth New York was advancing in the direction of the woods in an effort to consolidate and expand their position around the guns. What one participant later described as "a sharp and spirited skirmish" between the two forces ensued, which resulted in the Confederates falling back to the woods, leaving the Federals in "complete possession of the field."[12]

So pleased was McDowell that he personally rode to the top of the hill to congratulate Corcoran and his Irishmen on their accomplishment. As he glanced across the field, McDowell must have felt an immense sense of satisfaction, because at that brief, glorious moment, it appeared that, despite all the stumbles, fumbles, and delays, victory had finally been achieved on Henry Hill. The Hampton Legion and the five regiments of Jackson's brigade that had stood like a "stone wall" had shot their last bolt and were in no condition to put up much more of a fight. Bee was down with a mortal wound, Bartow was dead, and their commands were, if anything, in even worse shape than were Jackson's and Hampton's. All that was left now was for Howard to deliver the coup de grâce from Chinn Ridge to make the Federal victory complete.

Whatever satisfaction McDowell may have felt standing on Henry Hill at that moment would be short-lived, for just as his men had begun to consolidate their position around Ricketts's guns, another Confederate force was arriving on the other side of the field. It consisted of two regiments from Colonel Philip St. George Cocke's brigade, Colonel Eppa Hunton's Eighth, and Colonel Robert E. Withers's Eighteenth Virginia. Stationed at Lewis and Ball's Fords earlier that day and denied any role in the grand offensive Beauregard had planned, the morning of July 21 had been an anxious one for Hunton's and Withers's men, who feared they would miss out on the great battle. When the orders arrived shortly after 2 P.M. from General Beauregard instructing them to leave their positions along Bull Run, move to Henry Hill, and "go into action as speedily as possible," the men began their march to the field "so anxious to get at the Yankees that it [was] impossible to keep them in line."[13]

Cocke's men moved first to Portici and then to Henry Hill, where they went into position with Hunton's men on the right near the Robinson house and Withers's on the left. Withers and Hunton arrived just as the Fifth Virginia and Hampton Legion were falling back from Ricketts's guns. After rallying these troops, Hunton and Withers turned their men toward the Federal position on the other side of the plateau and ordered them to charge. The Federal position around Ricketts's battery, which only a few minutes earlier seemed to have been finally won, disintegrated as Cocke's men rushed forward like a massive tidal wave. As Sherman looked on, helpless to prevent it, the Thirty-eighth and Sixty-ninth New York broke and ran back down the slope to the Sudley Road.

As Hunton's men reclaimed the area around the Henry house, Withers's men gained possession of the eight guns of Ricketts's shattered battery for the South and turned them on the Federals. Finding the Sudley Road no longer a safe haven, Sherman's and

Willcox's men decided to abandon Henry Hill altogether and began falling back northward into the Young's Branch Valley. As Major George Sykes's battalion of regulars moved into the woods west of the Sudley Road to cover the Federal withdrawal from Henry Hill, Withers pushed his command down the slope from Ricketts's battery into the Sudley Road, where the men quickly became disorganized. They were soon joined by Colonel Joseph Kershaw's Second South Carolina and Colonel E. B. C. Cash's Eighth South Carolina from Bonham's brigade, who, during their advance to the field, had driven the last Federal troops from the woods on the south side of Henry Hill.

Ricketts's guns would change hands no more this day. The battle for Henry Hill was over.

NOTES

1. *OR*, 2:409.
2. *OR*, 2:406; Edwin C. Bennett, *Musket and Sword, or the Camp, March, and Firing Line in the Army of the Potomac* (Boston: Coburn Publishing Co., 1900), 17.
3. *OR*, 2:369.
4. Allen, "The Second Wisconsin at the First Battle of Bull Run," 228; Wert, *Brotherhood of Valor*, 46.
5. Wert, *Brotherhood of Valor*, 46.
6. *OR*, 2:370.
7. Lusk, ed., *War Letters*, 58.
8. Ibid., 59.
9. *OR*, 2:414.
10. David P. Conyngham, *The Irish Brigade and Its Campaigns*, edited by Lawrence Frederick Kohl (New York: Fordham University Press, 1994 [1866]), 37.
11. Scott, ed., *Forgotten Valor*, 295–96.
12. *OR*, 2:415.
13. Ibid., 2:546-47; Robertson, *18th Virginia Infantry*, 6.

Chapter Thirteen

"Hail, Elzey!"

WITH HIS MEN DEFEATED on Henry Hill, General McDowell's last
hope for victory rested with Colonel Oliver Otis Howard's brigade that was moving toward Chinn Ridge. If Howard could seize
the ridge, he would be on the western flank of Henry Hill and
could redeem the day by delivering a decisive stroke against the
far left of the Confederate line.

When Howard received his orders to advance to Chinn Ridge,
his brigade was back at Matthews Hill contemplating the wreckage of the fighting that had taken place there earlier. It had already been a long and exhausting day for Howard's men. The
last of Heintzelman's brigades to begin their march from their
camps at Centreville, they were destined to have a frustrating
and difficult morning. Although the sun had already been up for
an hour, Howard's New Englanders were in good spirits when
they finally commenced their march and began singing heartily
"John Brown's Body." By the time they had gone two miles, however, the blazing sun and brutal heat (a few weeks in Washington
had hardly been enough time to acclimate the New Englanders
to the joys of summer in northern Virginia) began taking their
toll and men began falling out by the side of the road. Then came
orders from General McDowell to halt several miles short of
Sudley Ford so they would be in a position to support either Tyler
or Hunter. There they stayed for several hours, baking in the sun
and denied the opportunity to slake their thirst and cool their
feet in Bull Run. To make matters worse, their commanding officer was hardly a model of calmness and confidence. As the
sounds of battle reached his command, Howard lingered anxiously by his horse and at one point cried out, "O God! Enable
me to do my duty."[1]

Finally, the eagerly awaited order to move to the battlefield via Sudley Ford came. Unfortunately, the officer sent back to Howard to escort his brigade to the field "in double time," as instructed by General McDowell, Captain Amiel W. Whipple, chose a route twice as long as the shortest one to the battlefield. The effect on Howard's New Englanders was devastating. Exhausted and dehydrated men fell out in such numbers that Howard later estimated that no more than half his men actually managed to reach and cross Sudley Ford. To add insult to injury, when Howard's men finally crossed Bull Run and began their advance south along the Sudley Road, they encountered a wise-cracking staff officer who, flush with excitement after the Federal victory on Matthews Hill, shouted to them: "You better hurry and get in if you want to have any fun."[2]

At approximately 3:00 P.M., McDowell's orders reached Howard instructing him to advance to Chinn Ridge. With Captain James B. Fry of McDowell's staff as their guide, Howard's men marched south to Dogan Ridge, then across the Warrenton Turnpike and Young's Branch into a ravine north and west of Chinn Ridge. There Howard deployed his men in two ranks. In front were Colonel Henry Whiting's Second Vermont on the right and Colonel Hiram G. Berry's Fourth Maine on the left, with Major Henry G. Staples' Third and Colonel Mark H. Dunnell's Fifth Maine in the second rank. With his men thus deployed, Howard ordered the first line forward to the crest of Chinn Ridge.

When Whiting's and Berry's men reached the top of the hill, they came into the view of Colonel Kershaw's South Carolinians posted in the Sudley Road a few hundred yards east of and at the bottom of Chinn Ridge. Since their arrival in the road in the wake of the successful charge of Cocke's brigade that had finally cleared Henry Hill of Federals, Kershaw's men, supported by Delaware Kemper's Alexandria battery of light artillery, had been exchanging fire with the battalion of Regulars under Major George Sykes that was covering the withdrawal of the rest of McDowell's forces to the north side of the Warrenton Turnpike. When Howard's men came into view, a firefight commenced between them and Kershaw's in which neither side was able to do much damage.

Meanwhile, two fresh Southern brigades were rushing to the field from Portici. The first and more important technically belonged to Colonel Arnold Elzey, but was actually being led to the battlefield by Brigadier General Edmund Kirby Smith, and was the last of the brigades to arrive from the Shenandoah Valley at Manassas Junction. From his headquarters at the Lewis house, Johnston had seen Elzey's three regiments come up from the station and immediately knew where he wanted to send them. When Smith arrived at Portici, Johnston directed him to take Elzey's men to the far left and "attack the right flank of the enemy."[3]

Smith and Elzey ordered their men forward following the same route Kershaw had taken to the battlefield. As Smith neared the field, he encountered Kershaw, who assured him the situation was stable in his front and advised him and Elzey to continue moving straight west to the high ground on the west side of the Sudley Road. Before they reached the road, however, Smith and his staff encountered a handful of isolated Federals who fired a volley at the oncoming Confederates. Smith was struck in the neck and, although not fatally injured, toppled from his horse.

With Smith down, Elzey immediately assumed command and led his brigade to Bald Hill, an eminence just south of Chinn Ridge. There he deployed his infantry with Colonel S. B. Gibbon's Tenth Virginia on the right, Lieutenant Colonel George H. Steuart's First Maryland Battalion in the center, and Colonel John C. Vaughn's Third Tennessee to the left. To Vaughn's left, Elzey posted the four guns of Lieutenant Robert F. Beckham's Culpeper Artillery.

Elzey and his men were soon joined by another brigade, one commanded by Colonel Jubal Early, which had begun the day posted in support of Longstreet's position at Blackburn's Ford, eagerly awaiting the commencement of the grand offensive against Centreville. That plan had, of course, fizzled and led to Johnston and Beauregard's calling Early to Portici. There Early was instructed by Johnston to follow Elzey and assist in the attack on the Federal right.

From his vantage point a mile away on Henry Hill, however, the sight of the dust clouds kicked up by Elzey's and Early's troops as they marched to the battlefield and a report from Captain Alexander that suggested it might be hostile filled Beauregard with "the keenest anxiety." Throughout the day, he and Johnston worried that, once the Federals learned that Johnston had slipped away from the Valley, they would duplicate his move and send Patterson's command to Manassas. If this had in fact happened, and it was Patterson's force that was riding up, Beauregard's entire line was in serious danger. Heightening Beauregard's anxiety was his inability to discern the identity of the oncoming troops because of the similarity of the Confederate and United States flags. Just as Beauregard began contemplating issuing orders to retreat, however, the breeze caught the colors of one of the lead regiments and exposed its identity. This enabled Beauregard to ascertain, to his great relief, "that the column was Early's gallant command, hurrying on, with all possible speed."[4]

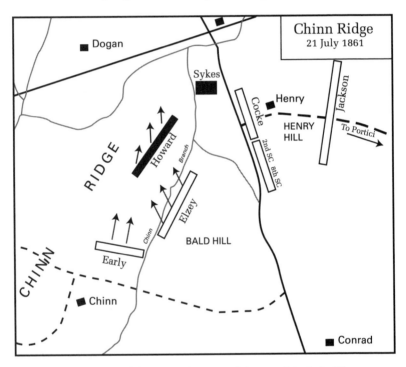

As Early moved his men into position on his left, Elzey was endeavoring to ascertain the identity of the forces he saw up on Chinn Ridge. When he caught sight of a U.S. flag at the top of the hill, he shouted ecstatically to his men: "Stars and Stripes! Stars and Stripes! Give it to them, boys!" His men then opened fire on the Federals on the top of the ridge. Beckham's artillery soon joined in the fight and made life extremely unpleasant for Howard's men. "The cannon balls and baum shels flew like hale stones," one of Whiting's Vermonters wrote shortly after the battle, "and there was an emensed show of rifle balls. . . . There was one of our men shot through the head by my side and three wounded and my canteen was shot of my side."[5]

Howard then rode back to the bottom of the ridge to order his second line forward. Much of the Fifth Maine, he found "in consequence of a cannon shot striking its flank and rear and a rush of our own retreating cavalry had been broken up and was gone." Howard managed, however, to get the remainder of Colonel Dunnell's command and Major Staples's Third Maine formed and led it up the ridge to help out Whiting's and Berry's men. When they reached the top, Howard decided to send Dunnell's men to the far right and instructed Staples to relieve Whiting's Vermonters, which were then placed in reserve. As Howard's men moved into position, Elzey's and Beckham's men continued firing at their position. "It was," Howard later recalled, "a hot place. Every hostile battery shot produced confusion."[6]

To relieve his men, Howard directed that one of his wings fall back and reform. Then, to his amazement, he saw his entire line begin to fall back. An agitated Major Frank Nickerson of the Fourth Maine then rode up to Howard and asked: "Did you order us to retreat?" Howard shook his head. Next, as if this was not bad enough, Colonel Dunnell rode up to Howard and informed him that his men could do no more and that, personally exhausted by illness, he could do nothing to stop their retreat. Howard, Nickerson, and several other officers made a gallant effort to rally the men and persuade them to stay on the ridge. But Howard quickly realized "I could effect nothing under fire," and he "at last ordered all to fall back to the valley and reform." The men from Vermont and Maine fell back through the thicket behind their former position at the top of the ridge, "not at first in a panicky manner," Howard remembered later, "but steadily, each according to his own sweet will."[7] Upon reaching the other side of the thicket, Howard and his subordinates successfully restored order to their ranks.

As the Federals were falling back, Elzey had come to the decision that the time had come to take Chinn Ridge and ordered his three regiments to charge up the hill. Elzey's men surged to the top of the hill, but found it devoid of the enemy. Elzey then ordered his men to advance in the direction of the thicket through which Howard's men had just passed. As they approached the thicket, Elzey's men were greeted by scattered small arms fire from some of Howard's men. Elzey then directed Beckham to train his guns on the thicket as Early began his advance farther to the west.

As shells from Beckham's guns began raining down on the Federal position, Elzey's men poured a devastating fire into the thicket. Within minutes, panic seized almost every member of Howard's brigade. Whatever order had been preserved vanished as Howard's command disintegrated. Men began fleeing northward back toward Sudley Ford, heedless of organization, and no amount of pleading or threatening by Howard or his subordinates could stop them.

In addition to securing Chinn Ridge for the Confederacy, Elzey's advance and Howard's retreat also had the effect of endangering the right flank of Sykes's Regulars, which had formed a square (a military formation traditionally employed to break up cavalry charges) and were sparring with the Confederate forces in the Sudley Road. To prevent being cut off from the rest of the army north of the Warrenton Turnpike, Sykes gave the order to retreat. Contemplating the scene of Union soldiers fleeing from the field, one of Sykes's lieutenants turned to his commanding officer and asked, "What do you make of this, Major?" "Looks very like a rout, Lieutenant!" Sykes replied.[8]

"Hail, Elzey, thou Blücher of the day!" a more cheery Beauregard shouted as he arrived on Chinn Ridge after a triumphant ride over from Henry Hill.[9] (As almost every Civil War general knew, Gebhard von Blücher was the Prussian general whose timely assault on the French flank sealed the fate of Napoleon's army at Waterloo.) The contest to see who had the longest reach to the west had ended just as had the struggle for Henry Hill, with the Confederacy in complete control of the entire field.

With Howard's retreat from Chinn Ridge, further effort, General McDowell quickly realized, had become useless. Even before the extent of Howard's rout was known, McDowell had sent orders to Colonel Dixon Miles at Centreville "to move up two of his brigades to the stone bridge" with an eye to having them ready should a retreat be necessary. He also instructed Miles to ask the War Department to "send on immediately all the troops that can be spared."[10] With Howard's defeat, a sense quickly spread among McDowell's men that they could accomplish no more that day on the west side of Bull Run. Although most of the regiments were hopelessly disorganized, only in a few units was there any sign of serious panic. It seemed the men had taken the attitude of a shopkeeper on a slow day rather than that of a beaten army, deciding, as one of McDowell's staff officers put it, "It was no use to do anything more and they might as well start home."[11]

NOTES

1. Howard, *Autobiography,* 1:154.
2. Ibid., 1:157.
3. *OR,* 2:476.
4. Alfred Roman, *The Military Operations of General Beauregard in the War between the States, 1861 to 1865, Including a Brief Personal Sketch and a Narrative of His Services in the War with Mexico, 1846–8,* 2 vols. (New York: Harper and Brothers, 1884), 1:107–8.
5. Hennessy, *First Battle of Manassas,* 112; Jeffrey D. Marshall, ed., *A War of the People: Vermont Civil War Letters* (Hanover, NH: University Press of New England, 1999), 38–39.
6. Howard, *Autobiography,* 1:159.
7. Ibid., 160.
8. Parker, "Personal Reminiscences," in *War Papers,* 2:222.
9. Hennessy, *First Battle of Manassas,* 117.
10. *OR,* 2:332, 746.
11. Fry, "McDowell's Advance to Bull Run," in *Battles and Leaders of the Civil War,* edited by Johnson and Buel, 1:191.

CHAPTER FOURTEEN

RETREAT

TO COVER THE RETREAT of the bulk of his army from the battle-field, McDowell selected Major George Sykes's battalion of regular infantry, Major Innis Palmer's battalion from the Second U.S. Cavalry, and Captain Richard Arnold's 4-gun battery from the Fifth U.S. Artillery. The other units of the army retraced their steps back to their original Bull Run crossings. Burnside's, Porter's, Willcox's, Franklin's and Howard's brigades crossed at the Sudley Road, Keyes's and Sherman's at Farm Ford. Although their ranks quickly "became intermingled, and all organization was lost," the Federals shared a common destination: their camps at the Centreville heights.[1] Once there, McDowell intended to take and hold a defensive position behind which his battered command could reform and perhaps, once reinforced, try again to break the Confederate army. In McDowell's mind, he was conducting a strategic withdrawal rather than a retreat, and he by no means considered himself the commander of a beaten army.

On the other side of the battlefield, exultation over the Federal withdrawal, exhaustion from the day's labors, and hopes that a vigorous pursuit might produce even more decisive results than simply holding good ground against an attack possessed the Confederates. Perhaps no one was as happy as Pierre G. T. Beauregard as he rode across the field ecstatically shouting to his men: "The day is ours!"[2] Cheering Confederate soldiers rushed to his horse as he rode along Henry Hill, and they eagerly grasped the hand of their triumphant commander as he contemplated a pursuit.

There was certainly material available for a vigorous pursuit. Of the forces on Henry Hill and Chinn Ridge, only "Stonewall" Jackson's brigade was so battered as to be incapable of further action. Over on Chinn Ridge, Arnold Elzey's and Jubal Early's brigades were winded, but relatively unbloodied after their rout of Howard, and they had a battalion of Stuart's cavalry and the four guns of Lieutenant Robert F. Beckham's Culpeper Artillery at their disposal. On Henry Hill, the four regiments of Philip St. George Cocke's brigade, augmented by the Second South Carolina from Bonham's brigade, were still relatively fresh after driving the last Federals from the hill. Also available downstream from the Stone Bridge were the brigades that had yet to see action.

Beauregard turned first to one of Cocke's regiments, Colonel Robert T. Preston's Twenty-eighth Virginia, and ordered it to lead the pursuit, followed by Early's brigade. Preston and his men quickly bounded down Henry Hill, across the Young's Branch Valley, and then marched up Matthews Hill, following the route to Sudley Ford that most of McDowell's men were taking in their retreat. Passing over the battlefield, Early found "unmistakable indications of the overwhelming character of the enemy's defeat, in the shape of abandoned guns and equipments."[3] However, neither he nor Preston moved quickly enough to negate the head start gained by the Federals, who in their desire to get away from the field demonstrated a fleetness of foot that, employed earlier in the day, might have reversed the outcome of the battle.

"The most pitiful feature," wrote one Union man of the retreat, "was the wounded men lying by the roadside who begged not to be left to the tender mercies of the rebels." Among the Federals left behind was John L. Rice of the Second New Hampshire, wounded in the chest during the fighting on Henry Hill. His comrades managed to carry him all the way back to the vicinity of Sudley Church where, not hearing a sound from him and terrified by rumors that the infamous "Black Horse Cavalry" was in pursuit, they left him under a fence, assuming he was dead. Two days later, however, Rice regained consciousness and was found by a local resident, Amos Benson, who with his wife ministered to Rice's wounds and brought him to the Confederate hospital at Sudley Church. Rice survived his wound and during a visit to Washington in 1886 decided to visit the battlefield and "visit his kind benefactors." To his great delight he found the Bensons still living near Sudley Church. But when Rice expressed a desire to repay them for their kindness, the Bensons made it clear they would not accept "any recompense for themselves." They did, however, say that "if you want . . . you can help us poor people here pay for our little church. . . . We owe two hundred dollars on it." Rice returned to Massachusetts and, with the assistance of a local newspaper, in only three days managed to raise $235 for the repair of Sudley Church.[4]

When it became clear that Early and Preston would not be able to catch Rice's fleeing comrades, Beauregard turned to Stuart. At his commander's order, Stuart led his approximately 150 cavalrymen dashing north toward Sudley Ford until they encountered the Federal rearguard. When Stuart's cavalry came into view Sykes directed his regulars to face about and open fire. The well-directed fire from Sykes's muskets, augmented by Arnold's guns, was sufficient to discourage Stuart's men from pushing too hard in pursuit of the rest of the Federal army as it crossed at Sudley Ford. Consequently, Stuart and his men then turned their attention to rounding up Federal soldiers who had been separated from their commands, a task that consumed enough manpower to effectively end their pursuit.

With a direct pursuit northward toward Sudley Ford yielding little in the way of results, Beauregard decided to push forces directly east across Bull Run at and below the Stone Bridge, with an eye to seizing the Warrenton Turnpike, the road the Federals would have to use to reach Centreville. He instructed Colonel Robert Withers's Eighteenth Virginia from Cocke's command to march back to Lewis Ford, cross Bull Run, and march to a position on the turnpike east of the stream, and Colonel Joseph Kershaw's Second South Carolina, Colonel E. B. C. Cash's Eighth South Carolina, and the 4-gun Alexandria Battery commanded by Captain Delaware Kemper from Bonham's command to march along the turnpike over the Stone Bridge and link up with Withers's command east of the bridge

Withers's, Cash's, Kershaw's, and Kemper's men managed to reach the left bank of Bull Run with little difficulty. There Kershaw spotted a large body of Federal troops in position on the high ground overlooking the bridge from the east, and decided along with Withers to halt their advance and deploy in line of battle to the right of the turnpike with Kershaw's men in front. Once deployed, Kershaw decided to send a staff officer back across Bull Run "to report to the first general officer he might meet that I had occupied the position; that the enemy was in front, and that I awaited orders." Before the aide returned, another staff officer rode up to Kershaw and informed him Beauregard wanted "pursuit of the enemy with a view to cut them off."[5]

As Kershaw formed his men into columns in order to comply with the commanding general's orders, a Union surgeon rode up to ask him why he was retreating. Kershaw quickly made him aware of his mistake and, after questioning the poor man about the force in front, sent him to the rear as a prisoner. A few minutes later, Cash's South Carolinians came upon a bigger prize: New York congressman Alfred Ely, whom they found cowering behind a tree and whose presence so infuriated Cash that his men had to talk him out of shooting Ely on the spot. Kershaw and his men then advanced along the turnpike until they came upon a house the Federals were using as a hospital, where to their surprise they were greeted by a battalion of Confederate cavalry under the command of Colonel R. C. W. Radford.

Radford's command had been pushed across Bull Run at Lewis Ford by General Johnston without Beauregard's knowledge. Radford and his men arrived at the turnpike approximately one half-mile west of its intersection with the road to Sudley Ford where Porter's and Heintzelman's men were just passing through. There Radford's men could see a number of Federal soldiers gathered in the yard of Mrs. Spindle and drinking from her well. As the Confederate cavalry approached, two guns from Captain Romeyn Ayres's battery arrived and deployed in the Spindle yard. Lieutenant Peter Hains, whose shot from a 30-pounder had begun the days's fighting nearly twelve hours earlier, was the first to spot the Confederate cavalry bearing down on the turnpike. He shouted to the men to rally and resist Radford's advance, but his shouts and fire from the Federal guns served only to frighten and confuse the Unionists. Radford's horsemen met little resistance when they charged. Terrified at the prospect of being cut to pieces by what they feared was Virginia's notorious (at least in Yankee imaginations) "Black Horse Cavalry," those Federals who could fled in what Radford later described as "wild confusion . . . and in the greatest disorder."[6] Dozens were taken prisoner, along with several wagons and pieces of artillery.

After dispersing the Federals around the Spindle house, Radford and his men moved east down the turnpike toward Cub Run, gathering prisoners and equipment as they went, until they encountered a strong Federal column of infantry. Radford halted his pursuit at the top of the ridge separating Bull Run and Cub Run to await the arrival of reinforcements, which soon came in the form of Kershaw's and Cash's infantry and Captain Kemper's artillery.

As they looked down into the Cub Run Valley, Radford, Kershaw, Cash, and Kemper could see that the effort to cut off the portion of the Federal army that had crossed at Sudley Ford before it reached the turnpike had failed. Nonetheless, as Kershaw contemplated the scene before him, he could see that the opportunities to make mischief for the Unionists on this July day had not yet been exhausted. The turnpike leading to the Cub Run bridge was packed with thousands of Federal soldiers, several civilian spectators, and innumerable wagons making their way there. Kershaw turned to Kemper and instructed him to take two of his guns south of the turnpike and fire on the bridge.

At approximately 6:00 P.M., Kemper wrestled his guns into position and granted the old Virginia secessionist fanatic, Edmund Ruffin, the honor of firing the first shot against the retreating mass of Federals. The shot could not have been more perfectly aimed. It exploded right above the Cub Run bridge with enough force to knock over a wagon on the crossing.

The sound of Kemper's artillery exploding overhead, the sight of the wagon tipping over, and the realization that their escape route was obstructed sent shock waves of panic quickly throughout the mob of Federals in the Cub Run Valley. Within seconds what had been a disorderly, but nonetheless relatively leisurely, withdrawal degenerated into a panicked flight to Centreville. "Before the third shell struck near us," one man recalled, "every man as far as the eye could reach seemed to be running for very life." Another wrote in his diary, "A panic seemed to seize upon every one. . . . I jumped into the run and holding my gun above my head struggled across with the water up to my waist." A Massachusetts man recalled: "Drivers, finding it impossible to cross the run with the wagons and artillery, took their horses, and sometimes cut the traces to expedite their movements. . . . The foot soldiers, alarmed by this strange conduct and the absence of general officers, double-quicked and ran; and hundreds cast aside muskets, axes, and equipments. . . . 'We have been sold,' was a common remark."[7]

By nightfall most of the Federal army had reached Centreville. There they were covered by Colonel Dixon Miles's division, which, despite the intoxication of its commander, put up a bold enough front to dissuade the Confederates from seriously contemplating an attack on Centreville. By the time the Federals reached their former camps around Centreville, their sense of panic had mostly subsided. Nonetheless, there was no disputing the fact that they had not just failed to carry the enemy's position but had been positively whipped. Few were in any condition physically or psychologically to do much more that night or at any time in the near future, a fact that their commander quickly realized as he pondered whether or not to stick to his original plan to remain at Centreville or continue the retreat.

It did not take McDowell and his subordinates long to determine that there was no way the army could or would remain at Centreville. After reaching the village, McDowell encountered General Tyler, who later recalled being "astonished at the demoralization which presented itself on every side" in Centreville. "Even the reserve seemed demoralized; its commanding general was maudlin drunk." "It was a terrible sight," one soldier wrote in his diary the next day, "to see the wagons coming in last night loaded down with dead, cut, torn & mangled in every possible manner & the wounded running or hobbling along with arms & legs dangling or hanging by shreds."[8]

At Tyler's suggestion, McDowell decided to call those brigade and division commanders near enough to be consulted to headquarters and solicit their opinions of the situation and the feasibility of remaining at Centreville. During the discussion, an exhausted McDowell fell asleep until one of his subordinates roused him to inform him that they could see no alternative to falling back toward Washington. McDowell then dispatched some aides to the various camps who found the decision to abandon Centreville "had been anticipated by the troops."[9]

McDowell then rode back to Fairfax Court House where he composed and sent off a telegram ruefully informing the War Department of his decision: "The men having thrown away their haversacks in the battle and left them behind," he wrote, "they are without food. . . . The larger part of the men are a confused mob, entirely demoralized." He advised Washington that, although "it was the opinion of all the commanders that no stand could be made this side of the Potomac," he would attempt to establish and hold a position at Fairfax. Before long, however, even McDowell had to bow to the inevitable. Soon after sending off this last message, he dispatched another to Washington, stating that the troops had decided they were not going to stop at Fairfax no matter what their commander wanted and, in any case, they were so disorganized and demoralized that, McDowell determined, "They could not be prepared for action by to-morrow even were they willing . . . I think now," he finally conceded, "as all of my commanders thought at Centreville, there is no alternative but to fall back to the Potomac, and I shall proceed to do so."[10]

Back in Washington, Winfield Scott had spent July 21 as he did most days, alternately napping and exchanging messages and reports with his frontline commanders. Early in the day, Scott sent McDowell a telegram warning him that positive information had been received that "a strong reinforcement left Winchester on the afternoon of the eighteenth, which you will have to beat also," but nonetheless he was confident that McDowell's offensive would succeed, especially after reports arrived of the success the Federals had achieved early in the day.[11] After directing that the reserve division under Theodore Runyon be forwarded to the front, Scott dozed off for his customary afternoon nap. He was awakened shortly after 3:00 P.M. by President Abraham Lincoln, who had stopped by that morning and, having been assured by Scott that McDowell would prevail, had headed off to church. After church, the president had spent the early afternoon at the Executive Mansion receiving telegrams from Fairfax Station until, alarmed over a message suggesting there were problems at the front, he headed over to the War Department and awoke General Scott. Scott assured the worried president that things were going well before dozing off again.

Scott received further encouragement when, at around 6 P.M., a message written two hours earlier arrived from one of

McDowell's staff officers. It requested that "all troops that can be sent from Washington to come here without delay," but also stated that McDowell had "driven the enemy before him." Almost as soon as this message arrived, however, reports of a major disaster for Federal arms began trickling into Washington, which were confirmed when a dispatch reached the War Department: "General McDowell's army in full retreat . . . the day is lost. Save Washington and the remnants of this army. . . . The routed troops will not reform."[12]

Scott's response, once he had fully accepted the validity of the reports of defeat, was to assume McDowell would rally his troops at Centreville or "at the worst" Fairfax Court House and to order Runyon to send forward troops to support the rally. By 1:00 A.M. on the twenty-second, however, the magnitude of the disaster and the fact that the Federal retreat would not stop until it reached the Potomac had become clear. Scott responded by canceling the orders to forward troops and instructed Mansfield to "man all the forts and prevent soldiers from passing over to [Washington]; their arrival would produce a panic."[13]

At the Executive Mansion, President Lincoln, for the first but not last time in this war, stretched out on a couch and hunkered down for a long sleepless night of reading and listening to reports of a military disaster. Over the next two days, McDowell's men, "so unexpectedly reduced to tramps and fugitives," wrote one observer, "fagged out, hungry, and dejected," would stumble their way to the safety of the Washington entrenchments as "rain commenced falling in torrents" on the city. The North was stunned. "Today will be known as BLACK MONDAY," wrote one man when news of the Federal defeat reached New York. "We are utterly and disgracefully routed. . . . If the secessionists have any dash in them, they will drive McDowell into the Potomac. . . . Only one great fact stands out unmistakably: total defeat and national disaster on the largest scale."[14]

Sober reflection on the events of July 16 to July 22 quickly replaced the sense of shock and depression that swept through the North after the debacle at First Manassas. Northerners naturally sought to know why their fine young men had suffered defeat in their first major tangle with the South. The easiest explanation was that the Union army was simply too raw and inexperienced. Men who had belonged to "the headlong 'forward to Richmond' school," like the Blairs, came under heavy criticism for urging the army onward before it was ready. Certainly General Scott believed that this approach was the source of the defeat. Shortly after the battle, he stated with great anguish in a meeting with Lincoln and members of Illinois's congressional delegation that "I am the greatest coward in America! . . . I have fought this battle, sir, against my judgment. . . . I deserve removal because I did not stand up, when my army was not in a condition for fighting, and resist it to the last!"[15]

The rawness of the troops certainly helped compromise Federal efforts. To be sure, in this regard, as Herman Hattaway and Archer Jones have noted, "The disadvantages were mutual and each could expect his opponent to fight with a degree of incompetence equal to his own."[16] Yet as the campaign developed, this proved to be a greater disadvantage to the Federals; to the great good fortune of the South, circumstances conspired to foil Beauregard's desire to fight on the offensive. Due to advances in military organization and weapons technology that enhanced the mobility and firepower of armies during the first half of the nineteenth century, fighting on the tactical defensive during the Civil War would prove to be a major advantage in any major engagement, especially ones fought by raw troops. (It is true that neither side at Bull Run was fully equipped with the rifled musket. However, the overwhelming advantage that armies fighting on the defensive enjoyed had been evident since the Napoleonic Wars, when armies were armed only with smoothbore flintlock muskets.) Although McDowell managed to turn the enemy's flank successfully and catch the Confederates at a disadvantage on the morning of July 21, the flexibility and maneuverability of the multidivisional army that enabled him to do this also made it possible for the Confederates to change their front and shift forces in order to successfully counter the Federal turning movement. Clearly, however, McDowell's plans and movements demanded more from his troops in the way of discipline, stamina, and the other qualities that distinguished veteran troops than did Beauregard's and Johnston's.

McDowell's performance during the campaign also came under some scrutiny, although it was difficult not to be charitable toward the defeated general. Certainly Lincoln was sympathetic. When he first encountered McDowell after the battle, the president assured him, "I have not lost a particle of confidence in you." McDowell replied, "I don't see why you should, Mr. President."[17] Whatever deficiencies in tact McDowell may have had, he was not without justification in feeling he had performed well the duty fate had thrust upon him.

In his plans and conduct of the campaign, McDowell demonstrated real ability. Although marching into what was for all intents and purposes terra incognita, the advance to Fairfax Court House and the plan for capturing the Confederate force there were as well conceived and conducted as could have been realistically expected. That the Confederates escaped McDowell's trap, although it was a source of frustration to McDowell, was probably inevitable given the impossibility of concealing the commencement and direction of the Federal advance from any reasonably alert foe. The plan to have Heintzelman turn the Confederate position at Manassas, while the other three divisions distracted Beauregard from the direction of Centreville was a good one, although the nature of the terrain over which Heintzelman was to operate would make it impracticable, a fact McDowell did not have until the campaign was in full swing.

In his conduct of the battle, however, McDowell made a number of decisions that are open to criticism, for they gave the Confederates time to respond to his well-conceived plan. The first was the decision to have Tyler's demonstration force lead the march west from Centreville along the Warrenton Turnpike, followed by the flanking force of Hunter's and Heintzelman's divisions, rather than the other way around, which cost the flanking force precious time in their march to Sudley Ford. The second was his decision not to push his command forward immediately to seize Henry Hill after overrunning the Confederates on Matthews Hill, which gave the Confederates time to establish a strong position from which they were able to thwart Federal attempts to seize the hill later in the day. The third of McDowell's mistakes was deciding to send Ricketts's and Griffin's guns to Henry Hill ahead of the infantry, which left them vulnerable to capture. Finally, in his efforts to reclaim those guns and drive the Confederates off Henry Hill, McDowell and his subordinates threw their men into the battle in a piecemeal fashion, failing to ever send more than two regiments at a time against the hill.

To be sure, these mistakes, as important as they were, might not have been fatal had Patterson successfully held some or all of Johnston's forces in the Shenandoah Valley. Of course, it could be argued that Patterson's mistakes would not necessarily have been fatal had McDowell not committed his mistakes. But Patterson clearly had the easier task, and his failure to carry it out diminished McDowell's margin for error at Bull Run to the point where the minor tactical errors he made were enough to give the Confederacy the time to respond to his skillful opening maneuver and get the last units from Johnston's army to the battlefield.

For Lincoln's counterpart, the evening of July 21 was a much more joyous occasion. Unable to sit in his office in Richmond as his countrymen met the Yankee invaders in combat, Jefferson Davis had boarded a train earlier in the day and headed north to Manassas Junction. Upon arriving at the station, he commandeered a horse and rode forward to Johnston's headquarters through crowds of stragglers whom he personally attempted to rally and lead back to the field. Late in the afternoon Davis finally arrived at Portici, where he encountered Johnston as the general was returning from Henry Hill where he had met with Beauregard to check on the state of the pursuit. To Davis's delight, Johnston reported that the Yankees had been whipped and were retreating back to Washington. Johnston informed the president that he had already instructed Milledge Bonham at Mitchell's Ford and James Longstreet at Blackburn's Ford to cross Bull Run and attack the Federals at Centreville. Davis then rode off to see how the pursuit was going, leaving Johnston to continue working on plans for its execution.

As it turned out, Radford's cavalry and the units Beauregard had pushed across would be the only Confederate force to press the Federals seriously. Bonham's and Longstreet's men would cross Bull Run as directed, but when reports arrived that the Federals were at Centreville in strength, they decided to fall back to the right bank of the creek. By the time darkness fell, all hopes for a successful pursuit that day were gone.

As this became clear, Johnston decided to ride back to Manassas Junction to check up on affairs there. However, President Davis and Beauregard managed to intercept Johnston along the road from Portici to Manassas and persuade him to meet with them at Beauregard's headquarters behind Mitchell's and Blackburn's Fords. The three men arrived at the McLean house at approximately 10:00 P.M. and began discussing plans for pursuing the retreating Yankees. As they talked, reports began arriving of the rapid disintegration of the Federal army, which led one of Beauregard's staff officers to suggest that President Davis personally issue orders for an immediate pursuit. Davis eagerly agreed, but almost as soon as he did so, a staff officer expressed deep reservations about the validity of the reports concerning the condition of the Federal army. Davis responded by merely ordering a reconnaissance in force to begin at first light the next morning. Heavy rains on the twenty-second proved to be the final nail in the coffin of the Confederate high command's hopes for a vigorous pursuit that might inflict more damage on the Federal army before it reached the safety of the Washington fortifications that evening.

After the war, an acrimonious debate over who was responsible for missing what was perceived to be a golden opportunity to follow up the great victory at Manassas, inflict even greater damage on the Federals, and possibly capture Washington would engage Johnston, Davis, Beauregard, and their partisans. The simple fact, however, is that on July 21 and 22 the Federals withdrew with such speed that, even had Johnston and Beauregard pushed their command more vigorously, it is highly unlikely that their raw troops could have caught up with, let alone inflicted much more damage upon, the Union forces. Most significant, however, the Confederates along Bull Run were in no condition to conduct a vigorous pursuit. A long day of desperate fighting, followed by wild celebrations when the enemy withdrew, left "our army," as Johnston would sum up the situation on the evening of July 21 several years later, "more disorganized by victory than that of the United States by defeat."[18]

Perhaps just as important as the state of the army's organization in frustrating President Davis's hopes for an immediate pursuit was the shock that came over the raw Confederate troops as for the first time they contemplated the human wreckage on a battlefield they had fought to possess. Wrote one man two days after the battle:

> I made an attempt to go over [the battlefield] some hours ago, and the smell of the blood made me sick, and I had to turn back, but this time succeeded, and may God grant that I may never see another. . . . I have often read descriptions of battle-fields, but never, until now, realized all the horrors that the word expresses. Here are mangled human bodies on every side, some pierced by a rifle or musket ball—others almost torn to frag-ments by shell. . . . Some have a look or expression as mild and calm as if they were only sleeping, others seem to have had a terrible struggle with the monster Death and only yielded after having suffered such pain as has caused their faces to assume expressions that are fearful to look upon, their features dis-torted, the eyeballs glaring, and often with their hands full of muck and grass that they have clutched in their last agony.[19]

Even had the organization been there for an effective pursuit, such scenes no doubt diminished the eagerness of Johnston's men for another battle for at least as long as it took McDowell's men to reach safety.

Nonetheless, the Confederate soldiers could take comfort in the fact that they had achieved a victory at Bull Run as complete as almost any Southern partisan could have hoped for. The con-fidence Southerners had in themselves soared and the contempt they possessed for Yankee manhood reached new heights. The notion that the products of a decadent Northern culture were no match for them seemed to have been confirmed. "Never again" would the Yankees dare "advance beyond cannon shot of Wash-ington," one Southern newspaper predicted after the battle. An-other saw in the battle evidence of "the breakdown of the Yankee race, their unfitness for empire" and asserted that the South could now "take the scepter of power. We must adapt ourselves to our new destiny."[20] Surely now, the Yankees would see the futility of trying to restore the Union by force of arms.

This great victory had cost the South, Johnston reported, ap-proximately 378 killed, 1,489 wounded, and thirty missing, for a total of just under 1,900 casualties. Federal casualties, McDowell reported, came to 2,896 altogether with 460 killed, 1,124 wounded, and 1,312 missing.[21] Thus, the Federals lost 1.5 soldiers for every Confederate casualty. If the North could take comfort in anything from the battle, it was that the casualty figures favored the Union if the North, with its 5-to-2 advantage in manpower, could continue trading lives on a 1.5-to-1 ratio. Thus, the South was hurt more than the North. If such rates of losses continued over several battles, the North would win by attrition.

That, of course, would only be relevant if the North, contrary to Southern expectations going in, possessed the steel to persist in the effort to restore the Union after suffering a defeat. Unfortunately for the South, it quickly became clear that the determination of Abraham Lincoln and the people of the loyal states to preserve the Union for their communities and future generations remained as strong as ever. In the weeks that followed Bull Run, this renewed determination would be manifest in new troops—raised for three years this time—pouring into Washington to receive the guiding hand of a master organizer and disciplinarian, George B. McClellan, who would forge them into a formidable army. Thirteen months later the North and South would meet again in battle on the plains of Manassas.

NOTES

1. *OR*, 2:321.
2. Hennessy, *First Battle of Manassas*, 117.
3. OR, 2:557.
4. Haynes, *History of the Second Regiment, New Hampshire*, 35–36.
5. *OR*, 2:524.
6. Ibid., 2:533.
7. Aldrich, *History of Battery A*, 23–24; Rhodes, ed., *All for the Union*, 30; Blake, *Three Years in the Army of the Potomac*, 26.
8. Tyler, "Autobiography," 62–63; Sears, ed., *For Country, Cause and Leader*, 58.
9. *OR*, 2:321.
10. Ibid., 2:316.
11. Ibid., 2:746.
12. Ibid., 2:747.
13. Ibid., 2:748, 754–55.
14. Wheeler, *A Rising Thunder*, 388; Strong, *Diary of the Civil War, 1860–1865*, 169.

15. *New York Herald*, July 26, 1861; Timothy D. Johnson, *Winfield Scott: The Quest for Military Glory* (Lawrence: University Press of Kansas, 1998), 228.

16. Hattaway and Jones, *How the North Won*, 43.

17. Russell, *My Diary North and South*, 301.

18. Joseph E. Johnston, "Responsibilities of the First Bull Run," in *Battles and Leaders of the Civil War*, edited by Johnson and Buel (New York: Century, 1884–88), 1:252.

19. Barrett, *Yankee Rebel*, 8.

20. McPherson, *Battle Cry of Freedom*, 347.

21. *OR*, 2:477; 51, part 1:17–19.

BIBLIOGRAPHICAL ESSAY AND RECOMMENDED READINGS

Any effort to understand the war in 1861 and the particular campaign and battle described in this book will benefit from a solid grounding in the general history of the Civil War. The following multivolume works have long been considered classics in the field: Allan Nevins, *The War for the Union*, 4 vols. (1959–1971); Shelby Foote, *The Civil War: A Narrative*, 3 vols. (1958–1974); and Bruce Catton, *The Coming Fury* (1961), *Terrible Swift Sword* (1963), and *A Stillness at Appomattox* (1967). Of the many single-volume treatments, a number stand out: James M. McPherson's *Ordeal by Fire: The Civil War and Reconstruction* (1982), offers a comprehensive treatment of the coming of the war, the war itself, and Reconstruction, although his more massive Pulitzer Prize–winning *Battle Cry of Freedom: The Civil War Era* (1987), omits any discussion of postwar Reconstruction. Readers can also consult the following fine works: Peter J. Parish, *The American Civil War* (1975); Russell F. Weigley, *A Great Civil War: A Military and Political History* (2000); and James G. Randall and David Herbert Donald, *Civil War and Reconstruction* (2001), a longtime classic that has recently been revised and updated by Donald, with the assistance of Jean H. Baker and Michael F. Holt.

Good brief histories include: Richard H. Sewell, *A House Divided: Sectionalism and the Civil War, 1845–1876* (1988); Charles P. Roland, *An American Iliad: The Story of the Civil War* (1991); Frank E. Vandiver, *Blood Brothers: A Short History of the Civil War* (1992); Allen C. Guelzo, *The Crisis of the American Republic* (1996); and Brooks D. Simpson, *America's Civil War* (1996). Readers will find much valuable information in the following reference works: Mark M. Boatner, *The Civil War Dictionary* (1959); E. B. Long, *The Civil War Day by Day: An Almanac, 1861–1865* (1971); Patricia L. Faust, ed., *Historical Times Illustrated Encyclopedia of the Civil War* (1986); Richard N. Current et al., eds., *Encyclopedia of the*

Confederacy, 4 vols. (1993); and David S. Heidler and Jeanne T. Heidler, eds., *Encyclopedia of the American Civil War*, 5 vols. (2000).

For a superb narrative and insightful analysis of the military history of the war, Herman Hattaway and Archer Jones, *How the North Won: A Military History of the Civil War* (1983), is unmatched. Both authors have also published shorter military studies that are of great value: Jones, *Civil War Command and Strategy: The Process of Victory and Defeat* (1992), and Hattaway, *Shades of Blue and Gray: An Introductory Military History of the Civil War* (1997).

In preparing this book, I found much of value in several previous works on the First Manassas Campaign. The best tactical study of the battle by far, informed by the author's many years of working at Manassas National Battlefield, is John J. Hennessy, *The First Battle of Manassas: An End to Innocence, July 18–21, 1861* (1987). I relied on it heavily in preparing my narrative of the battle. William C. Davis, *Battle at Bull Run: A History of the First Major Campaign of the Civil War* (1977), although not as good on the battle as Hennessy's book, provides a more complete study of the entire campaign and the events in Washington and the Shenandoah Valley that shaped it. Superseded by Davis's and Hennessy's books are Robert M. Johnston, *Bull Run: Its Strategy and Tactics* (1913), and Russell H. Beatie, *Road to Manassas* (1961). Joanna M. McDonald, *"We Shall Meet Again": The First Battle of Manassas (Bull Run), July 18–21, 1861* (2000), is a good later narrative. Readers seeking to follow the course of the battle will find the six "Troop Movement Maps" prepared by the National Park Service and the companion volume by Edwin C. Bearss, *First Manassas Battlefield Map Study* (1981), highly instructive. Bull Run's status as the first major battle of the Civil War is considered in W. Glenn Robertson's mistitled, but still useful, "First Bull Run, 19 July 1861," in Charles E. Heller and William A. Stofft, eds., *America's First Battles, 1776–1965* (1986). Readers will also find much valuable information in the August 2001 issue of *Civil War Times Illustrated*, which was devoted to the First Bull Run Campaign.

There are several published collections of invaluable primary material on the campaign. The most important is U.S. War Department, *The War of the Rebellion: The Official Records of the Union and Confederate Armies*, 70 vols. in 128 parts (1880–1901). In the past decade, Broadfoot Publishing has produced Janet B. Hewitt et al., eds., *Supplement to the Official Records of the Union and Confederate Armies*, 98 vols. to date (1994–). Further information is contained in essays by participants in Robert U. Johnson and Clarence C. Buel, eds., *Battles and Leaders of the Civil War*, 4 vols. (1887), and in the testimony given by Union officers to the U.S. Congress, *Report of the Joint Committee on the Conduct of the War*, 3 vols. (1863). Useful first-person accounts by Union veterans are sprinkled throughout the sixty-six volumes, handsomely reprinted by Broadfoot Publishing, of *Papers of the Military Order of the Loyal Legion of the United States* (1991–1996). For Confederate accounts, see J. William Jones et al., eds., *Southern Historical Society Papers*, 52 vols. (1876–1959), and *Confederate Veterans*, 40 vols. (1893–1932).

Memoirs, diaries, letters, and unit histories written by participants in the First Manassas Campaign abound, only a few of which can be listed here. Often cited in Ken Burns's memorable PBS series on the Civil War, Robert Hunt Rhodes, ed., *All for the Union: The Civil War Diary and Letters of Elisha Hunt Rhodes* (1985), is an excellent source for readers interested in a Unionist perspective on the campaign. Also of value, not the least because of the fine work of their editors, are Stephen W. Sears, ed., *For Country, Cause, and Leader: The Civil War Journal of Charles B. Haydon* (1993), and Thomas W. Cutrer, ed., *Longstreet's Aide: The Civil War Letters of Major Thomas J. Goree* (1995). A number of sequential primary accounts are strung together to form a readable narrative of the campaign and the events that preceded it in Richard Wheeler, *A Rising Thunder: From Lincoln's Election to the Battle of Bull Run: An Eyewitness History* (1994). Several editions of William Howard Russell's invaluable and justly celebrated *My Diary North and South* have appeared since its original publication in 1863; I have used the 1988 edition, which was ably edited by Eugene H. Berwanger. For further sources, the reader is referred to the notes after each chapter in the text.

Studies of the major military and political figures who shaped the course of the First Bull Run Campaign number in the thousands. Although both contain arguments that have been challenged by more recent scholarship, two works on the Union high command stand out: T. Harry Williams, *Lincoln and His Generals* (1952), and Kenneth P. Williams's at-times shrill *Lincoln Finds a*

General, 5 vols. (1948–1959). Works on Lincoln number in the thousands; space allows listing only a few here. Lincoln's own writings can be found in Roy P. Basler, ed., *The Collected Works of Abraham Lincoln*, 9 vols. (1953–1955). John G. Nicolay and John Hay, *Abraham Lincoln: A History*, 10 vols. (1890), is an admiring, but nonetheless invaluable work by Lincoln's wartime secretaries. David H. Donald, *Lincoln* (1995), is the best biography, although previous works by Mark E. Neely, Stephen B. Oates, Benjamin Thomas, James G. Randall, and Carl Sandburg remain valuable. An exceptionally fine study that focuses on Lincoln's presidency is Philip S. Paludan, *The Presidency of Abraham Lincoln* (1994).

Winfield Scott has been the subject of two biographies in the past few years: John S. D. Eisenhower, *Agent of Destiny: The Life and Times of General Winfield Scott* (1997), and Timothy D. Johnson, *Winfield Scott: The Quest for Military Glory* (1998). Unfortunately, neither work provides a very detailed—or particularly penetrating—treatment of Scott's role in the Civil War. The lives of Scott's most determined and influential critics within the Lincoln administration are chronicled in William E. Smith, *The Francis Preston Blair Family in Politics*, 2 vols. (1933); Rita Monroney, *Montgomery Blair: Postmaster General* (1963); and Elbert B. Smith, *Francis Preston Blair* (1980). Their debate is placed insightfully in an important context in Joseph L. Harsh's dissertation, "George Brinton McClellan and the Forgotten Alternative: An Introduction to the Conservative Strategy in the Civil War, April–August 1861" (1970); and in Mark Grimsley, *The Hard Hand of War: Union Military Policy toward Southern Civilians, 1861–1865* (1995).

Curiously, Irvin McDowell has yet to have a biography, although Thomas J. Rowland is reported to be working on one. Many of McDowell's senior subordinates slipped back into obscurity after Bull Run and have suffered the same neglect. Good studies of those who went on to bigger things in the war, which provide useful information both on their subjects and on the Bull Run Campaign, include William Marvel, *Burnside* (1991); Edward A. Miller Jr., *Lincoln's Abolitionist General: The Biography of David Hunter* (1997); and Mark A. Snell, *From First to Last: A Biography of Major General William B. Franklin* (2002). Robert Garth Scott, ed., *Forgotten Valor: The Memoirs, Journals, and Civil War*

Letters of Orlando B. Willcox (1999), provides much useful information on that Union officer. Readers interested in Oliver Otis Howard can consult *Autobiography of Oliver Otis Howard, Major General United States Army*, 2 vols. (1907); and John A. Carpenter, *Sword and Olive Branch: Oliver Otis Howard* (1964). The most famous of McDowell's subordinates, of course, was William T. Sherman, who has been the subject of several fresh studies, including Charles Royster, *The Destructive War: William Tecumseh Sherman, Stonewall Jackson, and the Americans* (1991); John F. Marszelak, *Sherman: A Soldier's Passion for Order* (1994); Michael Fellman, *Citizen Sherman* (1995); Stanley P. Hirshorn, *The White Tecumseh: A Biography of William T. Sherman* (1997); and Lee B. Kennett, *Sherman: A Soldier's Life* (2001). For Sherman's own take on things, see *Memoirs of General W. T. Sherman*, 2 vols. (1890); and Brooks D. Simpson and Jean V. Berlin, eds., *Sherman's Civil War: Selected Correspondence of William T. Sherman, 1860–1865* (1999).

The Confederate high command has been the subject of several perceptive analyses. Of particular value, although they disagree on several key points, are Steven E. Woodworth, *Davis and Lee at War* (1995); and Joseph L. Harsh, *Confederate Tide Rising: Robert E. Lee and the Making of Southern Strategy* (1999). Both are superlative, prize-winning works that are broader in scope than their titles suggest. Also valuable for anyone seeking to understand the Confederate war effort are Richard E. Beringer, Herman Hattaway, Archer Jones, and William N. Still Jr., *Why the South Lost the Civil War* (1986); and Gary W. Gallagher, *The Confederate War: How Popular Will, Nationalism, and Military Strategy Could Not Stave Off Defeat* (1999). Jefferson Davis has been the subject of a trio of massive biographies in the past few years: William C. Davis, *Jefferson Davis: The Man and His Hour* (1991); Felicity Allen, *Jefferson Davis: Unconquerable Heart* (1999); and William J. Cooper Jr.'s much-anticipated *Jefferson Davis, American: A Biography* (2000). Readers of Jefferson Davis's own writings can consult his *Rise and Fall of the Confederate Government*, 2 vols. (1881); and Lynda L. Crist, Mary S. Dix et al., eds., *The Papers of Jefferson Davis*, 9 vols. to date (1971–). A counterpart to Paludan's study of Lincoln is Herman Hattaway and Richard E. Beringer, *Jefferson Davis: Confederate President* (2002).

The best biography of Joseph E. Johnston is Craig L. Symonds, *Joseph E. Johnston: A Civil War Biography* (1992). Readers will also benefit from Alan C. Downs's interesting and rewarding dissertation, "Gone Past All Redemption? The Early War Years of General Joseph Eggleston Johnston" (1991); Downs's essay, " 'The Responsibility Is Great': Joseph E. Johnston and the War in Virginia," in Steven E. Woodworth, ed., *Civil War Generals in Defeat* (1999), 29–70, 202–9. and Johnston's own *Narrative of Military Operations* (1874). T. Harry Williams, *P. G. T. Beauregard: Napoleon in Gray* (1957), is an outstanding biography, although the Civil War scholarly field eagerly awaits T. Michael Parrish's forthcoming account. Beauregard's perspective on events is presented in ghostwriter Alfred Roman's *Military Operations of General Beauregard in the War between the States, 1861 to 1865*, 2 vols. (1884).

Johnston's and Beauregard's subordinates have received much more attention than McDowell's. Douglas Southall Freeman, *Lee's Lieutenants: A Study in Command*, 3 vols. (1942–44), remains unmatched in its treatment of these men and their role in the war from Manassas to Appomattox. Works on Thomas J. Jackson abound, but the best is James I. Robertson Jr.'s mammoth *Stonewall Jackson: The Man, The Soldier, the Legend* (1997), the magnum opus of one of the most celebrated modern Civil War scholars. Still valuable is Frank E. Vandiver, *Mighty Stonewall* (1957). The life and career of cavalryman James Ewell Brown Stuart have been superbly recounted in Emory Thomas, *Bold Dragoon: The Life of Jeb Stuart* (1986). James Longstreet is the subject of William Garrett Piston's *Lee's Tarnished Lieutenant: James Longstreet and His Place in Southern History* (1987), and Jeffry Wert's *General James Longstreet: The Confederacy's Most Controversial Soldier* (1993). Written to defend his career against attacks, but still informative, is Longstreet's *From Manassas to Appomattox: Memoirs of the Civil War in America* (1886). The life and career of one of Longstreet's postwar tormentors, Jubal Early, is chronicled in Early's own *Lieutenant General Jubal Anderson Early, C.S.A.: Autobiographical Sketch and Narrative of the War between the States* (1912); and in Charles C. Osborne, *Jubal: The Life and Times of General Jubal Early, CSA* (1992). The latter work will undoubtedly be superseded by a forthcoming publication by Gary W. Gallagher, who also edited the highly useful *Fighting for the Confederacy: The Personal*

Recollections of General Edward Porter Alexander (1989). Harold R. Woodman Jr., with his *Defender of the Valley: Brigadier General John Daniel Imboden* (1996), and Donald C. Pfanz, with *Richard S. Ewell: A Soldier's Life* (1998), offer fine accounts of their subjects.

Popular attitudes toward war and the military in the United States as it was heading into the Civil War are superbly described in Marcus Cunliffe's penetrating *Soldiers and Civilians: The Martial Spirit in America, 1775–1861* (1968). Philip S. Paludan skillfully integrates Cunliffe's arguments into his outstanding work, *"A People's Contest": The Union and the Civil War* (1988), the counterpart to which is Emory M. Thomas, *The Confederate Nation, 1861–1865* (1979). Also invaluable for understanding the mindset of Northerners during the Civil War is Earl J. Hess, *Liberty, Virtue, and Progress: Northerners and Their War for the Union* (1988). Popular attitudes on both sides are scrutinized perceptively in Randall C. Jimerson, *The Private Civil War: Popular Thought during the Sectional Conflict* (1993). Michael C. C. Adams considers the behavior of Northern soldiers during the First Manassas Campaign and the impact of the defeat on the North in a broader cultural context in *Our Masters the Rebels: A Speculation on Union Military Failure in the East, 1861–1865* (1978). Readers interested in the impact of notions of masculinity and femininity in nineteenth-century America on the war will find much to consider thoughtfully in Catherine Clinton and Nina Silber, eds., *Divided Houses: Gender and the Civil War* (1992).

Few topics in Civil War history have been the subject of so many fine works, or inspired more spirited debate in recent years, than the common soldier. Bell I. Wiley's masterly works, *The Life of Johnny Reb* (1943) and *The Life of Billy Yank* (1952), remain unmatched in their treatment of the life of the Civil War soldier. *Soldiers Blue and Gray* (1988) is a more concise and later study of the subject by Wiley's distinguished student, James I. Robertson Jr. Those seeking to understand the soldiers' mind-sets and how they reflected broader themes in nineteenth-century U.S. culture would be remiss if they did not consult Samuel J. Watson, "Religion and Combat Motivation in the Confederate Armies," *Journal of Military History* 58 (January 1994): 29–55; Steven E. Woodworth, *While God Is Marching On: The Religious World of Civil War Soldiers* (2001); and two stimulating and insightful works by

Reid Mitchell: *Civil War Soldiers: Their Expectations and their Experiences* (1988), and *The Vacant Chair: The Northern Soldier Leaves Home* (1993). William Garrett Piston, "The First Iowa Volunteers: Honor and Community in a Ninety-Day Regiment," *Civil War History* 44 (December 1980): 3–25, illustrates the importance of community ties to the 90-day soldiers who served west of the Mississippi. Piston also offers a useful introduction to the historiography of the common soldier in "Enlisted Soldiers," one of many superb essays in Steven E. Woodworth, ed., *The American Civil War: A Handbook of Literature and Research* (1996).

Recent debates over the cultural factors that motivated and shaped the experiences of Civil War soldiers have generally revolved around theses presented in Gerald Linderman, *Embattled Courage: The Experience of Combat in the Civil War* (1987). Linderman's arguments are challenged in Earl J. Hess, *The Union Soldier in Battle: Enduring the Ordeal of Combat* (1997), and in two works by James M. McPherson: *What They Fought For, 1861–1865* (1994) and *For Cause and Comrades: Why Men Fought in the Civil War* (1997). For discerning discussion of the debate among Linderman, McPherson, and Hess on combat motivation, see Mark Grimsley, "In Not So Dubious Battle: The Motivations of American Civil War Soldiers," *Journal of Military History* 62 (January 1998): 175–88.

INDEX

215